05/07

UNIVERSITY OF
WOLVERHAMPTON

Harrison Learning Centre
City Campus
University of Wolverhampton
St Peter's Square
Wolverhampton WV1 1RH
Telephone: 0845 408 1631
Online Renewals:
www.wlv.ac.uk/lib/myaccount

Telephone Renewals: 01902 321333 or 0845 408 1631
Please RETURN this item on or before the last date shown above.
Fines will be charged if items are returned late.
See tariff of fines displayed at the Counter. (L2)

VOICES IN TIMES OF CHANGE

Culture and Society in Germany
General Editors: Eva Kolinsky and David Horrocks

Volume 1: *Turkish Culture in German Society Today*
Edited by David Horrocks and Eva Kolinsky

Volume 2: *Sinti and Roma in German-Speaking Society
and Literature*
Edited by Susan Tebbutt

Volume 3: *Voices in Times of Change.*
Edited by David Rock

VOICES IN TIMES OF CHANGE

*The Role of Writers, Opposition Movements and the
Churches in the Transformation of East Germany*

David Rock

Berghahn Books
New York • Oxford

First published in 2000 by **Berghahn Books**

www.berghahnbooks.com

Library of Congress Cataloging-in-Publication Data

Voices in times of change : the role of writers, opposition movements and the churches
in the transformation of East Germany / [edited by] David Rock
   p. cm. -- (Culture and Society in Germany ; v, 3)
 Papers presented at a one-day symposium sponsored by the Centre for the Study of
German Culture and Society
 Includes bibliographical references and index.
 ISBN 1-57181-959-2 (alk. paper)
   1. Intellectuals--Germany (East) 2. Opposition (Political Science)--Germany (East) 3.
Church and state--Germany (East) 4. Dissenters--Germany (East) I. Rock, David. II.
Series.

DD287.3 . V65 2000
306'.09431--dc21

                                                        00-031191

British Library Cataloguing in Publication Data

A catalogue record for this book is available
from the British Library.

Printed in the United Kingdom on acid-free paper

ISBN 1-57181-959-2 hardback

Table of Contents

Preface and Acknowledgements

In October 1995, the German Section of the Modern Languages Department at Keele University welcomed Friedrich Schorlemmer as Visiting Writer. During his stay, he discussed his life and his work, talked to students about problems in the GDR and in the new Germany and generally inspired everyone with his sharp insights, his infectious enthusiasm and his impressive oratorical skills. To conclude his stay, the Centre for the Study of German Culture and Society held a one-day symposium focusing on issues related to Schorlemmer: the role of the GDR church and citizens movements in the transformation of Germany and the part played by GDR writers both before and after unification. Friedrich Schorlemmer himself gave his assessment of the importance of literature in the GDR before and after the 'Wende', Peter Hutchinson outlined Stefan Heym's responses to German Unification, the editor of this volume presented a paper on Christoph Hein and Jurek Becker, Detlef Pollack spoke on the citizens movements and Paul Östreicher looked at the problematic history of the church in the GDR and its role in events at the end of the 1980s.

Chaired by Stuart Parkes and Karl Cordell, the symposium confirmed what Friedrich Schorlemmer's stay as Visiting Writer had revealed: the present and the future for the former citizens of the GDR are marked by profound uncertainty. This is the theme of this volume. The new federal states are still undergoing unsettling changes in the wake of unification and some of the repercussions have been savage and will continue to be so, and *Voices in Times of Change* aims to contribute to the understanding of these radical changes by providing a multi-faceted picture of aspects of the new Germany related to its immediate past, showing the impact of individuals on events, with Friedrich Schorlemmer as the focal point.

Special thanks are due to the Deutscher Akademischer Austauschdienst for their generous support of our Visiting Writer programme and to Dr. Richard Schneider and the Goethe-Institut for their generous sponsorship of the symposium; to

Eva Kolinsky for arranging the latter, industriously supported by Val Elks; to the British Academy and to the Deutscher Akademischer Austauschdienst for research awards; to Eva Kolinsky and David Horrocks for their painstaking reading of the manuscript and their many helpful suggestions; and last but by no means least, to Friedrich Schorlemmer himself for his support in this undertaking.

David Rock

Abbreviations

BEK	League of Evangelical Churches
CDU	Christian Democratic Union
EKD	Evangelical Church of Germany
EKU	Evangelical Church of the Union
FDJ	Free German Youth (GDR)
FDP	Free Democratic Party
PDS	Party of Democratic Socialism
PEN	(Poets, Playwrights, Essayists, Editors, Novelists) International Writers Club
SED	Socialist Unity Party (GDR)
SDP	Social Democratic Party (GDR)
SPD	Social Democratic Party of Germany
VELK	United Evangelical Lutheral Church

Abbreviations

Introduction

Voices of Writers, Opposition Movements and the Churches: their Role in Preparing the Way for the Wende

David Rock

Writers

The GDR was a state which sought to control all aspects of society, and its *Kulturpolitik* (cultural policy) aimed to produce the kind of literature which the Party wanted, through censorship if necessary. Most of the writers in the early post-war period in the GDR were supportive, for they fervently believed in socialism and saw in the GDR the possibility of building a humane socialist society out of the havoc wrought by the fascists in the immediate past. Indeed, it was for this reason that returning exiles such as Bert Brecht, Anna Seghers and Arnold Zweig had chosen East Germany. In the fifties, writers broadly supported their official cultural task, declared at the 1949 congress of the SED (Socialist Unity Party): educating people to understand social reality, instilling optimism and enjoyment of labour, and revealing to ordinary people the significance of the Two Year Plan (Kolinsky and van der Will 1998: 12). Yet from the outset, too, the officially declared aesthetic doctrine of 'socialist realism' raised problems, because it demanded that writers should assert and illustrate certain fixed truths, with the emphasis always on collective experience, not the individual standpoint (Reed 1992: 216), the predominant aesthetic norms being commitment to the party, typicality and optimism (Reid 1990: 32–35). Though restrictions were relaxed in 1971 when Erich Honecker replaced Walter Ulbricht as First Secretary of the SED and declared, at the Eighth Party Congress, that there would be no 'taboos' for writers, his pronouncement contained an important proviso which still enabled the state to determine what would or would not be published: the writer's starting point had to be the 'festen Grundlagen des Sozialismus' (the solid fundamentals of socialism – Rüß 1976: 180–81). Yet literature by its very nature requires the freedom to question accepted values and explore new possibilities. And the situation of literature in the GDR was worsened as increasingly hard Stalinist lines in both ideological theory and political practice whittled away people's early hopes. The propaganda of 'really existing socialism' increasingly raised doubts as to what was really 'real', making it impossible for writers of integrity to go on proclaiming the bright future of socialism, and by the 1970s, authentic individual experience had replaced collective norms to become 'the touchstone for what was real' (Reed 1992: 216). Christa Wolf's *Nachdenken über Christa T.* (Reflections on Christa T., 1968), for instance, a narration of a young woman's attempt to achieve individual self-fulfilment, illustrates Wolf's dictum that the business of art is subjective experience. With younger writers, the freedom to live out individual yearnings found more mundane yet no less authentic expression in terms of youth culture, such as having long hair and wearing jeans, in Plenzdorf's *Die neuen Leiden des jungen W.* (The New Sufferings of Young W., 1972), and listening to loud rock music or playing a guitar in public[1] in Reiner Kunze's controversial work *Die wunderbaren Jahre* (The Wonderful Years, 1976), a collection of short prose pieces not published in the GDR, which exposes the repressive nature of the state in its attempts to extinguish any spark of independence in young people.

Two events were of particular significance for the increasingly oppositional stance of many leading East German intellectuals and writers. First, the invasion of Czechoslovakia by Warsaw Pact troops brought about a severe crisis in relations between many writers and the state, though few voiced this openly at the time. The loyalty of many writers, old and

young, was suddenly overtaken by political events: For Franz
Fühmann, who had been converted to from fascism to communism in a Russian prisoner-of-war camp, these events were
an existential turning point to which he responded in combat-
ive fashion, proceeding to fight for the very kind of socialism
which Prague represented (Tate 1997: 4). Jurek Becker, a child
survivor of the concentration camps who died in 1997,
described the invasion in 1968 as 'a sort of caesura in my relationship with the GDR' (Arnold 1992: 9),[2] adding in a later
interview: 'the basis for my loyalty was damaged or even
destroyed' (Heidelberger-Leonard 1992: 112).[3] With Becker,
any previous acquiescence in an intolerant system gradually
changed into a position of critical defiance, and the following
eight years which he spent in the GDR were a period of
'ständiger Nerverei und Zeterei' (perpetual nagging and moan-
ing, Heidelberger-Leonard 1992: 112), as he put it, during
which, in the protected position which his international reputation gave him, he felt increasingly obliged to speak out on
controversial issues. And for Christoph Hein, representative of
the younger generation of writers, the crushing of the Prague
Spring was, as he explained in 1991, the key moment of 'Illu-
sionsverlust' (loss of illusion, Hein 1991: 90).

The second event which clearly marked a rift between the
SED and critical GDR writers, and also signalled the end of
the 'era of no taboos' initiated by Honecker in 1971, was the
expulsion of the dissident poet-singer Wolf Biermann in
November 1976. Twelve leading intellectuals sent an open letter of protest to Honecker, asking the SED to reconsider its
decision. It was signed by Christa Wolf, Sarah Kirsch, Volker
Braun, Franz Fühmann, Stephan Hermlin, Stefan Heym, Günter Kunert, Heiner Müller, Gerhard Wolf, Jurek Becker, Rolf
Schneider and Erich Arendt (Reid 1990: 45). They demanded,
too, that it be published in *Neues Deutschland.* When the letter
failed to appear, it was publicised in the West, with many more
writers now adding their names to the original, including
Ulrich Plenzdorf, Klaus Schlesinger, Günter de Bruyn and
Helga Schütz. In the wake of Biermann's expatriation, a number of writers chose to move to the West, including Reiner
Kunze, Jürgen Fuchs, Sarah Kirsch and Günter Kunert. They
were followed by others in the 1980s.

Recent evidence, though, has questioned whether the qual-
itative difference in GDR cultural life did indeed last for as

long as the five years until Biermann's expulsion. Peter
Hutchinson, for instance, argues that the first real breach of the
'no taboos' policy occurred with the banning of Stefan Heym's
Fünf Tage im Juni (Hutchinson 1992). Dennis Tate goes even
further, viewing the events of November 1976 as the outcome
of a protracted political struggle within the SED rather than a
sudden change of direction, and citing evidence recently produced by Biermann himself from his Stasi files that, even as
early as 1973, the Politbüro had worked out a strategy to
deprive him of his citizenship when the circumstances seemed
right (Tate 1997: 2–3). Added to this, Tate notes the growing
body of new information about the massive intensification of
the surveillance of authors by the Stasi before the expatriation
of Biermann, in particular Joachim Walther's discovery of the
sinister change which had occurred by 1975 in the Stasi's
assessment of oppositional authors who were now viewed not
just as 'Saboteure der Kulturpolitik der Partei' (saboteurs of
party cultural policy) but as 'Gegner des Sozialismus
schlechthin' (opponents of socialism per se) who should be
treated accordingly (Walther and von Prittwitz 1993: 80).

Critical writers in the GDR, though, were not opponents of
socialism per se. On the contrary, the reason why most of
them chose to stay in the GDR was precisely their hope that
their country had the capacity to reform itself and that their
voices would have a crucial part to play in this process. For
instance, Stefan Heym was defiantly critical of the SED and
obliged to publish much of his work in the West, yet he maintained his commitment to socialism and remained in East
Berlin. Critical writers developed what Wilhelm Emmerich
has called the 'counter-discourse' (Emmerich 1991: 232): living in a state which, by labelling its society 'Realer Sozialismus' (Real Socialism), indicated that it wanted to be seen as
one where socialism had been achieved, many genuinely
socialist writers were by the 1970s experiencing contradictions
between their socialist utopia, their ideals, and socialism as it
actually existed in the GDR. For instance, the ambiguous title
of Volker Braun's *Unvollendete Geschichte* (Incomplete Story,
1975 – the word *Geschichte* can mean story or history) signals
not only an unfinished, tragic story of two young lovers who
founder on the rocks of hypocrisy, but also incomplete history
in the Marxist sense, indicating that the communist millen-
nium has not yet been reached in the GDR: it was an appeal

to the party to admit its mistakes and adopt a more critical Marxist approach. Other writers were even more radical in their criticism: for instance, the title of Jurek Becker's prose collection *Nach der ersten Zukunft* (After the Initial Future, 1980) announces in almost programmatic fashion the disappearance of his utopian hopes for the GDR, and Becker, equipped with a special ten-year visa and living in West Berlin, was already testing whether the 'second future' lay elsewhere.

The development of this counter-discourse is reflected in the works of Christoph Hein, one of the most significant and well-known GDR writers to emerge in the 1970s and 1980s and a spokesman for the younger generation – for his early work coincides with the critical point when socialist writers began to dissociate social reality from the socialist utopia. His play *Schlötel oder was solls* (Schlötel or What's the Point), first produced in 1974, is set in a factory and deals with the complete failure of a young intellectual, Schlötel, who embodies the socialist ideal. Hein demonstrates that GDR society destroys people who are committed to socialism as an idea. By 1982, though, like many other writers in the GDR at the time, Hein was shifting his attention from the individual as a social being to the individual psyche: in his novella *Der fremde Freund* (The Stranger-friend, 1982), he focuses on a 'successful' doctor whose life is devoid of any idealism, hope and sense of direction, being spent between a drab flat surrounded by prying neighbours and a hospital ruled by professional rivalry. This gloomy portrayal of GDR society examines the emotional vulnerability of a woman whose guilt-ridden memories of conformist betrayal in a childhood relationship lead her to disconnect her needs from those of the society around her. Hein's last GDR novel *Der Tangospieler* (The Tango Player), published early in 1989, was praised in *Der Spiegel* as 'ein Vorbote der Wende' (a harbinger of the big change to come). Set in the 1960s, it focuses on the Stalinist past which undermines both the present and the future, thereby exposing the empty promises of socialism as it 'actually exists'. In the last play which Hein wrote in the GDR, *Die Ritter der Tafelrunde* (The knights of the round table, 1990), he pokes fun at the many crabbed, mostly octogenerian members of the GDR's Politbüro: they appear as aged modern versions of the Knights of the Round Table, out of touch with ordinary people, and though Arthur and some of his Knights still believe in the original legend and in the virtues of the society which they founded, doubts now prevail even as to whether the Holy Grail of socialism really does exist. It was no doubt with works such as these in mind that Hein once claimed half-jestingly to have described the end of the GDR eleven times!

If Hein's works representatively chart the course of counter-discourse in the GDR, it is Franz Fühmann's letters, published in 1994 (Schmitt 1994), which offer new clues to the fluctuations in the cultural climate of Honecker's Germany and their impact on not only on authors, but also on broader sectors of the cultural intelligentsia, as Dennis Tate has shown (Tate 1997: 3–4). Three distinct periods emerge from the letters: a long build-up of conflict involving writers and other intellectuals in opposition to a renewal of repression in the mid 1970s, culminating in Biermann's expulsion; a steady intensification of hostilities between 1977 and 1979, characterised by an extraordinary commitment on the part of intellectuals to explore any channel of communication to keep the dialogue with the Party alive; and finally, increasing despair in the early 1980s, marked by intellectual alienation from the sources of power in the GDR, with the articulation of such feelings in literature becoming a central concern for some authors. Though the progression in Fühmann's literary works from humanistic optimism to bleak pessimism and virtually total embitterment may have been more extreme than many, his experiences were also representative. By the early 1980s, Fühmann's profound despair not only about the future of socialism but also about human relationships and the future of the planet itself, expressed in such works as *Vor Feuerschlünden* (1982) and *Saiäns-Fiktschen* (1981), marks the beginning of the end of any lingering hopes that the GDR still retained the capacity to reform itself, 'the point of no return in the process which led to its collapse in 1989' (Tate 1997: 10). During the first half of the 1980s, damning literary judgement of the GDR increased, culminating in outstanding prose-works by other major authors, such as Christa Wolf's *Kassandra* (1983), Günter de Bruyn's *Neue Herrlichkeit* (1984), and Volker Braun's *Hinze-Kunze-Roman* (1985), marking what Tate suspects are the limits of what GDR authors felt they could achieve in a dispiriting political context.

These critical voices were all published in the GDR, invariably after long delays and much controversy, and almost all had a big following. Despite this, however, their warnings about the extent of alienation from state authority predictably had no perceptible impact on GDR political life, even in the context of Gorbachev's reforms elsewhere (Tate 1997: 11). After all, these works were in such demand and writers themselves taken more seriously by their readers in the GDR than anywhere else in the world, with the exception of the Soviet Union, precisely because of the political content written 'between the lines': literature functioned as a limited outlet for dissent, becoming an 'Ersatzöffentlichkeit' ('substitute public medium' – Emmerich 1997: 436), the only published medium in the GDR where political debate was possible, since newspapers were merely the mouthpiece of the state. Yet critical writing in the GDR was not synonymous with the 'dissident literature' of other post-war Eastern European communist states: virtually to the end, most writers retained a certain loyalty and commitment to the socialist ideology of the society in which they lived, particularly *vis-à-vis* West German criticism, even if the Party itself refused to listen.

What writers wrote or did not write, though, had been ultimately determined by the censor. Only after 1989 did they have a really independent voice. Moreover, the role which writers both played and were expected to play put enormous pressure on them. Jurek Becker, for instance, admitted in 1989 that his reasons for leaving the GDR in 1977 were primarily his private concerns about his work, for he felt that he was no longer in full control of his writing, producing what he deemed to be substandard literature: 'In the end, I got the jobs of writer and resistance fighter mixed up' (Mehr 1989: 12).[4] The pressure from both the censor and also the expectations of his GDR readers, therefore, was like 'the continuous presence of a "huge eye": by this I mean not only the censor. By the "eye" I mean, too, the expectations of readers who expect from literature a certain sound-level' (Heidelberger-Leonard 1992: 116–17).[5] These and simliar sentiments were shared by other writers too, as we shall see.

Opposition Movements and the Churches

The pressures which the state exerted on the intellectual life of the GDR beyond the sphere of literature were arguably even greater: oppositional voices such as that of Friedrich Schorlemmer were never, of course, able to appear in print in the GDR before 1989, whereas it was precisely the international reputation of distinguished authors such as Stefan Heym and Jurek Becker, widely published in both East and West, that afforded them some degree of inviolability, not only in the early years of the Honecker era. Moreover, despite his more liberal stance *vis-à-vis* the arts at the start of the 1970s, Honecker soon sought to prevent the influence of Western values and ideas through a policy of *Abgrenzung* (demarcation) and also imposed a clampdown on his own critics on the Marxist left, such as Robert Havemann who was arguing for political pluralism and against the Soviet hegemony in the Eastern bloc. Havemann spent his final years under house arrest. As we have seen above, since the scope for intellectuals and citizens to articulate dissent was limited, literature took on what Jurek Becker called an 'Ersatzfunktion' (substitute function – Arnold 1992: 78), becoming the only public domain where real political debate could take place. True, in the later years of the GDR, there were other limited outlets for citizens' and intellectuals' discontent, namely the citizens' movements and the churches, though the latter had, from the outset, also been subordinated to the dictates of the SED and its attempts to create an atheistic Marxist-Leninist state. Yet it is doubtful whether it is at all correct to speak of an opposition in any usual sense, for prior to the opening of the Hungarian border in 1989, the GDR had no cohesive or broadly socially relevant opposition. It was largely a movement without leaders – there was certainly no one in the mould of Václav Havel in Czechoslovakia or Lech Walesa in Poland. The groups of 'dissidents' loosely associated with the Protestant church, activists in issues such as peace, human rights, women's rights and ecology, were informally structured organisations and did not really offer a platform for political action with specific reforms. Moreover, even the 'opposition' of 1989 was very much an ad hoc phenomenon rather than an organised political movement, as the various dissident groups came together in response to the pressure of events inside and, primarily, outside the GDR, with the mass exodus of GDR citizens via Hungary and Czechoslovakia.

Indeed, recent commentators such as Günter Minnerup (1994: 69) have noted that it is difficult to imagine the 1989 revolution in East Germany taking place at all had it not been prompted by events in the Eastern bloc outside the GDR. To many people, the SED's reaction to Gorbachev's reforms resembled an attempt to construct a wall within a wall, a communist enclave within the socialist bloc, as Jurek Becker commented at the time from the vantage point of West Berlin: 'With horror, we witness the GDR uncoupling itself from the developments in Eastern Europe and forming an actually existing socialist enclave, raising a new wall around the wall which is around it' (Mehr 1989: 12).[6] For Becker, the reason why young people were fleeing the GDR in droves was simple: they did not want to become like their parents, 'who have been pliant for thirty or forty years, either out of putative loyalty or out of cowardice' (Mehr 1989: 12).[7]

Two, brief oppositional challenges did materialise much earlier in the 1950s: firstly, under Walter Ulbricht, the first GDR supremo, austerity measures and the SED's decision to increase working norms and production quotas led to the June 1953 workers' uprising, put down in bloody fashion by Soviet intervention. Workers were unable to offer any further organised resistance to pressures of the regime, for their traditional structures of communication and action were subsequently disrupted when the 'German Stalin', backed by Khruschev in the aftermath of the Hungarian Revolution (1956/7), purged the Party intelligentsia of a second oppositional threat in the shape of liberal antagonists such as Wolfgang Harich, who had emerged after Stalin's death in 1953. A wave of arrests, sackings and expulsions ensued. The Writer's Union, too, was purged, and an atmosphere of intimidation and passive resignation eventually prevailed, affecting even such leading GDR literary figures as Johannes R. Becher and Bertolt Brecht (who died in 1956). Many were pressurised into emigrating to the West, including some of the most prominent names of the East German intellectual elite such as Ernst Bloch, Gerhard Zwerenz and Hans Mayer. From then on, until its eventual demise in 1989, the GDR regime would never again face a similar oppositional challenge (Minnerup 1994: 70–78), despite occasional 'thaws' in cultural policy such as Honecker's 'no taboos' speech in 1971.

However, one key event did later encourage opposition and civil rights' groups: the signing of the Helsinki agreements in 1974 had its impact in the GDR, too, in so far as it put human and civil rights firmly on the agenda throughout the Eastern bloc (Jackson 1994: 20–21). The GDR's signing of the Treaty inspired a number of civil rights campaigns, especially around the issues of peace, ecology, travel and emigration, and feminism. Something of a political counter-culture did thus emerge, even in the teeth of Stasi surveillance and harassment; yet the various groups were diverse in their mostly single-issue campaigns and only came together briefly during the final months of 1989.

One of the most prominent was the *Schwerter zu Pflugscharen* (Swords into Ploughshares) movement with which Friedrich Schorlemmer was associated; indeed, the pastor himself had suddenly come to prominence in 1983 when, following up the suggestion of a local smithy, Stefan Nau, he had invited the latter quite literally to forge a sword into a ploughshare during the Wittenberg Church congress. The movement itself had begun several months earlier, in February 1982, when some five thousand young East Germans gathered in a Dresden church to take part in a peace forum, wearing distinctive badges bearing the Biblical words 'Swords into Ploughshares'. Their oppositional stance *vis-à-vis* nuclear weapons, conscription and militaristic propaganda in GDR schools echoed some of the main sentiments of the 'Berliner Apell' (Berlin Appeal) of the previous month, with its subtitle 'Make Peace without Weapons'. Covering the whole spectrum of East German peace movement concerns, the Berlin Appeal had been formulated jointly by Robert Havemann and Rainer Eppelmann, an East Berlin pastor specialising in work with young people (Sandford 1983: 58–67). Supporters of such movements suffered in various insidious ways: conscientious objectors, for instance, waved goodbye to any prospects in higher education, and school pupils who wore Swords-into-Ploughshares badges suffered personal reprisals such as expulsion or non-admittance to colleges and apprenticeships (Sandford 1983: 72). Nevertheless, peace forums were supported by thousands of (mainly young) East Germans in the early 1980s. Increasing awareness of the catastrophic environmental damage done by heavy industries in the GDR also led to protest (Woods 1986).

The values evolved by this partly underground, partly fringe culture often ran counter to the squeaky-clean images and ideals purveyed by the party. Socialists most of these young people certainly were, but their purer socialist ideals were pursued in more unorthodox lifestyles. If the early 1980s saw the first signs of a mingling of cultures and attitudes, with even FDJ members marching loudly for peace, then gathering quietly for peace in a local church, their long hair and their parkas contrasting with their FDJ shirts tucked in their jeans (Sandford 1983: 80), then later on, insubordination became almost a value in itself, particularly with younger people: the GDR, too, had its rebels who often imitated the outlandish manners and fashions of punks and skinheads in the West. Indeed, the defiant attitudes of many teenagers in the GDR had been underpinned by Western icons such as jeans, Coca Cola and above all by the insolent stance of rock music (Wierling 1994). The rebellion of Fleischmann, for instance, the disturbed young hero of Ulrich Plenzdorf's prose piece 'kein runter kein fern' ('grounded, no telly', 1978), revolves around his rock-hero Mick Jagger, and even though Fleischmann's English is dire, the refrain of the Rolling Stones' hit 'Satisfaction' takes on a special meaning for him: 'EIKEN-NGETTNOSETISFEKSCHIN!', his personal phonetic transcription of the English text, becomes an expression of his own alienated condition and his frustration with the older generation. Fleischmann's authoritarian father is representative of the GDR state itself, a hierarchy dominated by old men. By the mid 1970s, the authorities in the GDR had recognised the powerful influence which rock musicians could exert as role models for the young and increasingly sought to accommodate popular culture through the development of a socialist concept of rock culture during the late 1970s and 1980s: 'Rock mit einem sozialistischen Gesicht' (rock with a socialist face, Wicke 1987: 153). The ultimate failure of this venture was signalled in events of autumn 1989: on 11 October, the Erlöserkirche (Church of the Redeemer) in Berlin was the venue for an unsanctioned rock concert ('Konzert gegen Gewalt' – Concert against Violence), details of which were reported in the West, but not in the GDR; and in November fifty leading rock musicians signed a resolution in support of the initiatives of the newly formed 'Neues Forum' (Watson 1993).

Increasingly during the late 1970s and the 1980s, the ruling Politbüro was seen as an antiquated gerontocracy, out of touch with ordinary people, particularly the younger generations, many of whom were applying in droves for exit permits in their boredom at the drab, claustrophobic atmosphere of everyday life in the GDR. Indeed, the question of the right to travel, even to emigrate, increased in importance during the

1980s to become the prime issue for protest in September 1989, when the authorities were suspected of dragging their feet in issuing exit permits. The Prayers for Peace, held regularly in the Nikolaikirche (Nicholas Church) in Leipzig, became the rallying point, too, for those demonstrating for the right to emigrate.

As we have already seen in the case of the emergence of the peace movement in the early 1980s, the Protestant Church had become one of the focal points for nonconformists and dissenting voices before 1989 (Cordell 1990). It had increasingly provided a forum for discussion of alternative values and even a sanctuary for criticism and protest. It achieved its peculiar status in the GDR by defining itself as a 'church in socialism' and thereby establishing a relationship with the SED based on reciprocal tolerance. The church accepted the humane principles upon which socialism and hence East Germany was founded, and sought and found common moral ground on issues such as social equality. Simultaneously though, with its Lutheran legacy of the autonomous individual conscience, it was a natural focus for conflict between the individual and a repressive authoritarian society. Hence, while proclaiming their support for socialism, the more radical Christians, such as Eppelmann, the Evangelical Student Congregations in some universities, and in particular the new generation of pastors (such as Friedrich Schorlemmer) who played such a vital role in the peace movements of the 1980s, did not accept the militarism and the discrimination against those of pacifist conviction practised by the particular socialist state in which they lived (Sandford 1983: 80).

It is now widely recognised that the church had a cohesive effect during the period leading up to the *Wende*, for it provided an ideology-free zone in a repressive totalitarian state, thus offering a haven, seemingly beyond the reach of the otherwise omnipotent Party, which met the needs of environmentalists, peace activists and critical theologians alike (Frank 1997: 9). Yet whilst the church thus provided a gathering point for dissent and, particularly towards the end, even a training ground for non-violent resistance, it was also no more able than any other sphere in the GDR to avoid infiltration by the Stasi which used church groups as a base to monitor opposition, a factor revealed only some time after unification (Jackson 1994: 22).

As several observers have commented, the men and women who played leading parts in the 'gentle revolution' of autumn 1989 had, in many cases, been members of GDR socialist organisations. They even included the offspring of high GDR officials, representatives of a younger generation of socialists whose frustrated idealism manifested itself in their involvement in peace, ecological and civil rights issues and in their alternative lifestyles. There were some 160 such groups of approximately 25,000 activists, with a hard core of only sixty according to Stasi estimates (Jackson 1994: 22).

It was the civil rights and church groups who challenged the official results of the municipal elections in May 1989: they proved that the figures had been blatantly falsified to produce the usual near-unanimity for the SED, concealing the large number of 'no' votes cast (Schorlemmer 1993: 29). But it was not until September 1989 that 'Neues Forum' was constituted as the first national platform for critical dissent and reform of the GDR along democratic socialist lines. Its members came from a wide mixture of opposition groups, including green and peace activists, left-wing Protestants, campaigners for legal reform and communist/socialist reformers. Predictably, 'Neues Forum' was classified by the authorities as 'staats-feindlich' (hostile to the state, Jackson 1994: 29), to which its members courageously responded with the demand for its legalisation. In September, too, another opposition group called 'Demokratie Jetzt' ('Democracy Now') was founded, most of whose members were civil-rights activists close to the church who demanded a 'demokratische Umgestaltung der DDR' (democratic transformation of the GDR, Jackson 1994: 28). 'Demokratischer Aufbruch' (New Democratic Departures), the group of which Friedrich Schorlemmer was one of the founder members, was established in October 1989 with the aims of uniting critical groups and individuals but also holding to the values of socialism and recognising GDR citizenship (Wimmer et al.: 1990). For many civil rights campaigners, and writers too, the mass demonstration at Berlin Alexanderplatz on 4 November 1989 seemed, at the time, to be the culmination of their efforts, the historic moment for 'das Volk' (the people) to realise their dream of 'true' socialism: Jens Reich of 'Neues Forum', for instance, called it 'the best thing produced by the GDR, the final political fireworks' (Emmerich 1997: 458).[8] The twenty six speakers included Ste-

fan Heym, Christa Wolf, Christoph Hein, Jens Reich, Gregor
Gysi and Friedrich Schorlemmer. Banners proclaimed the
advent of democracy and popular socialism; Heym declared
that the people were learning 'den aufrechten Gang' (to walk
upright); Christa Wolf spoke of a 'revolutionären Erneuerung'
(revolutionary renewal) rather than a *Wende* in the GDR; and
Friedrich Schorlemmer urged 'Toleranz und kritische Solidarität miteinander' (tolerance and critical solidarity with one
another) (Conrady 1993: 190). But the agenda in the mass
demonstrations which followed was changing, soon to be
dominated not by demands for a reformed, truly socialist
GDR but by calls for German unity in the hope that it would
bring democracy and, more significantly, Western economic
prosperity to East Germany.

Times of Change

The euphoria at the culmination of events in November 1989
soon evaporated, giving way to speculation and concern as to
what the future would hold now that the old restrictions were
gone – but also the old certainties. People were suddenly aware
of the possibility that, for the first time, they might have real
independence – and, in the case of writers, a really independent
voice – but they also recognised certain dangers in the new situation. In his speeches and essays, Friedrich Schorlemmer
stressed the significance of literature both for himself personally
and for the individual in general in the GDR (Schorlemmer
1992: 344–51). Could people now look to writers again for guidance in adjusting to new and possibly harsh realities? Or would
writers too fall prey to increasingly widespread feelings of disorientation and be unable to point the way forward?

In the new situation, GDR writers were suddenly forced to
question the implications and effects of the *Wende* on their role
hitherto and gradually to accept that their status as an avant-
garde and an elite was vanishing almost overnight after 1989
(Emmerich 1997: 457). One of the first voices to issue a note of
warning was Jurek Becker. In his three Frankfurt lectures *Warnung vor dem Schriftsteller* (Warning against Writers, 1990),
Becker, resident in West Berlin from 1977 until his death in
1997, and thus able to speak with a voice of some experience,
attacked West German literature for being primarily a

'Wirtschaftszweig' (branch of industry) and GDR literature for the extent to which it owed its influence to the existence of the censor: 'The books of authors who pick arguments with the censor are even read by people who would usually never pick up a book' (Becker 1990: 16).[9] And in his provocative essay bearing the ironic title 'Die Wiedervereinigung der deutschen Literatur' (The Reunification of German Literature), Becker predicted rather dismal prospects for former GDR writers after unification, for almost all works of literature written and published there had become vehicles for transporting the political concerns of their authors, which in turn made the public 'avid for books, to be more precise – for books by writers who deviated' (Arnold 1992: 78).[10] Such literature would no longer sell in the West since many GDR authors owed their fame and success to a combination of the censor and the existence of a second, hostile German state, where the West German public, like the East German one, was, as Becker put it, 'auf das Dissidentische scharf' (keen on things dissident). For this reason, books were often judged according to ideological rather than aesthetic criteria, with the result 'that the banning of a book often brought its author greater fame than normal publication would have done' (Arnold 1992: 80).[11] And in 'Die Wiedervereinigung der deutschen Literatur', Becker posed the teasingly provocative question: 'Is it ultimately not appropriate, however macabre it may sound, to mourn the censor?' (Arnold, 1992: 82).[12] For he added that the disappearance of the censor with the demise of the GDR would have several implications: former GDR writers, without this 'Orientierungshilfe' (help with their bearings), 'Wegweiser' (signpost) and 'Kompaß' (compass), would be left to their own devices and have to adapt to market forces. GDR literature would thus suffer the same fate as East German industry. Becker concluded his diatribe in the same provocative tone, directing it at the West German scene too: What was left of East German literature would 'unter neuem Firmennamen weiterbestehen' (carry on under a new company name), surviving not as 'deutsche' (German), but as 'westdeutsche' (West German) literature, whose dominant characteristics were, as he put it, 'currying favour, craving for admiration, vociferous marketing and simplicity of ideas' (Arnold 1992: 85).[13]

The pertinence of Becker's polemic on the role of the censor and market forces has been borne out by the experiences

of several prominent GDR writers since the *Wende*: albeit not
without irony, Helga Königsdorf has spoken of 'Überwachungsentzugssyndrom' (surveillance-withdrawal symptoms) and Christa Wolf of missing the part which the censor
played as 'heimlichen Adressat[en]' (secret addressee) to
which she had grown so accustomed (Emmerich 1997: 457).
Heiner Müller saw an impending cultural and moral vacuum
being created by money and market forces and Volker Braun
spoke of Western 'structures' enveloping the East like lava
(Emmerich 1997: 436). Coming so suddenly after a situation
when literature was 'Ersatzöffentlichkeit', and critical writers
and 'das Volk' (the people) had often been political bedfellows, the central problem for authors was now, as Wilhelm
Emmerich has commented: 'facing a public which was more
and more losing its distinct contours as each day passed, having first defined itself as "the people" and then suddenly as
"one people"; it now seemed to have completely different concerns to that of letting writers show them how to save washed-
out socialism by reforming it' (Emmerich 1997: 457).[14] Thus
Stefan Heym, seeing his hopes for reformed socialism dwindling so swiftly, could only express irritation at the sight of 'the
people' rushing out not to buy the books, but the bananas and
pairs of tights of which they had been so long deprived.

Structure and Themes

Voices in Times of Change considers not only the fate of GDR
writers, it also explores the wider scene by surveying the
responses of intellectuals, writers, opposition groups and the
churches to the new situation and attempting to assess their
role in the tranformation of East Germany taking place before
and after 1989. Stuart Parkes (Chapter 1) examines initial
responses to the events of autumn 1989 and shows that,
although GDR intellectuals were at the forefront of the
demands for reform and democratisation of the GDR, their
position appeared to be quickly superseded by the rapid popular movement towards German unity. Refuting the false
impression that the transformation of East Germany was
effected by Western politicians, Parkes demonstrates the
importance of considering what preceded the events of
1989/90 and what has happened since unity in October 1990.

He outlines, too, the criticism which GDR intellectuals have faced from the Western media, namely a general questioning of their role during the existence of the GDR and scathing condemnation of any endorsement of that state's socialist ideals (particularly during the autumn of 1989) as support for totalitarian dictatorship. Some Western critics post 1989 went as far as attempting to discredit critical GDR authors (quite unjustly, as Heinrich Mohr has indicated, Mohr 1995: 16) with the perverse argument that their criticism provided a release valve for collective discontent and so had a stabilising effect for the SED regime. Parkes argues that, on the contrary, because of the relative freedom which they enjoyed, critical GDR writers and intellectuals actually helped to undermine the authority of the regime and contributed to its collapse.

Parkes shows how the atmosphere of controversy and recrimination has continued since unification as intellectuals have responded to the changes in the former GDR and the increased status of the Federal Republic. Western intellectuals, too, have expressed their concerns, particularly about a ruthless take-over in the East and a rebirth of German nationalism, and whilst some Eastern intellectuals have continued to identify with their former state, others have been accused of being part of a new right-wing climate within united Germany. Although concerns about increasing nationalism are not borne out by political developments, by maintaining their vigilance intellectuals may well be contributing to the strengthening of democracy in the new Germany.

Moving from this broad canvas to a more specific focus, Karl Cordell assesses the extent of the role played by the Evangelical church in the transformation of East Germany, with special emphasis on the events and developments in the two cities which emerged as centres of opposition in the GDR, namely East Berlin and, in particular, Leipzig. Cordell explains the unequal partnership between state and church in the GDR and shows how, with the emergence of dissent, the church offered sanctuary when East Berlin and Leipzig became centres of the dissident movements. However, as an uneasy coalition between clergy and citizens' movements developed, and because the church was trying to fulfil different needs, it was pulled in different directions. Though the church was important for supporting the beginnings of a civic culture in the GDR, its perceived political strength was largely illusory and such illusions arose from the compromise between church and SED state. Whilst it is true that political power began to ebb away from the SED when, in October 1989, local authorities offered to enter into dialogue with the church and citizens' movement, and though the shared commitment of the latter two was evidenced by their role in the Round Tables in late 1989, the church was gradually marginalised from the process of change with the *Wende* and since unification, its political role has greatly diminished for various reasons. Nevertheless, the church still performs a range of valuable socioeconomic tasks, alongside its traditional pastoral function. Of significance for the future of the Evangelical church and its function in East Germany are the relationship between West and East German branches, the response of the church to post-unification social problems, and the issue of secularisation.

In Chapter 3, Detlef Pollack examines the changes in attitude of former leading members of the civil rights groups and opposition movements in the GDR. After the downfall of the socialist system, the politically alternative peace, environmental and human rights groups of the former GDR were forced to adapt to social and political circumstances which radically differed from the circumstances under which their political activities arose. After 1989, the grass-roots groups whose actions were orientated to social changes in the GDR had to cope with changes that proceeded faster and were more comprehensive than they had intended and that went in a different direction from the one they had wanted. This study examines whether or not the representatives of the former politically alternative groups were able to readjust to the new conditions, and if so, then how.

The chapters on Friedrich Schorlemmer focus on one individual voice, shedding further light on the central issues of the book from his personal perspective as pastor, dissident and man of letters. The importance of his writings for Germans in both East and West has already been recognised in the new Germany (he was, of course, unable to publish in the GDR), but he has also been much criticised by West German commentators for being a prime example of so many of the 'dissidents' from within the East German Lutheran church: very sincere, almost charismatic, but also rather ignorant of the involved political culture of a complex pluralist society, with a tendency to sympathise with the underdog and to blame the big Western brother for all the ills and problems encountered in the new Germany by former citizens of the GDR, with whom he took too soft a line. In his *Spiegel* article of March 1999, 'Keine Opfer, keine Täter' (No victims, no perpetrators), for instance, Matthias Matussek declared that, some ten years on, GDR reality had become the 'Gegenstand von Mythen' (subject of myths). His provocative subtitle, 'what remains is one single big gap in people's memories',[15] was a deliberately ironic allusion to the title of the Christa Wolf story *Was bleibt* (What Remains) which had sparked off the big literary controversy of the early 1990s, the *Deutsch-deutscher Literaturstreit* (the intra-German literature conflict – see Chapter 1)). Here, Matussek offered a brief summary of what he saw as the part played by Schorlemmer in this process of myth-making; the irony and sarcasm inherent in the journalist's remarks leave little doubt as to his attitude to the often irascible red-headed pastor from Luther's Wittenberg:

> Schorlemmer reads Luther, preaches Luther, is Luther. He is ever the 'fireball', he is 'pugnacious' and 'powerfully eloquent' and, of course, 'courageous'! He is partial to flinging ink-pots in the direction of the capitalist West, and on each occasion, there is an enormous splash in the arts sections of the newspapers. He has casually tried to ignore the stink in his own household about the fact that he abuses his job primarily for building up his own personal image. / Schorlemmer argues for coalitions with the PDS. He was against reunification. Above all, however, there was his hymnic proposal to make a 'bonfire out of Stasi-files'. Forgiveness for the weak. Great! cheered the weak and all the others whose covers had not yet been blown. With this courageous intervention, he picked up the 'Peace Prize of the German Book Trade'. / No one seemed to hit upon the fact that with this, Schorlemmer, only four years after the *Wende*, was intending to let people off by drawing a line under the GDR dictatorship. It applies today more than ever. The pastor who, in an emotionally charged essay, recently accused Martin Walser, a writer grown tired of guilt, of repressing history [in relation to the Nazi past – *editor*], doesn't like anybody poking around in GDR history one little bit. Or at least not beyond the narrow pastoral framework of murmured repentance and beaming forgiveness.[16]

In contrast to this albeit typically one-sided view, Roger Jones, with the benefit of geographical distance from the often fraught East/West German political scene, redresses the balance somewhat in Chapter 4, concentrating on the positive aspects of Schorlemmer's contribution and giving an account of Schorlemmer's life and works, and, in particular, the central ideas in his thinking. Chapter 5 draws on an interview with Friedrich Schorlemmer conducted during his stay in England as Keele Visiting Writer in October 1995. The interview covers aspects of his life as a dissident in the GDR: the difficulties faced by a pastor's son in the GDR; his work in the church and his role in the citizens' movements; his view of the role of the churches and writers in the GDR; and his views on German unification and its effect on the political and social future of Germany, particularly the Eastern part.

Beginning with the political significance of Prague 1968 and of Gorbachev's Paris speech (1985), Friedrich Schorlemmer himself focuses on issues such as the church in the GDR, literary developments and hopes/fears for the new Germany, presenting them from his personal angle. He explains what inspired GDR intellectuals to fight for a more just socialism, and recounts his view of significant events in October 1989 in Berlin and Leipzig. He examines, too, the realities of the 'peaceful' unification in terms of the extent to which democratic hopes have been fulfilled; discusses current disillusionment with promises of material happiness, and the dangers attending 'Siegermentalität' (victor mentality); and in terms of 'was bleibt' (what remains), he assesses the achievements of GDR writers before and after the *Wende*.

Chapter 7 focuses on another individual voice, this time the most internationally prominent of all former GDR writers, and demonstrates that Stefan Heym's activities, both pre- and post-*Wende*, were as intensive as those of any intellectual, and that his widely respected and long-standing opposition to the GDR leadership meant that his speeches and writing carried weight. Yet, like so many other intellectuals, he was dismayed by the direction of the post-*Wende* GDR, and his analysis of the developing situation, conveyed in speeches, journalism and fiction, was sharp, fearless – and unpopular. His negative prognosis of the new politics, social development, and an economically-driven 'unification' was inspired by an unbowed belief in socialism; but the collapse of that ideology in the GDR could have led him to greater balance in some of his arguments, as Peter Hutchinson demonstrates. Heym's natural role, however, is that of courageous gadfly, and it is in this capacity that his principal contribution to the transformation may be seen to lie.

The last two chapters consider responses of other prominent and some less well-known former GDR writers to the GDR past and to the new situation in Germany. Chapter 8 examines initial responses to the *Wende* from representative critical literary voices who remained in the GDR until the end, conformist GDR authors and also emigrant writers able to comment from the vantage point of the West. Whilst the breakdown of the SED regime in 1989 was welcomed by the majority of critical GDR writers, most initially remained loyal to their own utopian notions of socialism. Hence much of the writing of former GDR writers in the first few years since the *Wende* has been concerned not so much with the new realities, but with coming to terms with the loss of utopian hopes. Views of the function of literature in society are rapidly changing, with some reaffirming their belief in its potential for guidance and others now rejecting the notion that art should have a social or political message. The chapter concludes with notable examples of writers who have bucked the aforementioned trend and confronted the new Germany in their works, responding to monumental historic events with satire, irony and humour and operating in more than one artistic medium.

In the final chapter Martin Kane discusses *Von Abraham bis Zwerenz,* published by the Bonn Ministry of Education, Science, Research and Technology in 1995. Bonn's declared aim with this anthology underlines its relevance to the themes of *Voices in Times of Change*: 'The anthology aims to contribute to the intellectual and cultural unification of East- and West- Germany. … To do justice to the aim of bringing closer together people in East and West with their different concerns, wishes and hopes, and to awaken mutual understanding, texts were included which give insights into past and, in particular, present problems and situations, social conditions and everyday life past and present' (Boeger and Lancaster 1995: 7–8).[17] *Von Abraham bis Zwerenz* brings together over three hundred contributions by 104 writers from East and West Germany and offers many insights into how writers have responded to developments since 1990, casting light on the historical, social and psychological problems that they face. Considering lesser-known but worthy former GDR writers, Martin Kane examines the ways in which many of these writers have portrayed, and reacted to, an unsettling passage of recent German history, paying special attention to the question of identity and also to the humorous perspective on events which writers have been able to bring to bear. The chapter stresses the importance of two aspects of the historical context in which the anthology appeared, namely the wholesale clear-out of millions of East German books, which is cited as an example of the attempted eradication of the identity of the vanquished by the vanquishers; and secondly, the acrimonious debates within the East and West German PEN about which former GDR writers should or should not be allowed to be a member in view of past loyalties. Kane also considers writers who operate in satirical and comic mode in their responses to the savage repercussions of unification. Yet here, too, what emerges most strongly is the preoccupation with the peculiarity of the East German experience, and the insistence on an East German identity, whether positive or negative. This sense of separateness, temporarily drowned out during the euphoria of late 1989, was now recognised as something worth holding on to at a time when the culture of the GDR was being consigned by many Western commentators to the dustbin of history. This is the principal achievement of the anthology: capturing and giving expression to the rapidly fading singularity of the GDR, and thereby both contributing to the general understanding of what it was to be a German living beyond the Elbe and helping East Germans to understand themselves.[18]

Notes

1. For the Party, these were both emblems of American imperialism and a protest against the state-propagated image of the conservatively dressed, model young socialist, cf. Dorothee Wierling 1994: 409–11.
2 '... dieser Einmarsch 1968 war eine Art Zäsur in meinem Verhältnis zu(r) DDR'.
3. 'Die Loyalitätsbasis ... wurde ... angeschlagen oder sogar zertrümmert'.
4. 'Zum Schluß habe ich die Berufe Schriftsteller und Widerstandskämpfer miteinander verwechselt'.
5. '... die ständige Gegenwart eines "großen Auges": Damit meine ich nicht nur den Zensor. Mit dem "Auge" meine ich auch die Erwartung einer Leserschaft, die eine bestimmte Lautstärke von Literatur erwartete'.
6. 'Man sieht mit Grauen, wie die DDR sich von der Entwicklung in Osteuropa abkoppelt und eine realsozialistische Enklave bildet, um die Mauer, die um sie herum ist, eine neue Mauer zieht'.
7. '... die sich seit dreißig oder vierzig Jahren verbiegen, entweder aus vermeintlicher Loyalität oder aus Feigheit'.
8. 'das Beste, was die DDR hervorgebracht hat, ein politisches Schlußfeuerwerk'.
9. 'Die Bücher der Autoren ... , die sich mit dem Zensor anlegen, werden selbst von denen gelesen, die sonst nie ein Buch in die Hand nehmen würden'. A variation on this sentiment appears in the novel *Amanda herzlos* in the reference to the Russian journal *Sputnik*, proscribed in the GDR: 'prior to this not a soul knew it, now everyone is missing it' ('kein Mensch kannte sie vorher, jetzt vermissen sie alle') (Becker 1992: 379).

10. '… begierig auf Bücher, genauer – auf die Bücher der Abweichler.'
11. '… daß das Verbot eines Buches dem Autor oft eine größere Bekanntheit einbrachte, als die normale Veröffentlichung es getan hätte.'
12. 'Ist am Ende, wie makaber das auch klingt, Trauer um die Zensur gebracht?'
13. 'Anbiederung, Gefallsucht, Marktschreierei und Schlichtheit der Gedanken.'
14. '… als Autor einem Publikum gegenüberzustehen, das täglich mehr seine festen Konturen verlor, indem es sich erst als *"das* Volk", dann plötzlich als *"ein* Volk" definierte und ganz andere Sorgen zu haben schien, als den maroden Sozialismus mittels Reformation zu retten und sich dabei von Schriftstellern anleiten zu lassen.'
15. 'was bleibt, ist eine einzige große Erinnerungslücke.'
16. 'Schorlemmer liest Luther, predigt Luther, ist Luther. Stets ist er ein "Feuerkopf", ist "streitbar" und "wortgewaltig" und "mutig" sowieso. Er schmeißt Tintenfässer mit Vorliebe nach dem kapitalistischen Westen, und jedesmal gibt es eine Riesenkleckerei in den Feuilletons. Den Stunk im eigenen Haus darüber, daß er seinen Job vorwiegend zu persönlichem Imagebildung mißbraucht, hat er lässig weggesteckt./ Schorlemmer plädiert für Koalitionen mit der PDS. Er war gegen die Wiedervereinigung. Vor allem aber war da sein hymnischer Vorschlag, ein "Freudenfeuer aus Stasi-Akten" zu veranstalten. Vergebung für die Schwachen. Prima, jubelten die Schwachen und all die anderen, die noch nicht enttarnt waren. Er strich mit diesem mutigen Einsatz 1993 den "Friedenspreis des deutschen Buchhandels" ein. / Keinem schien aufzustoßen, daß Schorlemmer damit bereits vier Jahre nach der Wende den schonenden Schlußstrich unter die DDR-Diktatur zu ziehen gedachte. Das gilt heute mehre denn je. Der Pfarrer, der dem schuldmüden Schriftsteller Martin Walser jüngst in einem glühendem Essay Geschichtsverdrängung vorwarf, mag das Stochern in DDR-Vergangenheit überhaupt nicht. Zumindest nicht, wenn es den engen seelsorgerischen Rahmen aus gemurmelter Reue und hirtenstrahlender Vergebung verläßt.'
17. 'Die Anthologie will zur geistig-kulturellen Einigung zwischen Ost- und Westdeutschland beitragen. … Um der Absicht der Anthologie gerecht zu werden, die Menschen in Ost- und Westdeutschland mit ihren unterschiedlichen Sorgen, Wünschen und Hoffnungen einander näher zu bringen und gegenseitiges Verständnis zu wecken, wurden vor allem Texte aufgenommen, die Aufschluß geben über vergangene und insbesondere gegenwärtige Probleme und Befindlichkeiten, gesellschaftliche Zustände und den Alltag von damals und heute'.
18. In view of the number of specialist works on women-centred issues which have already appeared, no specific chapters deal with the feminist contribution to either the shaping of the GDR or its destabilisation and demise. For publications in English dealing with women in the social and political transformation of the GDR, see, for instance, Eva Kolinsky's three works: *Women in Contemporary Germany* (Oxford: Berg, 1993); *Social Transformation and the Family in Post Communist Germany* (London: Macmillan, 1998); and the essay 'Women, Work and Family in the New Länder: Conflicts and Experiences', in: Eva Kolinsky and Chris Flockton (eds), *German Politics, Special Issue: Recasting East Germany: Social Transformation after the GDR,* vol.7, no. 3, December 1998, pp.101–25. For the importance of the contribution of women writers, see, for instance, Chris Weedon, *Post-War Womens's Writing in German. Feminist Critical Approaches* (Oxford/New York: Berghahn, 1997); and Elizabeth Boa and Janet Wharton (eds), *Women and the Wende. Social Effects and Cultural Reflections of the German Unification Process, German Monitor* 31 (Amsterdam/Atlanta: Rodopi, 1994).

References

Arnold, Heinz Ludwig, ed. 1992. *Jurek Becker: text und kritik*. Munich, Verlag edition text + kritik.

Baumann, Eleonore, et al., eds. 1990. *Fischer Weltalmanach. Sonderband DDR*. Frankfurt am Main, Fischer Taschenbuch Verlag.

Becker, Jurek. 1980. *Nach der ersten Zukunft*. Frankfurt am Main, Suhrkamp.

——. 1990. *Warnung vor dem Schriftsteller, Drei Vorlesungen in Frankfurt*. Frankfurt am Main, Suhrkamp Verlag.

——. 1992. *Amanda herzlos*. Frankfurt am Main, Suhrkamp.

Boeger, Wilhelm and Lancaster, Helga, eds. 1995. *Von Abraham bis Zwerenz*. Fulda, Parzeller.

Braun, Volker. 1975. *Unvollendete Geschichte* in *Sinn und Form*, 27, pp.941–79.

——. 1985. *Hinze-Kunze-Roman*. Halle / Leipzig, Mitteldeutscher Verlag.

de Bruyn, Günter. 1984. *Neue Herrlichkeit*. Halle, Mitteldeutscher Verlag.

Conrady, Karl Otto. 1993. 'Deutsche Wendezeit', in Karl Otto Conrady, ed., *Von einem Land und vom andern*, Frankfurt am Main, Suhrkamp, pp.173–248.

Cordell, Karl. 1990. 'The Role of the Evangelical Church in the GDR'. *Government and Opposition*, 21, 1, winter, pp.48–59.

Emmerich, Wolfgang. 1991. 'Status melancholicus. Zur Transformation der Utopie in der DDR-Literatur', in Heinz Ludwig Arnold and Frauke Meyer-Gosau, eds., *Literatur in der DDR. Rückblicke: text und kritik*, Munich, Verlag edition text + kritik, pp.232–45.

——. 1997. *Kleine Literaturgeschichte der DDR: Erweiterte Neuausgabe*. Leipzig, Gustav Kiepenheuer Verlag.

Frank, Helmut. 1997. 'Kreuz des Ostens'. *Die Zeit*, 26, 6 June, p.9.

Fühmann, Franz. 1981. *Saiäns-Fiktschen*. Rostock, Hinstorff.

——. 1982. *Vor Feuerschlünden. Erfahrungen mit Georg Trakls Gedicht*. Halle, Mitteldeutscher Verlag.

Heidelberger-Leonard, Irene. 1992. *Jurek Becker*. Frankfurt am Main, Suhrkamp Verlag.

Hein, Christoph. 1982. *Der fremde Freund*. Berlin, Aufbau Verlag.

——. 1986. *Schlötel oder Was solls. Stücke und Essays*. Darmstadt, Neuwied.

——. 1989. *Der Tangospieler*. Berlin (East)/Weimar, Aufbau.

——. 1990. *Die Ritter der Tafelrunde und andere Stücke*. Berlin (East)/Weimar, Aufbau.

——. 1991. 'Ich bin der Leser, für den ich schreibe', in Heinz, Ludwig Arnold, ed., *Christoph Hein: text und kritik*, Munich, Verlag edition text + kritik, pp.89–91.

Hutchinson, Peter. 1992. *Stefan Heym. The Perpetual Dissident*. Cambridge, Cambridge University Press.

Jackson, Paul. 1994. *DDR – Das Ende eines Staates*. Manchester, Manchester University Press.

Kolinsky, Eva and van der Will, Wilfried. 1998. 'In Search of German Culture', in Eva Kolinsky and Wilfried van der Will, eds., *The Cambridge Companion to Modern German Culture*, Cambridge, Cambridge University Press, pp. 1–19.

Kunze, Reiner. 1976. *Die wunderbaren Jahre*. Frankfurt am Main, Fischer.

Matussek, Matthias. 1999. 'Keine Opfer, keine Täter'. *Der Spiegel*, 10, 8 March, pp.120–42.

Mehr, Max Thomas. 1989. 'Eine nicht ganz vollzogene Scheidung. Gespräch mit Jurek Becker über die DDR, die Partei, die Flucht und die Schwierigkeiten der Opposition'. *tageszeitung*, 25 September, p.12.

Meyer-Gosau, Frauke. 1992. '"Fortschritt kann auch in Ernüchterung bestehen"': Gespräch mit Jurek Becker', in Irene Heidelberger-Leonard, ed., *Jurek Becker*, Frankfurt am Main, pp.108–24.

Minnerup, Günter. 1994. 'The Political Opposition in the GDR'. *German Monitor: Reassessing the GDR*, 33, pp.67–82.

Mohr, Heinrich. 1995. 'Einleitung in die Anthologie', in Wilhelm Boeger and Helga Lancaster, eds., *Von Abraham bis Zwerenz*, Fulda, Parzeller, pp.12–17.

Plenzdorf, Ulrich. 1973. *Die neuen Leiden des jungen W.* Rostock, Hinstorff.

———. 1978. 'kein runter, kein fern', in Marcel Reich-Ranicki and Ernst Willner, eds., *Klagenfurter Texte zum Ingeborg Bachmann-Preis 1978*, Munich, List, pp.13–31.

Reed, T.J. 1992. 'Another piece of the past: Writing since the 'Wende', in Axel Goodbody and Denis Tate, eds., *Geist und Macht: Writers and the State in the GDR*, Amsterdam/Atlanta, Rodopi, pp.215–29.

Reid, J.H. 1990. *Writing without Taboos.* New York/Oxford/Munich, Berg.

Rüß, Gisela, ed. 1976. *Dokumente zur Kunst-, Literatur- und Kulturpolitik der SED 1991–1974.* Stuttgart, Seewald.

Sandford, John. 1983. *The Sword and the Ploughshare. Autonomous Peace Initiatives in East Germany.* London, Merlin Press.

Schmitt, Hans-Jürgen. 1994. *Fühmann, Franz: Briefe 1950–1984. Eine Auswahl.* Rostock, Hinstorff.

Schorlemmer, Friedrich. 1992. 'Kunst. Was soll das?', in Friedrich Schorlemmer, *Versöhnung in der Wahrheit*, Munich, Knaur.

———. 1993 'Training des aufrechten Gangs – Die Rolle der Kirchen bei der demokratischen Emanzipation in der DDR', in Friedrich Schorlemmer, *Bis alle Mauern fallen*, Munich, Knaur.

Tate, Dennis. 1997. 'Keeping the Biermann Affair in Perspective. Repression, resistance and the articulation of despair in the cultural life of the Honecker era', in Robert Atkins and Martin Kane, eds., *Retrospect and Review: Aspects of the Literature of the GDR 1976–1990*, Amsterdam/Atlanta, Rodopi, pp.1–15.

Walther, Joachim and von Prittwitz, Gesine. 1993. 'Mielke und die Musen. Die Organisation der Überwachung', in Heinz Ludwig Arnold, ed., *Feinderklärung. Literatur und Staatssicherheit: text und kritik*, Munich, Verlag edition text + kritik, pp.74–88.

Watson, Roger. 1993. 'Flüstern und Schreien: punks, rock music and the revolution in the GDR'. *German Life and Letters*, vol. XLVI, no.2, April, pp. 162–75.

Wicke, Peter. 1987. *Anatomie des Rock.* Leipzig, Deutscher Verlag für Musik.

Wierling, Dorothee. 1994. 'Die Jugend als innere Feind. Konflikte in der Erziehungsdiktatur der sechsziger Jahre', in Hartmut Kaelble, Jürgen Kocka and Hartmut Zwahr, eds., *Sozialgeschichte der DDR*, Stuttgart, Klett-Cotta.

Wimmer, Micha, Proske, Christina, Braun, Sabine and Michalowski, Bernhard, eds. 1990. *'Wir sind das Volk!' Die DDR im Aufbruch* (We are the people! The GDR in a time of new departures). Munich, Heyne.

Wolf, Christa. 1968. *Nachdenken über Christa T.* Halle, Mitteldeutscher Verlag.

———. 1983. *Kassandra.* Berlin / Weimar, Aufbau Verlag.

Woods, Roger. 1986. *Opposition in the GDR under Honecker 1971–85.* Basinstoke/London, Macmillan.

CHAPTER 1

Intellectuals and the Transformation of East Germany

Stuart Parkes

On 4 November 1989, with Erich Honecker having been removed from office just over two weeks previously on 18 October and demands for a major reform of the GDR becoming increasingly insistent, a crowd that was estimated at around a million gathered on the Alexanderplatz in Berlin for a demonstration organised by figures from the city's cultural life. Among the speakers were Stefan Heym, Christa Wolf and Christoph Hein, three of the most famous names in GDR literature. Heym spoke in praise of those who had gathered 'for freedom and democracy and for a socialism worthy of the name'[1] (Görtz 1990: 115), whilst Wolf spoke of 'revolutionärer Erneuerung' (revolutionary renewal) (Vinke 1993: 11). For a moment GDR intellectuals appeared to be at the forefront of a popular movement for change that would democratise the ossified structures of a state that had previously been characterised by political and ideological rigidity. Five days later the Berlin Wall fell. The original slogan 'Wir sind das Volk' (We are the people), praised by Wolf as the most significant statement of renewal, was increasingly superseded by 'Wir sind ein Volk' (We are *one* people) so that the petition launched at the end of November by GDR intellectuals, 'Für unser Land' (For our Country) and signed by Wolf, Heym and Volker Braun among others, was doomed to failure even before the signatures of leading GDR politicians associated with the old system, in particular Honecker's short-lived and entirely unconvincing successor Egon Krenz, totally destroyed its credibility. In short, the agenda was now dominated not by demands for a reformed GDR but by calls for German unity, which would, it was hoped, bring democracy and, just as significantly, Western prosperity to the Eastern part of Germany. The end of November 1989 also saw the publication of Chancellor Kohl's 'Ten-point Plan' which envisaged a series of steps leading to eventual German unity. As things turned out, events moved much more quickly than many had expected. Free elections in the GDR in March 1990 brought success to the pro-unification 'Allianz für Deutschland' led by the Eastern CDU, the former GDR satellite party[2] behind which, after some hesitation, Chancellor Kohl put the weight of his own party of the same name. There followed negotiations between the two German states, and between the German states and the four wartime Allies who retained a residual responsibilty for Germany as a whole, with the result that German unity was completed on 3 October 1990. The crowds that had gathered on the Alexanderplatz eleven months earlier had apparently disappeared without trace, along with the agenda of those intellectuals who had demanded a reformed GDR rather than German unity. Not only had their plans for the transformation of the GDR come to nothing; in the eyes of many Western observers they were discredited by their commitment to any concept of a second German state. It was not without *schadenfreude* that the news magazine *Der Spiegel*, which had quickly begun to steer a pro-unity course during the events of 1989/90, reported in its edition of 11 November 1995 (*Der Spiegel* 45/1995: 72–79) that the November 1989 demonstration had in fact been organised with the acquiescence of the all-powerful GDR Stasi secret police, which, it was claimed, had partially stage-managed the event, by including its own speakers, specifically the former top intelligence agent Markus Wolf, and excluding dissidents who were totally at loggerheads with the previous GDR regime.

The only possible conclusion to be drawn from the events described above might be that intellectuals played almost no part in the transformation of East Germany. The successful initiatives were those of Western politicians, in particular Helmut Kohl, 'the Chancellor of German Unity', who recognised the moment and acted accordingly. However superficially attractive, such a viewpoint would be extremely restrictive. It limits the period of transformation to less than one year and thus ignores what went before the events of 1989/90 and what has happened since the achievement of unity in October 1990, during the continuing process of change. Moreover, it consigns all intellectuals to a single failed group, when in reality questions relating to the GDR and to the future of Germany as a whole had been of interest in both German states – and continue to be in united Germany – to many intellectuals with very different views. To consider this question adequately, it is necessary to bear in mind not only these views but also the role of intellectuals in the GDR, specifically their relations with the state and with the people, who, given the nature of the political system, were largely excluded from influence and power.

The first point to remember is that in the GDR there was no public sphere, as that term is understood in Western democracies. This can be most easily illustrated by reference to the role of the mass media in relation to issues of topical concern, for example the environment. Whatever their shortcomings, Western media provide a forum for the discussion of a question such as environmental pollution, with intellectuals being likely to play a significant part in the debate. In the GDR, all media were strictly controlled by the state whose policy was, with few exceptions, to restrict them to trumpeting the unparalleled achievements of the country and to criticism of the ideological enemy. Accordingly, there was no place for full discussion of the widespread pollution caused by the state's policy of exploiting its industrial capabilities regardless of the costs to the environment. The only potential place where more searching questions might be asked was within the framework of literary fiction – and possibly film – or within the Church, which, as will be seen later, did enjoy a degree of freedom or at least non-interference. It is, of course, true that literature too was subject to censorship; however, almost by definition, literature invariably presents a variety of voices. This means that there must be the expression of a number of views, even if this is restricted, at a most basic level, to the character cast in the role of 'villain' stating or representing the undesirable.

In the case of the GDR there are also other factors to be borne in mind. As part of the general effort to increase the state's prestige, great store was set on literature as an expression of national achievement; in this regard it can be compared with sport through which the GDR also sought (and achieved) acclaim. Moreover, discontented authors who were the victims of censorship could attempt to have their writings published in the Federal Republic. The publication of such works of literature solely in the West not only exposed the GDR as an illiberal state; there was also the possibility that what was published there would be an exceptionally damning indictment of conditions in the GDR, as the fear of any kind of ideological censorship preventing the work reaching an audience was now removed and the author could write more freely. It is true that the audience was not initially the GDR public, for whom such a work might have been primarily intended, but, given the accessibility of Western broadcasting media, knowledge of critical works could not be suppressed. Under such circumstances it was, on occasion, in the interests of the censor to enter into discussions with a writer and hold out the promise of publication if the harshest criticisms were toned down.[3] The result of this state of affairs was that at least some degree of social criticism could be expressed through literature and that literature was important for this reason to the large number of people who were discontented with the society in which they lived. To this extent it replaced the public sphere as it exists in a more open society. To return to the example of the environment: there was no full discussion of the issues in the media, but there was poetry in which regret about the destruction of beloved landscapes could be expressed.[4]

The nature of the criticism expressed and its relationship to the events of 1989/90 will be discussed shortly. Firstly, it is necessary to consider the role of the church in the GDR which in many ways parallels that of literature. The church, which, given the religious traditions of the area, means almost exclusively the Lutheran Church, was the only body to enjoy some degree of institutional independence within the GDR, since the state could hardly run a body whose fundamental beliefs were counter to official atheist ideology. As the church also had its own publications, it was, at least potentially, another replacement for the otherwise nonexistent public sphere, rather than just forming one part of it, as it does in democratic societies on the occasions when it expresses views on matters of social and political interest. In short, the same or similar concerns to those expressed in literature could be voiced through the church. Alongside writers, leading representatives of the church were the group of intellectuals who could comment on developments in the GDR more freely than, for example, academics, who were employed within the state-controlled system of higher education. One issue that concerned the church in the GDR in the 1980s was the increased militarisation of society, that led, for example, to the introduction of paramilitary exercises into the school curriculum; parallel to this, in the meeting between Eastern and Western writers in West Berlin in April 1983, the GDR novelist Günter de Bruyn complained that 'education is being taken over more and more by the military'[5] (*Zweite Berliner Begegnung* 1983: 89). In the same year Christa Wolf published her story *Kassandra*, which uses the historical example of the Trojan War to warn about the contemporary nuclear threat. The links between the church and literature can be seen at another level in the use of church premises for literary readings; before his expulsion in 1976, the poet and singer Wolf Biermann had circumvented the official ban on public appearances by giving occasional concerts in church buildings, which could be used more freely than state venues. Accordingly, the church, as an institution, was able, through its physical resources, to provide a focus for the protest movement that developed in 1989. The Gethsemane Church in Berlin and the Nikolai Church in Leipzig became world famous at that time as the places where protesters gathered to express their demands for change.

One of the main differences between literature and the church is clearly that literature is not an organised institution but the sum of the works of individual writers. Moreover, throughout much of recent history, writers and the church have often been at loggerheads, with the church seeking to curb aspects of literary freedom. However, in the unusual conditions that prevailed in the society of the GDR, both found themselves as mouthpieces of popular concern that could not be expressed in other ways. No doubt, many of those that gathered on the Alexanderplatz in November 1989 had previously attended protest gatherings in churches. Prior to the events of 1989, church figures and writers were faced with similar dilemmas, specifically how to respond to the pressures placed on them by the state authorities who sought to suppress or at least curtail freedom of expression. Since unification, both groups have faced criticism for compromising too much or even acquiescing in the policies of the state. In the case of writers and intellectuals, this is the key question in any attempt to assess their role in the transformation of East Germany.

In general terms, it is possible to speak of three major groups of writers in connection with the GDR in the 1970s and 1980s. One consists of those who gave more or less unstinting support to the state both in their literary work and in their public statements. The most obvious example of such a writer is Hermann Kant, who was President of the Writers Union and frequently photographed in the company of a smiling Erich Honecker. How far he (and others) were prepared to go can be illustrated by the events surrounding the expulsion of a group of nine writers, including Stefan Heym, from the Writers Union, a step which effectively excluded them from official literary life in the GDR. The campaign started with an open letter to Honecker by the novelist Dieter Noll, which appeared in the official SED party newspaper *Neues Deutschland* on 22 May 1979. Using shamelessly demagogic language, Noll described Heym and some of his like-minded colleagues as 'kaputte Typen' (broken wrecks) and 'sogenannten Literaten' (so-called literati) (Walther 1991: 97). This was followed by a meeting of the Union's executive committee during which Hermann Kant prepared the ground for the expulsions, which took place at a meeting of the Berlin group of the Writers Union in June 1979. After the meeting, the Berlin group wrote a cringingly servile letter to Honecker that referred to the need for a socialist literature 'which gives expression to the new human relationships and the humanist values of our society and serves the greatness of our cause'[6] (Walther 1991: 130). It goes without saying that those who behaved in such a way played no conscious part in the transformation of the GDR.

At the other extreme were those authors who were totally at odds with the political system. It is possible to include two sets of writers in this category. Firstly, there are the young writers associated with the run-down Prenzlauer Berg district of Berlin, who expressed their alienation from the only state they had known by their apolitical stance and their use of literary forms totally at odds with the official literary doctrine of 'socialist realism'. The second group consists of those who left the GDR in increasing numbers following the expulsion of Wolf Biermann. This event marked a caesura in the intellectual life of the GDR. It increasingly became official policy to allow discontented intellectuals to leave, both writers and those involved in unofficial peace movements, such as Roland Jahn, a member of a group in Jena, who was expelled to the

Federal Republic in 1983. Among the authors who left (estimates put their numbers between fifty and a hundred) were the prose writers Monika Maron and Hans-Joachim Schädlich, neither of whom had been allowed to publish, and the poet Günter Kunert, whose increasingly resigned view of human nature was totally at odds with official ideology. Incidentally, this exodus of intellectuals was matched by the departure of increased numbers of 'ordinary citizens', not least in 1984 when 40,900 exit visas were granted. With hindsight, it is clear that the use of exit visas for intellectuals and others as a kind of safety valve to relieve pressure was a failure. Getting rid of supposed malcontents in this way was the equivalent of chopping off one of the nine heads of the Hydra (the serpent of Greek mythology which immediately replaced such losses).

Given their numbers, the GDR regime could not pretend that its exiled or unpublished opponents did not exist. It is, of course, impossible to know how many copies of works only printed in the Federal Republic illegally found their way into the GDR or how many people read the writings of the Prenzlauer Berg poets who frequently published their work privately in small magazines with minute print-runs. However, the important point remains that the existence of the dissidents was known, not least because of the attention they received in the Western media – it again has to be remembered that GDR citizens were avid watchers of Western television – which in turn provoked angry responses from the official GDR media. In the case of writers who had published in the GDR and then left for the West, one example is Jurek Becker, so prominent in the Western media that many people must have been aware of what had occurred. Even if those that were gagged could not freely articulate their discontent, their existence helped to undermine the legitimacy of the GDR.

It is the group of intellectuals between the two extremes of loyalty and rejection that has attracted particular attention. It includes the authors already referred to in connection with the Alexanderplatz demonstration and, in generational terms, with the exception of Stefan Heym, it is dominated by writers who were born before the creation of the GDR but whose adult life was spent entirely in that state. In addition to Heym, the three most important names are (arguably) Christa Wolf, Volker Braun and Christoph Hein, born in 1929, 1939 and 1944 respectively. What characterises these writers is their commitment to the socialist ideals of the GDR, but their rejection of many aspects of its reality. In so far as all had problems with the censor, they can be classed to some extent as dissidents; on the other hand, their less than total rejection of the socialist system distinguishes them from, for example, Alexander Solzhenitsyn in the Soviet Union or Václav Havel in Czechoslovakia. Wolf's first major work *Der geteilte Himmel* (The Divided Sky) of 1963 is, in fact, an endorsement of the socialist project of the GDR, even though it does contain criticism of dogmatic elements within society. The decision of the heroine Rita not to follow her fiancé to the Federal Republic in the summer of 1961 shortly before the building of the Berlin Wall is fully endorsed and a vision of a new kind of society based on truth presented.

The tone adopted by Volker Braun in his 1975 story *Unvollendete Geschichte* (Incomplete Story) is very different. In this work a young couple fall foul of the authorities, who suspect their political loyalty. Because of the crude and heavy-handed methods employed against them, their lives are almost ruined. What is more, Braun does not show any resolution of the young couple's problems; as the title implies, the story is left open-ended. Clearly, Braun is playing on the two meanings of *Geschichte* (story and history); the story can only have a happyending if the state changes its repressive treatment of its citizens and begins to fulfil its – in Marxist terms – historical role of creating a communist utopia. Thus, Braun's work can be intepreted as a warning not heeded, which the events of fifteen years later were to prove.

At the time of unity, the criticisms of the GDR made by this group of writers were frequently discarded. What counted to their detractors was that they had endorsed the idea of the GDR and had continued to do so in the autumn of 1989. The greatest opprobrium was heaped on the head of Christa Wolf, whose publication of the text *Was bleibt* (What Remains) in early 1990 set off what became known as the *Deutsch-deutscher Literaturstreit* (The intra-German literature conflict). The work itself deals with a day in the life of a GDR author, recognisable as Wolf herself, who is under surveillance from the Stasi. What infuriated certain critics had little to do with the literary merit of the work; it was the way that Wolf had chosen not to publish the story, which had mostly been written over a decade earlier, until the old GDR regime had been largely swept away. Ignoring indisputable facts in Wolf's biography, for instance her criticisms of the ideological crackdown in the area of culture that took place in 1965 following the 11th Plenary Meeting of the Central Committee of the SED, and her protests against the expulsion of Biermann, the critic of the weekly newspaper *Die Zeit*, Ulrich Greiner, labelled her the 'Staatsdichterin' (state poet) of the GDR (Anz 1991: 66). The controversy became even more intense when it came to light early in 1993 that for a short time in the 1950s and early 1960s she had been recruited as an informant by the Stasi. However, her cooperation with that body was minimal, which was also the case with the Stasi involvement of the dramatist Heiner Müller, who had similarly shown scant enthusiasm for German unity and to this extent can be compared with Wolf. In fact, members of all the three groups decribed in this essay had Stasi connections. That Hermann Kant acted as an informant under the code-name Martin can be viewed as logical given his ideological stance; much more surprising was the discovery in 1995 that Monika Maron had worked with the Stasi, albeit more out of a sense of devilment than ideological commitment. Nevertheless, that she did not openly admit this aspect of her biography, thus behaving in the same manner as the other writers whose past was revealed, was enough to discredit her in the eyes of other former GDR intellectuals. A strident critic was the dissident Bärbel Bohley, who had been exiled for a period from the GDR in 1988 but thereafter chose to return. That she was no friend of German unity shows the fluidity of the boundaries between the second and third group of intellectuals spoken of here. What is certainly clear is that it is impossible to separate GDR intellectuals, as the critics of Wolf have tried to do, at least by implication, into the acceptable, who damned the GDR outright, and the unacceptable, who favoured some kind of second German state.

What then can be said of those GDR intellectuals, including Wolf, Heym, Hein and Braun, who wished for the continued existence of a reformed GDR? Viewed in absolute terms, their identification with the GDR can be regarded as misguided. It is true that there were historical reasons for the creation of a German state after 1945 that sought its legitimacy in a total break with the past. Moreover, given the extent of continuity between the Third Reich and the Federal Republic, for example in the areas of politics, the economy and the judiciary, there was reason to view that state with suspicion. Nevertheless, the GDR never offered an alternative, since from the out-set it was a rigid authoritarian state that was incapable of reform. The arbitrary nature of the SED's dictatorial regime should also have been particularly apparent to those involved in cultural activity. In the case of literature, depending on the prevailing mood, periods of relative liberality were invariably followed by crack-downs. Only five years after Honecker had spoken of no taboos on his accession to power in 1971, the exodus of writers following the Biermann case began. This does not mean that the reformist writers are to be condemned out of hand and that they played no part in preparing the transformation of the GDR. Christoph Hein has claimed, for instance, that his work includes many descriptions of the end of the GDR. One example might be the 1989 novel *Der Tangospieler* (The Tango-player), which covers the events of 1968, a seminal year in the development of the GDR, because its troops took part in the invasion of Czechoslovakia and thus put an end to any hope of achieving 'socialism with a human face' not only in Czechoslovakia but in the GDR as well. The piano-playing hero had been dismissed from his university job some years earlier for his role in a critical cabaret. This and his subsequent imprisonment have turned him into a cynic, a state of mind that paradoxically helps him to be reinstated follow-ing the 1968 invasion. The implication is that the GDR has become a moribund state in which any idealism is totally out of place. After unification Hein claimed to have lost faith in the GDR long before it collapsed and that his pro-GDR actions in 1989 were only a charade. If this is hard to swallow, it does not mean that his criticisms and those contained within works by Wolf, Braun and Heym had no effect. There is, in fact, no doubt that their writings struck a chord with many readers, who eagerly sought out the limited editions of their works that were available. It must be remembered in this con-text that, if critical literature was published at all, the rigidities of the planned economy meant that the supply never matched demand. How far critical GDR literature had been important to the country's citizens, and continued to be so after unifica-tion, can be further illustrated from an unlikely source. On the death in 1994 of the novelist and dramatist Erwin Strittmatter, a former pupil of Brecht who became increasingly disillu-sioned with the GDR, the notorious right-wing mass-circula-tion *Bild-Zeitung*, in its Eastern editions of February 2 at least, felt compelled to mark this event with a front-page paean of praise beginning with a sentence that itself did not lack literary pretentions: 'A great poet's heart beats no more'.[7] There can be no doubt that through the criticisms which they articulated GDR writers contributed to the events of 1989/90.

The transformation of the former German Democratic Republic was far from completed with the formal unification of the two German states in October 1990. Over half a decade later the process of adaptation is still continuing and it is likely to be some considerable time before the constitutional requirement of 'gleiche Lebensverhältnisse' (equal conditions of life) is realised. Equally, the problem of the continuing lack of a sense of unity on the personal level, what has been dubbed the 'Mauer im Kopf' (the Wall in the mind), shows that much remains to be done before the process of unification is welcomed on all sides. It is not possible to discuss here in full the benefits and disadvantages of unity for citizens in both East and West. In the case of many intellectuals, they have tended to stress what they perceive as negative aspects, problems that came to the surface before the benefits, visible, for instance, in the very high rates of economic growth achieved in the mid-1990s, began to be felt.

The root of the concern felt by intellectuals is the view that unification was nothing more than the take-over of the GDR by the Federal Republic, which ruthlessly imposed its own model on all areas of life. Particular wrath was reserved for the activities of the *Treuhand* privatisation agency which was seen as being responsible for the destruction of GDR industry or its sell-off at knockdown prices to rapacious Western interests. This body was created in early 1990 by the GDR government under Hans Modrow prior to the free elections in March of that year. Its brief was to sell the state's assets, which, given the nature of the GDR system, meant virtually the whole of industry, that is to say both the manufacturing and service sectors. In the changed economic circumstances brought about by unification, what had originally been seen as valuable proved in many cases unsaleable. The *Treuhand* had therefore to preside over the closure of much of GDR industry; where it could find buyers, these were, in the vast majority of cases, Westerners, the only people likely to be in possession of the necessary capital. This state of affairs led to huge unemployment and a sense of betrayal among many ex-GDR citizens, which was compounded by evidence of criminal collusion between *Treuhand* officials and purchasers when it came to fixing the value of the enterprises being sold and by suggestions that Western firms were acting out of the desire to destroy potential competitors. The terrorist murder of the head of the *Treuhand*, Detlev Karsten Rohwedder, in 1991 was incorporated by the invariably controversial Western dramatist Rolf Hochhuth into his play about the 'take-over' of the former GDR by Western interests, *Wessis in Weimar* (Westerners in Weimar) (Hochhuth 1993). This play consists largely of a series of scenes, characterised in the subtitle as 'Szenen aus einem besetzten Land' (Scenes from an occupied country), in which East Germans fall foul of Western interests; for instance, an elderly married couple on a farm who are shown preparing their joint suicide. It was, however, the first scene in which a young woman discusses the situation of the former GDR with a character based on Rohwedder and called 'Der Präsident' that caused the greatest stir because it was seen as a justification of murder.[8] What is undeniable is that the scene ends in crude melodrama. After the President has been warned that he will not survive his activities a shot rings out. In fact, much of the play contains the usual weaknesses of Hochhuth's writing, in particular the invariably didactic tone that results in much of the work resembling more a diatribe than dramatic dialogue. Nevertheless, notwithstanding the author's disapproval of it, the production of *Wessis in Weimar* at Brecht's former theatre, the Berliner Ensemble, under the direction of Einar Schleef, has proved to be one of that theatre's few successes since unification. Ironically, Hochhuth's subsequent behaviour towards the Berliner Ensemble, the decision to buy it to ensure the continued performance of his play about the Holocaust, *Der Stellvertreter* (The Representative), is reminiscent of the take-over mentality he criticises in *Wessis in Weimar*.

Undoubtedly Hochhuth's play reflects the sense of alienation among citizens in the East, one of whose results has been, in the area of politics, the continuing success of the *Partei des Demokratischen Sozialismus* (Party of Democatic Socialism), the successor of the SED. At the 1994 Federal Election it gained 19.8 per cent of the vote in the Eastern states and four years later 21.6 per cent. In some respects, this organisation can be described as an intellectuals' party; its voters include many former GDR academics, who lost their jobs during the reorganisation of GDR higher education in the early 1990s, another policy that created bitterness in the East. As late as 1995, according to an article in the 11 December edition of the magazine *Der Spiegel* (*Der Spiegel* 50/1995: 84/5), about half the students at the Humboldt University in (East) Berlin, who had participated in the Berlin state elections of that year, had given their vote to the PDS. It can be safely assumed that one motive for such a vote is alienation caused by the changes in academic life. As for the PDS parliamentary group after the 1994 election, it included not only – for a time – Stefan Heym but also the novelist and biographer Gerhard Zwerenz, who had been a pupil of the unorthodox Marxist philosopher Ernst Bloch at Leipzig University in the 1950s and, following his move to the Federal Republic in 1957, made necessary by his critical journalism, had retained his left-wing views.

Disquiet about the process of unification has been expressed particularly forcefully by Germany's most famous writer Günter Grass. From the outset he opposed unification, initially for moral reasons. He believed that the Germans had forfeited the right to a single state because of the horrors of Auschwitz, a view that was shared by the President of the (West) Berlin Academy of Arts, Walter Jens, a critic and writer who had previously been Professor of Rhetoric at Tübingen University. Grass was also worried about the Western takeover of the GDR which he described as a 'snip' for western interests in the title of a volume of essays, *Ein Schnäppchen namens DDR* (A Snip by the Name of GDR) (Grass 1990). His ultimate worry was that a unified Germany might assume the arrogance of past German states with the same or comparable catastrophic results.

These concerns lie behind the massive novel *Ein weites Feld* (Too Far A Field) that Grass published in 1995. The title refers to a favourite phrase of the eponymous heroine's father in Theodor Fontane's nineteenth-century novel *Effi Briest.* Grass's hero, Theo Wuttke, was born exactly a hundred years after Fontane in 1919 in the same town of Neuruppin. He is also a devoted Fontane scholar, who gave lectures on the author within the GDR's system of adult education, identifying himself so much with his subject that he is universally known under the nickname 'Fonty'. During the primary narrative of the novel, which is set at the time of the unification process, Wuttke is working at a menial level for the *Treuhand* agency. Grass's attitude to the *Treuhand* is already visible when he points out

that the same word was used for the body that administered
Jewish property under the Nazis (Grass 1995: 484). He goes on
to describe it as a Moloch charged with changing the whole of
the GDR, which is to be regarded as an 'Anschlußmasse' (a
mass to be incorporated) (Grass 1995: 485). However, the main
historical parallel he wishes to draw is with post-1871 Germany.
The biography and works of Fontane are used to suggest that
the forces that propelled that state into the catastrophe of 1914
might be awakened by the events of 1989/90.

Grass's novel met with an almost universally negative reception.[9] Aesthetic criticisms were made, but much of the venom
was reserved for the political dimension of the novel, both the
portrayal of the GDR and of the unification process. The first
aspect is not important here, and in fact Grass is anything but
an apologist of the GDR system. The real question is whether
his view of the dangers lurking in the unification process is at
all justifiable. What is specifically relevant in the present context is whether, following unification, German intellectuals
have moved to the right and are beginning to preach the
nationalism that characterised many parts of intellectual and
academic life in Germany prior to 1945. In 1993 *Der Spiegel*
published three essays that to many reflected the return of
rightist thinking.[10] It is true that they were all written by Westerners; nevertheless they could be linked indirectly to the
changes in the East and the existence of a new, more powerful
German state. In a piece that attracted unparalleled attention,
entitled 'Anschwellender Bocksgesang' (The Swelling Song of
the Goat), the novelist and dramatist Botho Strauß repudiated
many aspects of the liberal pluralist society and saw virtue in
traditional values, including those of the military (Strauß 1993).
Whilst Strauß adopted the distant tone of the prophet, Martin
Walser, in his essay 'Deutsche Sorgen' (German Worries)
turned more specifically to aspects of contemporary German
society, in particular the outbreaks of right-wing violence that
had occurred since unification. He did not lay the blame so
much at the door of the perpetrators of such violence as at
Western intellectuals who had rejected the concept of the
nation and refused to enter into dialogue with those with less
internationalist views (Walser 1993). Such a viewpoint was consistent with Walser's previous campaign for German unity during the 1980s at a time when it appeared to be a pipe-dream.
His demand at that time that Germans should enjoy the same

rights of self-determination as other nations had brought accusations of crude nationalism on someone who had previously been seen as an archetypal leftist intellectual. The third essay, 'Ausblicke auf den Bürgerkrieg' (Views of Civil War) by Hans Magnus Enzensberger (1993) was less directly related to the changes that had taken place in Germany; in any case in 1990 he had seen the fall of the Berlin Wall not as a matter of deep political significance but rather as a joyous occasion for the people (Enzensberger 1990).

Two years later, accusations of a rightwards drift moved to the former GDR. They centred around the dramatist and, at the time, co-director of the Berlin Ensemble, Heiner Müller, and the Director of another prominent (East) Berlin theatre, the *Volksbühne*, Frank Castorf, both of whom had previously been at odds with the GDR authorities. Müller was accused by his co-director Peter Zadek of 'faschistoid' (fascistic) productions that were preparing the way for a new nationalism, whilst Castorf was confronted with the 'fascist' views he had allegedly developed during the existence of the GDR.[11] With Castorf, it quickly became clear that the accusations did not hold water. He had merely been attracted at a theoretical level to the dynamic ideas of Friedrich Nietzsche and Ernst Jünger at a time when he felt frustrated by the institutional immobilism of the GDR. His more substantive support of different political ideals was shown in 1995 when he was actively involved in the campaign to prevent any renaming of the Rosa-Luxemburg-Platz in Berlin, the location of his theatre. Previously, at the end of 1994, the theatre had been used by leading PDS politicians for a hunger strike in protest against attempts to confiscate the party's assets. This episode may have smacked of crude stage-mangement and theatricality in the most negative sense, since it still remains incongruous for leading PDS politicians to cast themselves as hapless victims, given the history of the party's forerunner, the SED. Nevertheless, it does suggest that Castorf is anything but a right-wing extremist. The whole extremism debate seems, at least in his case, to have been little more than an intellectual storm in a teacup.

It is more difficult to be quite so categorical in the case of Müller, as the views he expressed at the time of unification and subsequently appear at times to have been quite contradictory. Indeed, there seems little doubt that he enjoyed adopting a variety of masks, a point made by Wolf Biermann in his obitu-

ary of Müller in *Der Spiegel* (*Der Spiegel* 2/1996, 154–61). What
seems clear is that Müller was no supporter of unification, nor
of the social order of the Federal Republic. This rejection of the
Federal Republic appears at times to be based on politics. He
argues, for instance, that it is just as possible to speak of terror
in the case of the Federal Republic as it was with the GDR:
'The terror in a Swabian small town is only different from the
terror that existed in Strausberg but equally bad'[12] (Müller
1992, 360). The difference, according to Müller, is that in a
Western system the terror is based on financial rather than
political repression. Earlier, at the time of unification, his objec-
tions to the Federal Republic had been somewhat different,
based more on aesthetics than politics. He had complained that
the incorporation of the GDR into the society of the Federal
Republic would only offer the writer uninspiring 'Stille' (still-
ness) (Müller 1990: 97). This is perhaps the core of Müller's dis-
like of unification. Once he had abandoned any youthful
support for the GDR system, his major interest was in the clash
between East and West and the possibility of mutual destruction. The aesthetic attraction of destruction for him can be seen
in the title of his play *Germania Tod in Berlin* (Germania Death
in Berlin) and his statement that he had been privileged to
experience the destruction of two political systems, but would
probably not live long enough to experience the collapse of the
Federal Republic (Müller 1992: 362). This fascination with
destruction and with war, reflected in the remark: 'Without the
possibility of waging an aggressive war, Europe is only an
empty cartridge case'[13] (Müller 1990: 42) is reminiscent of
right-wing ideology, for instance Ernst Jünger's glorification of
war and Oswald Spengler's cultural pessimism. On the other
hand, Müller was no conventional nationalist. This is shown
not only by his attitude to unification, but also by the last scandal in which he was involved before his death in December
1995. During a visit to Verdun, he attacked military memorials
that glorify patriotism and spoke of the cruelty of war, a view
somewhat at odds with his previous attitudes.[14] Given this variety of views, some of which are admittedly at first sight
extremely bizarre, it seems impossible to claim at all seriously
that Müller was a fascist in any real sense.

Some five years after unification it is clear that fears about
the return of nationalist attitudes in Germany are a major concern among many intellectuals. This raises the key question of

whether such concern is misplaced and whether those intellectuals who, in the view of many, failed to understand the events of 1989/90 are continuing on a wrong track. What does seem clear is that the post-unification Federal Republic, whilst undoubtedly more powerful, is not pursuing aggressively nationalistic policies but remains wedded to the ideals of European cooperation. Equally, the rightist intellectuals who may draw inspiration from a writer like Strauß remain a peripheral group. The newspaper *Junge Freiheit* (Young Freedom) associated with such people is hardly affecting the increasing numbers of young Germans who are refusing military service. How far the prevailing anti-nationalist ethos in the Federal Republic has to do with the warnings of intellectuals is an impossible question to answer. What can be said is that they are fulfilling one of the intellectual's roles: to warn against and to criticise undesirable social and political developments. It would be much more worrying if they had stood on the sidelines and merely expressed delight about all the changes that have taken place in Germany since 1989.

Notes

1. '... für Freiheit und Demokratie und für einen Sozialismus, der des Namens wert ist'.
2. On assuming supreme power in 1945, the Soviet Union quickly allowed the formation of political parties in its zone of occupation. One of these was the Christian Democratic Union (CDU). However, political life in the Soviet Zone and the GDR soon came to be dominated by the Socialist Unity Party (SED) that was formed in 1946 with the enforced merger of the Communists and the Social Democrats. The CDU continued to exist, but only under the control of the SED.
3. The extent and nature of the censorship process in the GDR was the subject of an exhibition in Berlin after unification. It gave rise to the volume: *Zensur in der DDR: Geschichte, Praxis und Ästhetik der Behinderung von Literatur*, ed. Ernest Wichner and Herbert Wiesner, Literaturhaus Berlin, 1991.
4. For a survey of poetry concerned with ecological and environmental themes see: Axel Goodbody, '*Deutsche Ökolyrik*. Comparative Observations on the Emergence and Expressions of Environmental Consciousness in West and East Germany Poetry', in *German Literature at a Time of Change*, ed. Arthur Williams, Stuart Parkes and Roland Smith, Peter Lang, Bern, 1991, 373–400.
5. '... die Erziehung immer mehr vom Militär übernommen wird'.
6. '... die den neuen menschlichen Beziehungen und den humanistischen Werten unserer Gesellschaft Ausdruck verleiht und der Größe unserer Sache dient'.
7. 'Ein großes Dichterherz schlägt nicht mehr'.
8. The controversy was sparked by an interview Hochhuth gave to the *Manager Magazin*. It can be followed in *Deutsche Literatur 1992* (Görtz et al. 1993, 49–51).

9. The review in *Der Spiegel* (*Der Spiegel*, 34/1995, 162–69), which was given the status of a cover story, was by the doyen of German literary criticism, Marcel Reich-Ranicki. In the form of an open letter, in which he skilfully adopted the tone of speaking more in sorrow than in anger, Ranicki condemned all aspects of the novel, but paid particular attention to Grass's political stance. There were three articles on *Ein weites Feld* in the weekly newspaper *Die Zeit*. In her review Iris Radisch (*Die Zeit* 35/1995, 43/4) condemned the book out of hand. Günter Hofmann (35/1995, 1), whilst conceding the book was a failure in aesthetic terms, praised Grass as an intellectual for his contribution to public debate. This prompted a reply by Helga Hirsch (36/1995, 55), who accused Grass of being out of touch with the reality of contemporary Germany.

10. For a wider survey of this debate see: Stuart Parkes, 'Postmodern Polemics: Recent Intellectual Debates in Germany', in *The New Germany. Literature and Society after Unification*, ed. Osman Durrani, Colin Good and Kevin Hilliard, Sheffield Academic Press, Sheffield, 1995, 92–108.

11. This controversy can be followed from articles that appeared in *Die Zeit*: Rolf Michaelis, 'Oberlehrer überall' (*Die Zeit* 3/1995 ,46); Robin Detje, 'Landschaft mit steinernen Gästen' (*Die Zeit* 5/1995, 51/2); and Helmut Schödel, 'Das trunkene Schiff' (*Die Zeit* 15/1995, 69/70).

12. 'Der Terror in einer schwäbischen Kleinstadt ist nur anders schlimm als der Terror in Strausberg war'.

13. 'Ohne die Möglichkeit, einen Angriffskrieg zu führen, ist Europa nur noch eine leere Patronenhülse'.

14. For details of this affair see *Fachdienst Germanistik*, vol.13 (1995), 12/1.

References

Anz, Thomas, ed. 1991. *Es geht nicht um Christa Wolf.* Munich, edition spangenberg.

Enzensberger, Hans Magnus. 1990. 'Gangarten'. *Kursbuch 100*, pp.1–10.

——. 1993. 'Ausblicke auf den Bürgerkrieg'. *Der Spiegel*, 25, pp.170–75.

Görtz, Franz Josef et al., eds. 1990. *Deutsche Literatur 1989*. Stuttgart, Reclam.

—— eds. 1993. *Deutsche Literatur 1992*. Stuttgart, Reclam.

Grass, Günter. 1990. *Ein Schnäppchen namens DDR*. Frankfurt am Main, Luchterhand.

——. 1995. *Ein weites Feld*. Göttingen, Steidl.

Hochhuth, Rolf. 1995. *Wessis in Weimar*. Berlin, Verlag Volk & Welt.

Müller, Heiner. 1990. "Zur Lage der Nation". Berlin, Rotbuch.

——. 1992. *Krieg ohne Schlacht. Leben in zwei Diktaturen*. Cologne, Kiepenheuer und Witsch.

Strauß, Botho. 1993. 'Anschwellender Bocksgesang'. *Der Spiegel*, 6, pp.202–7.

Vinke, Hermann, ed. 1993. *Akteneinsicht Christa Wolf*. Hamburg, Luchterhand Literaturverlag.

Walser, Martin. 1993. 'Deutsche Sorgen'. *Der Spiegel*, 26, pp.40–47.

Walther, Joachim et al., eds. 1991. *Protokoll eines Tribunals*. Reinbek bei Hamburg, Rowohlt.

Zweite Berliner Begegnung. Den Frieden erklären. 1993. Darmstadt und Neuwied, 1983. Luchterhand.

CHAPTER 2

Changing Fortunes: Church and Society in Eastern Germany Before and After the *Wende*

Karl Cordell

An Unequal Partnership

During the forty-one years of rule in the German Democratic Republic (GDR) by the Socialist Unity Party of Germany (SED), religious organisations such as the Evangelical (Lutheran) Church were subordinated to the dictates of the state and as such were expected to take a 'constructive' view of the SED's attempt to create an atheistic Marxist-Leninist state. Designated religious organisations coexisted precariously alongside the party/state. On the one hand, the state demanded that the churches accept the political status quo as irreversible. On the other, from the early 1970s, the state afforded them a degree of autonomy forbidden to any other organisation in the GDR. Given the de facto monopoly of political power on the part of the SED, the relationship between religious organisations and the state was no partnership of equals: the former were dependent upon the goodwill of the latter for their continued survival (Goeckel 1990).

The example of the largest church in east Germany, the Evangelical church, is illustrative of church–state relations during the period of SED rule. By far the largest religious organisation in the GDR, the church claimed the (notional) support of up to 90 per cent of the population, though it must be added that at no point in the forty-one year existence of the GDR was anywhere near such a figure in active communion with the church. Given the clear difference in *Weltanschauung* between church and state, a clash was bound to occur. As the SED enjoyed the aforementioned monopoly of power and the backing of the Soviet occupying power, it was equally clear that it would emerge as the victor in any such clash.

From the late 1940s through to the late 1970s, the state incrementally succeeded in eroding the position of the Evangelical church, and in forcing it to agree to a number of barely palatable measures. At an organisational level this involved, wherever possible, the gradual but systematic exclusion of Christians from all positions of societal authority and influence. The only exceptions made were for those Christians who were coopted by the SED via their membership of the East German Christian Democratic Union (CDU). These steps were complemented by a series of measures which served to weaken the churches' links with its communicants, such as the dissolution of the Christian youth organisation *Die junge Gemeinde* in 1953. The church was also forced to give its assent to the state's secular confirmation service, the *Jugendweihe*, by 1960 and – most controversially of all – the church was unable to halt the introduction of *Wehrkunde* (defence studies) in GDR schools from 1978.

The biggest blow suffered by the church had come earlier in 1969 when the Evangelical church in the GDR was forced to withdraw from the all-German Evangelical Church of Germany (EKD). In its stead, and in order to meet the requirements of the SED, The League of Evangelical Churches in the GDR (BEK) was constituted. The BEK itself acted as a coordinating body for two distinct Protestant conglomerates: Reformed (Calvinist) and a majority of Lutheran congregations which were organised into the Evangelical Church of the Union (EKU). This organisational cooperation between the two churches stemmed from the basic similarity of their theologies, and facilitated the continued autonomy of the Reformed Church within a mutually beneficial framework (Sievers 1993). The remaining Lutheran congregations were grouped within the United Evangelical Lutheran Church (VELK).

In return, the state finally recognised the legitimacy of the Evangelical church in GDR society in 1971 via the development of the 'Church in Socialism' formula. Under this formula the state recognised the right of the church to assume pastoral care over its congregation, whilst in return the church recognised the socialist nature of the GDR and the right of the SED to rule and define the contours of society (Cordell 1990 a: 49). This move on the part of the state can also be viewed as part of a wider strategy aimed at securing greater legitimacy for the SED, and at creating a specific GDR national consciousness (Nowak 1992).

Evidence of how the church was coopted into this strategy can be seen, for example, from an examination of the SED's attitude towards the celebration in 1983 of the five-hundredth anniversary of Martin Luther's birth. The party was so convinced of the importance of this event that Erich Honecker himself was announced as head of the state committee in charge of the celebrations. In this capacity, he was charged with the task of ensuring that everything ran according to plan and with coordinating activities between church and state. It is through the prism of the *Lutherjubiläum* that we receive the first clear indications that some within the church were not happy with what they viewed as too cosy a compromise with the SED. Despite the known disapproval of the church authorities, a group of young Christians in Leipzig insisted on staging a silent candlelight demonstration on the occasion of an ecumenical meeting in November 1983. The reaction of the police was as predictable as it was inevitable, and the six participants were arrested.

Despite the aforementioned compromise, the church and its communicants remained subject to discrimination and harassment. There was, however, a cautious rapprochement between leading figures in the BEK and the SED. This was epitomised above all, by the meeting between delegations of the party and church, respectively led by Erich Honecker and Bishop Albrecht Schönherr in March 1978. Although this rapprochement resulted in some limited gains accruing to the (Evangelical) church, the party/state was not prepared to make concessions in areas which it considered vital, such as *Wehrkunde*. It was perhaps disappointment with the results of this controlled dialogue that caused increasing numbers of pastors and Christian activists to pursue alternative strategies. Nevertheless, the Evangelical church, along with all other churches, had gained what eventually proved to be a vital degree of autonomy from the state. Such autonomy was of crucial importance to the process of change which had begun in the early 1980s, and which dominated the political discourse of the GDR from the summer of 1989 (Grabner et al. 1990: 12).

Appreciation of this autonomy is necessary in order to understand why the church was of such importance as dissent began to emerge. When it did emerge, two issues above all others came to the fore. The first was the question of the renewed arms race between the superpowers. The second was the political maturation of a younger generation of clergy, particularly within the Evangelical church, who, unencumbered by the burden of history, were not prepared publicly to support the SED's line on nuclear weapons, and who were increasingly unhappy with the conduct of domestic politics in the GDR.

The Emergence of Dissent

Under the terms of the compromise reached between church and state the church was free to use its premises for whatever purposes it saw fit, as long of course as these purposes did not clearly contradict the GDR's legal statutes. Those who wished to register their disapproval of the SED did so from the early 1980s through the holding of prayers for peace and through participation in the 'Swords into Ploughshares' movement of the early 1980s (Kaufmann et al. 1993: 5). Within this embryonic dissident movement, East Berlin and Leipzig emerged as the centres of opposition.

The reasons why these two cities became both the physical and spiritual centres of the emergent opposition movement are varied and complex. As much as anything else, their size, anonymity and relatively cosmopolitan nature facilitated their emergence as oppositional centres. In Leipzig dissidence may inadvertently have been facilitated by the comparatively tolerant attitude of leading elements within the city administration. Pastor Hans-Jürgen Sievers of the Reformed church in Leipzig has identified three further factors which he believes demonstrate why Leipzig and its clergy came to play such a pivotal role in the *Wende*. The first was the high level of environmental damage wrought upon the city and surrounding areas. The second was the related degeneration of buildings throughout the entire city, which by the 1980s gave the city an altogether shabby appearance (Sievers 1991: 25). The third factor he identifies is the destruction on political grounds of the *Paulskirche* by the authorities in 1968, which acted as a spur for Christians of all denominations to band together in the face of a common threat (Sievers 1993).

With regard to East Berlin, the situation was slightly different. As capital of the GDR, and therefore the SED's showpiece, the extent of physical and environmental degradation was not as great as it was in Leipzig. However, the demand for change that was finding such clear expression in Leipzig, was also expressed in East Berlin. More than anything else, East Berlin can be differentiated from Leipzig by virtue of the fact that it was even more secularised than Leipzig. In East Berlin, the secular Citizens' Movement was correspondingly stronger, and the church weaker than in Leipzig.

Having identified these factors we now need to examine other issues which affected Leipzig and East Berlin. With the benefit of hindsight we can now say that it was not the Evangelical church or any other churches *as institutions* which played such a decisive role in the events of 1989/90, rather, as will be shown, it was the actions of an increasing number of individual pastors and previously isolated dissidents which were of crucial importance. Leipzig and, to a lesser extent, East Berlin were to constitute the locomotive of change. Yet, we should not forget that the ideas being expressed in these two cities were supported by increasing numbers of (junior) clergy throughout the country.

Making clear a distinction between senior and grass-roots clergy is central to aiding our understanding of the situation of the Evangelical and other churches in Leipzig and elsewhere both during the *Wende* and today. Although the senior clergy in the Evangelical church sanctioned semi-official prayers for peace from the early 1980s, the behaviour of the church authorities was governed by two factors. The first was long experience of authoritarian and totalitarian rule coupled with first-hand knowledge of what the practitioners of such rule were capable. The second, and secondary, factor was an innate conservatism. Experience coupled with conservatism led the church authorities to be wary of any activities that might incur the wrath of the SED. Indeed the difference in attitudes towards the state help in understanding why the churches as institutions exhibited a range of aspirations *vis-à-*

vis the *Wende* instead of presenting an all-inclusive programme for change.

As mentioned earlier, in 1971 church and state had reached a compromise on the nature of their relationship through the formula of 'The Church in Socialism', and the SED had recognised the legitimacy of the Evangelical church as an institution. Both sides gained from this compromise: political pressure upon the church was reduced, and the SED gained greater domestic and international legitimacy for the GDR. Although an uneasy compromise, it nevertheless worked reasonably well up until 1978.

In that year two seemingly unrelated events occurred. First of all, on 6 March there was the aforementioned meeting between Honecker and Bishop Schönherr of the BEK. The meeting signalled the extent of the rapprochement between church and state in more than a symbolic way. Between 26 and 28 May the Saxon *Landeskirche* held its quadrennial *Kirchentag* in Leipzig. For the first time in years the church was allowed publicly to display material which advertised its existence and activities to the general public. In retrospect the spring of 1978 can be viewed as the high point of church–state relations, for in the autumn of the same year the SED announced the introduction of *Wehrkunde* into the GDR's schools. The church was powerless to stop what it saw as the incursion of the military into a forum where it had no right to be. Yet the SED's obstinacy was to have unforeseen consequences.

It was in November 1978 that one of the first actions of public protest against the SED's defence and related policies occurred in the Leipzig district of Plagwitz, when a placard appeared outside a church-owned building protesting against such policies. The response of the state was swift, albeit fairly low-key. During a meeting with the civil authorities on 23 November the Plagwitz parish priest, pastor Fritzsche, together with other like-minded members of the clergy, were told that their views would be best expressed through the state-sponsored 'Working parties of Christian groups'. The diplomatic reply from the clerics was that they were unsure of the efficacy of such institutions. In retrospect, this event can be seen as having lit the slow-burning fuse which ignited the eventual explosive showdown between church and state in the GDR.

We have already alluded to the renewed arms race as having been a factor in the gradual deterioration of church–state relations. Indeed, it was the December 1979 'dual-track' decision of Nato to station Cruise and Pershing-2 missiles which provided a major stimulus for both church-based oppositional activity in the GDR, and a consequent further deterioration of church–state relations. On 9 November 1980, the Evangelical church began its annual official 'Prayers for Peace' campaign. The slogan/symbol adopted by the participants was that of 'Swords into Ploughshares'. The decision to adopt this motif was deliberate: it was felt (erroneously as it turned out) that its association with the United Nations would cause the SED to act with circumspection *vis-à-vis* the campaign. Growing frustration among both practising Christians and non-Christian would-be dissidents at the renewed arms race, the nonimplementation of Basket Three of the Helsinki Accords and environmental damage in the GDR led previously isolated individuals to come together and cooperate on an increasingly regular basis.

These new dissident groups were concerned with precisely the topics which the SED was unwilling and unable either to compromise on or deal with in an imaginative way: peace and the environment, freedom to travel, education, military service, and the position of the church. One of the first dissident groups to be established was the 'Working Group on Environmental Questions', which was formed by a number of young Christians in the Leipzig area in the New Year of 1981. The group had been formed under the protective umbrella of the church, and attracted the immediate interest of the security services (Kaufmann et al. 1993). Yet, and this is significant here, the state was either unwilling or unable to eradicate such oppositional activity. Similarly, with regard to the 'Swords into Ploughshares' activists, the authorities demanded that display of this symbol be discontinued by the church-centred peace movement whose very existence alarmed them. These demands were initially ignored, and by 1983, a modus vivendi had been reached whereby unostentatious displays of the symbol, though not sanctioned, were tolerated.

The peace movement itself received a further boost when, in 1981, pastor Rainer Eppelmann of the Evangelical church in (East) Berlin launched his Berlin Appeal, in which he proclaimed the struggle for peace to be a civic duty. The Berlin Appeal is important to our study for two reasons. First, in common with the embryonic dissident movement which was operating under the protection of the church, pastor Eppelmann via the Appeal was calling for the church to oppose the state more clearly, and as such for a revision of the 'Church in Socialism' formula (Tismaneanu 1989: 90). Secondly, pastor Eppelmann's more assertive approach matched that of pastor Christian Führer based in Leipzig.

Pastor Führer was appointed to the *Nikolaikirche* in Leipzig in 1980. At this time the situation of the church in Leipzig *vis-à-vis* the putative dissident movement was already different from that which existed in other cities such as Erfurt and Dresden. Many of the senior clergy such as *Superintendent* Richter of the Evangelical church and *Probst* Hanisch of the Catholic church had known one another for many years. Good interpersonal relations in turn fostered a spirit of ecumenical cooperation which individuals such as Christian Führer were able to build upon (Hanisch 1993). As with pastor Eppelmann, pastor Führer translated his personal commitment to pacifism into public and practical action, and in so doing helped transform Leipzig into a centre of revolutionary change. From 1982, pastor Führer began to hold Monday prayers for peace in the *Nikolaikirche*. Until 1988 the prayer meetings constituted little more than an irritant for the state, given the small number of participants (Joppke 1993: 404). However, as will be shown, from 1988 these prayer meetings underwent a transformation, and became a focalpoint for both Christians and non-Christians alike. The common desire of both parties was to promote the renewal of society in the GDR.

In 1982 the *Nikolaikirche* was the only public forum available in Leipzig where open debate on the need for reform of the GDR could be discussed without fear of immediate arrest. The main themes were environmental and peace issues. Many young Christians were attracted to the idea of a 'third way' between Washington and Moscow, and were interested in the application of liberation theology in Nicaragua. This provided them with a degree of common ground with the largely leftist non-Christian dissidents. Yet we must acknowledge that the attitude of secular dissidents towards the church was primarily instrumental. The church was still the only institution in the GDR which had any autonomy from the party/state. This autonomy in turn helped to create an environment in which young Christians, and theology students in particular, developed a sociological and political critique of the SED's form of socialism (Bohse et al. 1990: 288). In effect, through these activities and debates, the church was returning to its ancient role of providing sanctuary from the civil authorities. For their part the church authorities expressed doubts about the opening-up of church premises to embryonic dissident groups. Yet they sought to pursue a flexible approach which would facilitate the growth of a climate of discussion. The experience of pastor Christian Führer is illustrative of the general state of affairs. Throughout the 1980s pastor Führer faced up to pressure coming from two seemingly opposite directions. The first was from the state which, particularly in the aftermath of the 'Star Wars' furore in 1984, was keener than ever to maintain the façade of societal unity. For their part the church authorities, in the guise of *Landesbischof* Hempel, were wary of pushing the state too far. Shortly after their inception in 1982, it was suggested by the authorities that the prayers for peace be moved to a less conspicuous site away from the city centre. Some of the church authorities were also unhappy when, in 1986, pastor Führer opened up his church to oppositional activists of all faiths and none. The example of pastor Führer's activities is instructive on two counts: first, it gives us a flavour of the activities and attitudes of pastors as individuals. Secondly, it illustrates the caution which typified the clerical authorities and which in August 1988 led the church leadership to issue a futile demand that nonreligious groups be banned from using church premises (Joppke 1990: 404).

At this juncture we should consider why the SED did not move to crush the activities of pastors such as Christian Führer and those who sought sanctuary within the church. By the late 1970s, the GDR and in particular cities such as Leipzig had become more open in the sense that there were more Western visitors coupled with a greater level of Western media penetration. In addition the GDR government had signed the Helsinki Accords in 1975 and in so doing had committed itself publicly to the maintenance of commonly agreed human rights. Whether the SED was serious in its intent is immaterial. More to the point is the fact that the unlikely (and uneasy) coalition of clergy and embryonic Citizens' Movement was determined to end violations of international accords to which the SED had expressed its adherence in its own media. By the same token the SED was eager to avoid actions which might interrupt the mini-*détente* between the GDR and the Federal Republic which, for the SED, had as its ultimate prize Erich Honecker's state visit to Bonn in September 1987.

Throughout the 1980s in Leipzig and elsewhere the state played its game of cat-and-mouse with the proponents of reform. More importantly, as the decade drew to a close the ramifications of the advent of Mikhail Gorbachev became ever clearer to all who had a direct stake in the future of the Soviet bloc. The SED found itself to be incapable of making a positive response to the policies of renewal espoused by the new Soviet leadership. Ultimately what was at stake in Germany was not only the capacity of the SED to rule as it saw fit, but also the continued existence of the GDR as a state.

The Evangelical church was also struggling to come to terms with the changed situation. With the balance of power in the GDR being undermined from within the Soviet Union itself, the relationship between church and state in the GDR was being called into question. At the 1987 synod of the Evangelical church in Görlitz, the applicability of the 'Church in Socialism' formula was questioned. Debate centred around the issue of whether the church should pursue a path of critical solidarity with a regime that was unwilling to respond to the challenge of societal renewal (Kaufmann 1993: 24). Indeed, it has been argued that from the end of 1987 the Evangelical church as an institution began to assume for itself an overtly sociopolitical role, which reached its zenith in November 1990 (Grabner et al. 1990: 26).

By the late 1980s the Evangelical church was facing increasing pressure from two separate and opposing forces. On the one hand, the dissident groups which the church had nurtured were demanding that the church be less circumspect in its dealings with the state. On the other, the state was putting increasing pressure on both the church as an institution and on individual pastors to disown and rein-in the opposition.

The catalyst for change appears to have come in January 1989. On 12 January in Leipzig the security forces arrested a total of eleven dissidents who were planning to distribute leaflets on 15 January at the annual (official) commemoration of the deaths of Karl Liebknecht and Rosa Luxemburg in 1919. All of the arrested were connected with dissident groups which met at the *Lukaskirche* in Leipzig. Despite the efforts of the authorities, the unauthorised action did go ahead with between 150 and 200 people gathering in the centre of Leipzig. A total of fifty-three of the demonstrators were arrested, and none other than Erich Mielke, the head of the

Stasi, recommended that both *Landesbischof* Hempel and *Superintendent* Magirius of the East Leipzig diocese be informed of the consequences to the church if it continued to offer support to such individuals (Mitter and Wolle 1990: 10–12). The result was not the one intended by Mielke. By way of protest at the actions of the state in Leipzig and elsewhere, vigils for the arrested were held in Evangelical churches in over thirty towns and cities throughout the GDR.

A change in the mood of the wider population now began to sweep through the GDR. The *Nikolaikirche* in concert with other Evangelical churches in Leipzig acted as a beacon for the ever-larger and ever-more disparate groups of people who sought a resolution to the crisis consuming the GDR. As the Citizens' Movement gathered strength, so it gradually distanced itself from the church. It also assumed a qualitatively different character as it began to mobilise the previously apolitical mass of society. As for the church itself, it appeared to go from strength to strength. The first of the Monday demonstrations in Leipzig occurred on 13 March 1989, when around 300 mostly would-be migrants attempted to march from the *Nikolaikirche* to the nearby *Thomaskirche*. The SED, rather than entering into dialogue, continued to behave as if nothing was amiss. To compound the worsening situation, the results of the local elections in May were falsified. This action was completely counter-productive, and had the effect of reaffirming the relationship between the church and the Citizens' Movement (Grabner et al. 1990). However, it was the decision that month of the Hungarian government to relax controls on Hungary's border with Austria, and the consequent mass flight of GDR citizens, that was finally to bring matters to a head.

With the inter-German border becoming an increasing irrelevance and the SED in disarray, the demonstrations gradually became bigger and more widespread over the summer months. Following large demonstrations in East Berlin, which had been broken-up by the security services, the breakthrough came following the mass demonstration in Leipzig on Monday 9 October 1989. On that night, approximately 70,000 people protested against the policies of the SED, with around 5,000 taking part in simultaneous prayers for peace in the *Nikolai, Thomas, Michaelis* and *Reformierte Kirche*. The local authorities, recognising that the protest movement was representative of various social forces (*Friede und Freiheit* No. 6: 1990), offered to enter into dialogue with the church and the Citizens' Movement. With that, political power in the GDR finally and decisively began to ebb away from the SED (Kaufmann et al. 1993: 25). By this time most other Evangelical churches such as the *Thomaskirche* had opened their doors to the reform movement as had the main Roman Catholic and Calvinist churches in the city (Magirius 1990: 99). Regardless of whether the demonstrators desired reform or simply wanted to leave the country, or even wished for the destruction of the GDR as a state, those who protested did so under the aegis of the church. Just as Leipzig stood coequal with East Berlin as the focus of this revolutionary movement, increasingly the churches as institutions came to serve as a focus for the aspirations of the people. Despite this, the churches as institutions, together with prelates as individuals, were wary of becoming too closely identified with any one particular party. Rather, the churches sought to act as facilitators in the establishment of plural political institutions (Grabner et al. 1990: 28). As a consequence, to this date there is still debate over the extent to which the influence of either church or clergy was decisive in the process of change which overtook the GDR in 1989/90 (Cordell 1990b; Lease 1992).

The Protestant Dimension

Although the influence of the clergy is undeniable, the *Wende* cannot be interpreted as having been a Protestant revolution. Christian Führer himself has publicly acknowledged that the church was at one level simply part of a broad coalition, united in a common desire to promote change (Führer 1990a). For him the church was the only organisation that was capable of affording the necessary protection to dissident groups, secular or otherwise. According to pastor Führer, the initial momentum for change had been created by the Gorbachev reforms, and the church responded according to its Christian mission (Führer 1990b). The point has also been made that many of the original peace and environmental groups that began to emerge in the early 1980s were never *of* the church as such, but rather were based around it (Noack 1990: 20). To both students and casual observers of the GDR, such statements should come as no surprise. Neither should the attitude of Jochen Lässig, one of the co-founders of *Neues Forum* in Leipzig, who has characterised the initial alliance of the dissident groups with the church as being one of necessity (Lässig: 1990). Moreover, relations between the Citizens' Movement and those who wished to leave the GDR and also sought the sanctuary of the church were even less close.

Nevertheless, a shared commitment to democratisation by both the church and the Citizens' Movement was evidenced by their role in the 'Round Tables' which sprang up in late 1989, and played a prominent, albeit ephemeral, role in the democratisation of GDR society (Grabner et al. 1990: 27). Moreover, the view has been expressed from within the church itself that the main credit for the *Wende* lies with those ordinary people who eventually took to the streets in the autumn of 1989. Such individuals had little interest in the churches' spiritual mission, and their involvement in the *Wende* signalled both the changing natures of the revolution and the gradual marginalisation of the church from the process. The church, having so performed its role, has since early 1990 retreated to its previous somewhat marginal position (Hänisch 1993). One fact does, however, remain clear. It was the actions of those such as Christian Führer which transformed Leipzig into the fulcrum of the *Wende*. At this time within the leading circles of the SED there were some who were willing to contemplate the use of military might, particularly in October 1989. Without the part played by Christian Führer and other members of the clergy, the *Wende* would have taken another, almost certainly bloodier, course.

In the Wake of the *Wende*

Thus far we have established that the Evangelical church in Leipzig, in common with other religious organisations throughout the GDR, suffered from a large degree of official discrimination. We have also offered some observations as to why Leipzig served as a focus for the *Wende*, and the role of the church and church personnel in the promotion of change. However, what is of real interest some time on from the unification of Germany is the current role of the Evangelical church in Leipzig and elsewhere in East Germany. There are many superficial similarities between East German cities such as Leipzig and their West German counterparts. Such similarities are matched by an all-round retreat of the church from the political sphere within which it had briefly been of such importance.

Before undertaking such an examination, a few words on the organisational structures of the Evangelical church are appropriate. The East and West German Evangelical churches were formally reunited within the *Evangelische Kirche Deutschlands* on 1 July 1991 (Beckley et al. 1994: 173). Since 1975, the Evangelical church in Leipzig has been divided into two dioceses: Leipzig East and Leipzig West. From 1975 Leipzig West has been headed by *Superintendent* Johannes Richter. Between 1982 and 1995, Leipzig East was headed by *Superintendent* Friedrich Magirius, who played a pivotal role in negotiations with the authorities during the *Wende*. However, at the time of writing (December 1996), the post is vacant. Below each *Superintendent* stand fifty-four pastors who administer to a total of thirty-seven individual parishes, and above them all stands the *Landesbischof.*

Given the destruction of the GDR, and the political principles and structures that sustained it, there has been much debate on whether or not there should be a reorganisation of the internal structures of the church. Although there have been various proposals to alter the structures in the wake of unification, partly because the current system functions reasonably well, and partly because of internal church politics, there have as yet been no major changes.

Sceptics would perhaps argue that the churches have once more been edged towards the sidelines of political life and that despite their multifarious social functions and charitable works, they cannot be considered to be major actors in civil society. Such a view might appear to be vindicated by an examination of the degree of religious devotion evinced by the inhabitants of Leipzig. As of 1994 the Evangelical church possessed 67,762 members, from a total population of 481,120. In other words, only 14 per cent of the wider population declared themselves to be affiliates of the church. The number of communicants for 1994 represents a fall of over 64,000 from an estimated 132,000 parishioners in 1991 (*Stadt Leipzig* 1995). Whilst the 1991 estimate is almost certainly too high, no-one disputes that the church is suffering from a continued seepage of support (*Der Sonntag* 29 January 1996). With over 80 per cent of the population having declared themselves as having no religious affiliation, the remaining percentage of believers is split between a number of other denominations, such as the Roman Catholic, Methodist and Reformed churches (Hänisch 1993). Moreover, not all the Evangelical churches' communicants actually pay the church tax. Overall these figures indicate that for a large majority of the citizens of Leipzig the churches are organisations with which they do not identify. However, the view has also been expressed by some prelates that despite the drop in the number of communicants, the Evangelical church in particular is active in community affairs and hence is in reasonable health. From this perspective, what has altered above all is media interest in the church. With Leipzig no longer being a motor for revolutionary change, the consequent lack of media interest results in outsiders gaining the impression that Leipzig has undergone a rapid process of secularisation (Richter 1993). We shall return to this theme later, but at present we can note that evidence for the existence of a living church may be considered through examination of its activities and social standing, and not simply through the examination of a set of statistics.

Although the figures quoted in the previous paragraph may not fully represent the number of practising Christians in Leipzig, there is no reason to dispute them as not being representative of the number of communicants. Interestingly enough, in the months following unification, the numbers who initially paid the (new) church tax in this historically overwhelmingly Protestant city comprised some 30 per cent of the adult population. Why then this initial surge of enthusiasm? And why was the church unable to build upon its earlier success? As we have already noted, the Evangelical church above all others, via the action of some of its prelates, gained a great deal of kudos during the *Wende*. However, the euphoria that surrounded unification has long since dissipated in the sometimes painful transition towards the introduction of an alien socioeconomic and political system. The surge of interest in the church was consequent partly upon admiration for individual pastors, and partly upon the role which the churches played in the destruction of SED rule. Given that the immediate expectations of the benefits that unification would bring were unrealistic, it is of no real surprise that the church has suffered from the backlash that unfulfilled expectations have brought.

The Impact of Secularisation

During the momentous events of 1989/90 it was easy for the casual observer to gain the impression that East Germany was as religious a society as Poland. Nothing could be further from the truth. The influence of the church in East Germany, as in much of Europe, has been on the wane for decades (Gross 1990: 34). The aforementioned lack of parishioners is not solely or even primarily a consequence of the *Wende*. Structural explanations have more to offer. We need also to be aware of two phenomena which have contributed to the reduced role of the church in public affairs. The first of these is the fact that the church is no longer the primary or sole repository of alternative ideas in a uni-ideological state. The second is that the church exists within a secularised society and did so prior to the *Wende*. It is now apparent that, in effect, the SED inadvertently created a set of circumstances which allowed the church to exercise an influence over society which was disproportionate to its real strength. Indeed, as soon as it became clear in the autumn of 1989 to the previously apolitical mass of society that real change could be effected, the influence of the church began to wane. Once the issue was transformed from a question of how to achieve the democratisation of the GDR, into one of how best to unify Germany, so the church began to lose stature (Beckley et al. 1994: 171). The most important ramification of this change in direction was the fact that East German society has had spontaneously to develop the social supports which are necessary in order for liberal democracy to flourish. Despite the fact that prior to the *Wende* organisations such as the *Kulturbund* were able to develop initiatives that did not fully conform to the dogmas of the SED, civil society as understood in the old Federal Republic simply did not exist in the GDR (Schorlemmer 1992: 369). The church had been important in nourishing the first flourishing of the seeds of a civic culture. With the rush for instant wealth under way, the ramifications for the structure of East German society that unification would have were all but ignored.

With the formal transition to liberal democracy accomplished, the church finds itself further reduced in status. The remaining politically motivated and socially interested groups and individuals now have alternative ways of expressing their dissatisfaction with the prevailing status quo. They no longer need to express their discontent either by seeking sanctuary within the church, or by using it as a protective umbrella. The church had gained a position of relative privilege in the GDR as a result of its explicit acceptance of the SED's right to rule. In the period of transition from GDR to Federal Republic, the church became one of the myriad organisations which existed within what some commentators see as a poorly developed civil society. Alongside pressure groups, political parties and the media, it stands as an alternative frame of reference to the orthodoxies of the day, but now it is simply one voice among many.

Nevertheless, it would be wrong to consider the church as ever having constituted a unified ideological monolith. From as early as the autumn of 1989 it became apparent that both pastors and prominent lay figures had differing ideological perspectives. Thus Rainer Eppelmann took *Demokratischer Aufbruch*, which had originally been considered to be part of the Citizens' Movement, into the *Allianz für Deutschland*, Wilhelm Ebeling entered the right-of-centre *Deutsche Sozial Union*, and others such as Manfred Stolpe and Markus Meckel joined the Social Democrats. There has been a debate within the Evangelical church over the extent to which some of these ideological positions are actually compatible with the church's theology (Punge 1990: 54). Yet it is also reasonable to argue that a church founded on the idea of tolerance should be able to cater for differing ideological positions. It is also plausible to suggest that the flowering of democracy in East Germany during the *Wende* helped to nurture this diversity of views within the church. We should not however, delude ourselves into thinking that the pews have suddenly emptied because 'actually existing socialism' has fallen by the wayside. As we mentioned earlier, we need also to take into account the phenomenon of secularisation.

Leipzig, like so many cities in Northern and Western Europe, is essentially a secularised city. How then has this process come about? Part of the answer lies in the rule of the SED, which sought to eradicate the churches' influence through a combination of threat, force and stealth, in order to create an atheistic society. Unsurprisingly, given the dissemination and weight of atheistic propaganda, coupled with the police actions of the state, links between the church and its communicants became somewhat loosened during the years of SED rule. However, this effect was not uniformly felt throughout the former Marxist-Leninist world, as was most vividly demonstrated in Poland. Neither have such heavily secularised countries as Sweden and The Netherlands ever fallen under the sway of a Marxist-Leninist party. These latter examples demonstrate that secularisation is not contingent solely upon the experience of Marxist-Leninist rule. This indicates, in turn, that SED rule was in itself only partially responsible for the current state of affairs. We need now to identify the other main causes of secularisation. The answer would appear to be fairly simple. Over the past two hundred years or so, Leipzig has in many senses been no different from any other predominantly Protestant city in Northern and Western Europe. In the wake of the Enlightenment, industrialisation and urbanisation, belief systems based around religious faith have been replaced by secular ideologies. Except in isolated areas such as the *Vogtland*, the *Eichsfeld* and the *Erzgebirge*, the church in Leipzig as elsewhere in Eastern Germany had essentially become a church of the middle classes by the middle of the nineteenth century (Richter 1993). In Leipzig itself, the onset of widespread secularisation began during the period 1860–80, at precisely the time in which the city acquired an industrial base and witnessed the rapid growth of an urban-based, industrial working class. The churches failed to follow their flocks into this new and alien environment. By the time they did, the links had been broken, and their message was perceived as being out of step with either the needs or expectations of the working class (Sievers 1993).

The cumulative consequence of these factors is that today relatively few young people are being received into the church. It would also appear to be the case that in the absence of a religious revival, the number of communicants is set to decline, given the difficulty the church has in reaching children from secularised families. Although the churches are involved in a number of schools in Leipzig, there is only one denominational school. Religious instruction, even when taught in school, is available only as an option. There is a lack of teachers trained in religious education, and where such lessons are available they are often given by the laity. In many schools the main involvement of the church comes primarily through the staging of special exhibitions and at Christmas. On the other hand, the Evangelical church is conscious of its recent experience with the SED, and is wary of too close a relationship between church and state. As such it is opposed to the introduction of compulsory religious education in the state system. Such opposition does not, however, preclude conflict between the churches and the secular authorities concerning the role of religion in schools. Indeed, as of May 1996 no agreement had been reached between church and state on the form such education ought to take (*Der Sonntag* 14 April 1996).

Ironically, although the SED and GDR are extinct, approximately 40 per cent of young people in East Germany still take part in the *Jugendweihe* (coming of age) ceremony, thus demonstrating the extent to which secularisation has penetrated society at large. In fact in 1995 a post-*Wende* record was created when 86,000 East Germans went through the ceremony (*Die Zeit* 19 April 1996). Apart from anything else, this indicates the continued existence of a distinct value system among large sections of East German society. The church is at something of a disadvantage when it comes to combating the pressures brought upon it by secularisation. It is attempting to remedy the situation not only via the Christian example set by charitable work, and via the pulpit, but also by making use of the mass media.

Each *Landeskirche* publishes a weekly newspaper and a range of other publications and, since April 1991, *Sachsen-Radio* has broadcast a Sunday morning service and has devoted further sections of its Sunday schedules to issues of a religious orientation. In addition, the national terrestrial television networks broadcast a service every Sunday together with a range of religiously orientated programmes. Thus the written word is now complemented by the broadcast media. Turning to the youth of Leipzig (and East Germany in general), unsurprisingly we find that *die junge Gemeinde* (the young community) has been reformed. Despite the fact that members tend to be active rather than passive, given the general decline of organised youth movements, secular or otherwise, together with the more general onslaught of secularisation, the question as to what extent youth can be reached through *die junge Gemeinde* remains open.

We now need to ask how the church views this situation, and which functions the churches actually perform in Leipzig today. The activities undertaken in Leipzig may be taken as being indicative of the churches' activities in East Germany as a whole. We must also remember that the Evangelical church is increasingly subject to financial constraints. Here, the Saxon *Landeskirche* is better off than some others, and as such is able to perform a more comprehensive range of tasks.

These themes are inevitably entwined with the modus operandi of the churches themselves. No one church in a given city can in isolation do anything meaningful to reverse the process of secularisation. On the other hand, although the level of communicants is low, it may be argued that in contrast to the position of many West German Lutherans, membership of a church in Leipzig as elsewhere in East Germany can be seen as being a clear testament of faith. This applies also to the Reformed and Catholic congregations. It should not be forgotten that during the years of SED rule, for those who were not coopted via their membership of the CDU, maintaining a commitment to Christianity was in effect an act of opposition (Richter 1993).

Interestingly enough, the failure of the Evangelical church to gain a greater number of communicants, is not matched by similar problems in the sphere of social policy. The church continues to affirm its commitment to social and charitable work, especially in fields which are relatively new to East Germany, such as aid to the unemployed. On the other hand, the conditions under which such work is undertaken in Leipzig and the remainder of East Germany have undergone an obvious and radical change in the wake of unification. The most important change is that the political atmosphere is more conducive to the church performing such work than in the SED's day. This has led the churches to assume a more consistent public profile than they could ever attain during the years of Marxist-Leninist dominance. On the other hand, all such work must be carried out according to new standards imported from West Germany. This of itself necessitates greater capital expenditure on the part of churches, both Catholic and Protestant, that are not particularly wealthy in their own right (Hanisch 1993). The church must also work within a more commercial environment and alongside long-established relief and welfare agencies (based in West Germany), which may be better resourced and more professional in their techniques (Richter 1993).

Having noted the general environment within which the church performs its mission, let us now examine such work itself. The church organises religious activities such as Sunday schools, Bible classes and the like. It is also actively engaged in a number of ecumenical projects in Leipzig, Germany as a whole and throughout Europe (*Der Sonntag* 29 January 1996). To complement such work, the Evangelical church, often in partnership with the other major denominations, offers support networks to such groups as the unemployed, the handicapped, the homeless, pensioners, prisoners, and just about any other group that has found it difficult to compete in the free-market society currently under construction in East Germany. In Leipzig, the churches are particularly active in these fields.

By way of illustration we can highlight a project which, since 1991, has in south-west Leipzig provided day care for the elderly and infirm. Currently it is led by a trained nurse, who is assisted by a team of trainee nurses and young men who have opted for community service as an alternative to conscription. It is of interest to note that whereas such work is part of the churches' internal mission, each individual parish has a great deal of autonomy in deciding upon the nature and level of activity which it chooses to undertake. The church sets great store by the welfare work carried out by pastors, the laity and by volunteers, and sees the expansion of its welfare role since the *Wende* as being one of its main achievements. This is particularly true of the services provided to the elderly, and in the provision of *Kindergärten*. However, given financial constraints and a lack of trained personnel, such projects do not reach all who could benefit from them.

Finally, with regard to the churches' social work activities, we can note that in addition to providing services to the vulnerable, since 1996, and after much debate, the Evangelical church in East Germany has been offering pastoral care for members of the armed forces stationed in the former GDR (*Der Sonntag* 21 April 1996). Neither should we forget that such ecumenical activities have their lighter side. By way of example we can highlight the May 1996 street party in the Connewitz district of Leipzig, which was jointly organised by the local Evangelical and Catholic churches (*Der Sonntag* 14 April 1996). In addition, and in order to try and meet the needs of young people, the church also runs a number of youth clubs in and around Leipzig.

The Future: Constraints and Limitations

The direction in which the Evangelical and other churches proceed in the coming years is naturally of interest and importance but unfortunately also a matter of some speculation. Clearly a church without parishioners is not a church at all. Ultimately, a church derives its raison d'être above all from its missionary function (Hänisch 1993). Yet the various clerical, social and charitable functions performed by the church require finance. The churches also need funds for the maintenance of buildings, capital projects, and the payment of salaries. Ideally they should for the most part be financed from within the cities themselves. With only approximately 10 per cent of the population making regular financial contributions to the various churches, the bulk of the finance must come from external sources and by far the largest external source is, of course, West Germany.

It was acknowledged as early as 1990 that, with unification, the massive subventions from the EKD would cease to be given in the way in which they were whilst the church in East Germany laboured under the rule of the SED (Punge 1990: 107). The main worry is how long their West German counterparts will continue to dole out money to their poorer Eastern brethren without taking an active interest in how the money is spent. This is a matter about which the church in Leipzig is concerned (Hänisch 1993). The situation in other parts of East Germany is even worse, with Bishop Huber of the *Landeskirche* in Berlin-Brandenburg warning of a deficit of DM 92 million in the financial year 1996–97 (*Der Sonntag* 21 April 1996). Indeed, some quarters within the East German wing of the EKD feel that the relationship between the East and West German wings mirrors the overall pattern of relations between the two halves of Germany. In other words, they feel that they are living with the consequences of annexation rather than unification. Perhaps it was the acknowledgement of such concerns which led to Leipzig being chosen as the site of the Evangelical churches' 1997 *Kirchentag*, the first time Leipzig has staged this event since 1954.

The position of the Evangelical church in Leipzig, as elsewhere in East Germany, has greatly changed in recent years. In the space of six short years it has experienced much. From being a barely tolerated and marginalised institution in the GDR, the Evangelical church became above all, a tribune of the people during the *Gotterdämmerung* of that state and now it finds itself a legitimate member of the expanded Federal Republic, but once again somewhat towards the margins.

The hope expressed in some church circles that the process of democratisation which took place in West Germany after 1945 could be replicated in East Germany post-1989 has not as yet been realised. If the Evangelical church is to recover its fortunes and continue to contribute to the creation of civil society in East Germany, the task lies primarily with those clerics who faced down the threats of the SED throughout the 1980s. At one level they seem content to be out of the glare of publicity and able to continue with their religious and secular work. In order for prelates to re assume such a role they would first have to rid themselves of a certain air of melancholy and resignation that has taken root in recent years. Indeed for those who claim that the *Wende* began as a Protestant revolution aimed at Protestant renewal, disappointment with its consequences is most keenly felt. According to this perspective the revolution was in some way hijacked by the better resourced West German political parties who were then able, with the help of sympathisers from among the Citizens' Movement and the Evangelical church, to steer the revolution in a direction of their own choosing. It may well be true as, Manfred Punge has suggested, that 'the revolution devoured its fathers' (Punge 1990: 52).

At another level, both clerical and lay figures within the church are keenly aware of two problems which Leipzig shares with the rest of (East) Germany. The first is apathy born of disappointment. The second is hostility towards foreigners. Friedrich Schorlemmer among others has been prominent in highlighting the problems which confront East German society. He argues that East Germany has been transformed from being a society which was constantly subjected to pressures 'from above' into one which has new freedoms and responsibilities which it finds difficult to come to terms with. He goes on to describe a society which in some ways has been 'crippled' by years of dictatorship, a society which is keen to blame '*die da oben*' (those on high) for their problems as if decades of dictatorship had not been actively and passively supported or at least tolerated by ordinary people. Schorlemmer is also keen to point out that the naive materialism which enveloped the GDR's revolution was not simply the consequence of a refusal on the part of those who could have exercised responsibility to act in a responsible manner. Rather, West German business was all too keen to pander to the naivety of East Germans. The result has been the creation of widespread apathy, particularly among those who have felt the consequences of long-term unemployment. In short, in exchange for the D-

Mark, GDR society divested itself of what made it different from that which existed in the Federal Republic (Schorlemmer 1992: 357–61). The consequence has been apathy, alienation and nostalgia for an idealised picture of life that existed prior to the *Wende.*

Unsurprisingly, others have sought fundamentally anti-democratic solutions to these problems. Through the conjunction of a variety of factors, some of which may be located in the nature of the unification process, the radical right in Germany as a whole and especially in East Germany, assumed a greater public profile in the early 1990s (Richter 1990). Space does not permit us to examine this phenomenon in great depth, but the opinions of *Superintendent* Richter may be taken as being indicative of those of the Evangelical church as a whole. According to *Superintendent* Richter, the leftist authoritarianism of the SED paradoxically acted as an incubus for a latent right-wing authoritarianism. This was achieved through the creation of a thoroughly anti-democratic sociopolitical system which reinforced rather than challenged previous patterns of socialisation (Schorlemmer 1992: 361).

This anti-democratic culture was complemented by deliberate arrogance on the part of the SED, which from the 1980s was quick to point to the certainties of life in the GDR, as opposed to the disorder which characterised Poland and the Soviet Union. The inference was clear: that Slavs could not hope to compete with Germans. Such stereotyping simply served to act as an incubus to latent neo-Nazi sentiments within East German society which became all too apparent in Rostock, Hoyerswerda, and in numerous towns on the Polish border. Despite the long-established presence of non-Germans in the GDR, a semi-official policy of social apartheid meant that although Germans and non-Germans shared the same space, they lived alongside and not among one another. As a consequence both were strangers to one another. Many East Germans either did not understand that tolerance applied to all resident in the newly united Germany, or simply viewed and still view foreigners as a parasitic alien element.

The Evangelical church, together with other churches, has attempted to face up to these problems. They believe that they have an obligation through their religious and secular work to show that there is an alternative to the politics of illiberal nationalism or racial violence. For *Superintendent* Richter, as much as anything else the articulation of and support for fascism can be seen as a cry for help (Richter 1993). On the other hand, as indicated above, there are also deep-seated structural problems which need to be addressed.

Probst Hanisch has pointed out that what began as a demand for democratisation culminated in the demand for the D-Mark. In the absence of a thoroughgoing democratisation process and in the midst of disorientation, the radical right was able to make political capital, and the issue of negative stereotyping of immigrants and foreigners was side-stepped (Hanisch 1993). In the GDR, the SED claimed a leading role and a de facto monopoly on the truth. In turn, the certainties of life in the GDR have been replaced by the partially unanticipated uncertainties of the unification process. The problem is further compounded when those former figures of authority for young people such as schoolteachers, who for years eulogised the SED, suddenly reveal themselves to have been closet liberal-democrats. With credibility being stretched and social tensions coming to the fore, the radical right with its glib answers and appeal to *Machtpolitik* gains an audience (Sievers 1993). Although the extreme right has made little electoral impact, hostility towards foreigners remains commonplace. In the long run, the answers to such problems can only come from a much broader coalition of responsible social forces and not from the churches alone.

By way of conclusion we can note that ultimately the future of the churches in Leipzig (and elsewhere in East Germany) depends upon the ability of the clergy and laity to demonstrate the relevance of their faith to the remainder of society. In other words, to make the word of God relevant to people who are experiencing rapid and unexpected social change. Above all, this involves the churches in coming to terms with the fact that the church in civil society cannot hope or claim to represent all 'unofficial' interests (Punge 1990: 85). The Evangelical church, in concert with all other churches, must find ways of inculcating its values into a largely secular society. Given the nature of East German society, the challenge is formidable.

This piece is dedicated to the memory of Helga Kaufmann

References

Beckley, R. et al. 1994. 'Germany's Reconstruction: The Role of the Eastern German Church before and after Reunification', in W. Swatos jr., ed., *Politics and Religion in Central and Eastern Europe*. London, Praeger.

Bohse, R. et al. 1990. *Jetzt Oder Nie-Demokratie!*. Berlin, Forum Verlag.

Cordell, K. 1990a. 'The Role of the Evangelical Church in the GDR', *Government and Opposition*, vol.25, No.1, pp.48–59.

——. 1990b. 'Political Change in the GDR', *International Relations*, vol. 10, No.2, pp.161–66.

——. 1995. 'The Church: Coming to Terms with Change', in *Between Hope and Fear*. Keele, Keele University Press.

Elvers, W. and Findeis, H. 1990. 'Die politisch alternativen Gruppen im gesellschaftlichen Wandel', in W.J. Grabner et al., *Leipzig im Oktober*. Leipzig, Wichern-Verlag, pp.97–113.

Falkenau, M. 1990. 'Verspielte Erfahrungen?' in R. Schulze, ed., *Nach der Wende*, Berlin, Wichern-Verlag, pp.107–15.

Friede und Freiheit, No. 6, September 1990.

Führer, Christian. 1990a. Address given at the demonstration at the Großenstingen atomic weapons base, 8 April 1990.

——. 1990b. Interview with pastor Christian Führer, 4 May 1990.

Goeckel, R. 1990. *The Lutheran Church and the East German State*. London, Cornell University Press.

Grabner W.J., et al. 1990. *Leipzig im Oktober*. Leipzig, Wichern-Verlag.

Gross, J. 1990. *Begründung der Berliner Republik*. Stuttgart, Deutsche Verlags-Anstalt.

Hänisch, Gottfried. 1993. Interview with Pastor Hänisch, Head of the Evangelical Church Office for Community Service, 24 April 1993.

Hanisch, Günther. 1993. Interview with Probst Hanisch of the Catholic Church in Leipzig, 12 November, 1993.

Henkys, R. 1990. 'Die Kirchen im Umbruch der DDR', in W.J.Grabner et al., *Leipzig im Oktober*, Leipzig, Wichern-Verlag, pp.26–31.

Hildenbrandt J. and Thomas G., eds. 1990. *Unser Glaube mischt sich ein*, Berlin, Evangelische Verlaganstalt.

Joppke, C. 1993. 'Why Leipzig? "Exit" and "Voice" in the East German Revolution', *German Politics*, vol.2, No.3, pp.393–414.

Kaufmann, K. et al., ed. 1993. *Sorget nicht was ihr reden werdet*. Leipzig, Evangelische Verlaganstalt, draft manuscript.

Lässig, Jochen. 1990. Interview, 5 May 1990.

Lease, G. 1992. 'Religion, the Churches, and the German Revolution of November 1990', *German Politics*, vol.1, No.2, pp.264–73.

Magirius, F. 1990. 'Selig sind, die Frieden stiften', in J. Hildenbrandt and G. Thomas, eds., *Unser Glaube mischt sich ein*, Berlin, Evangelische Verlaganstalt, pp.92–99.

Mitter, A. and Wolle, S. eds. 1990. *Ich liebe euch doch alle! Befehle und Lageberichte des MfS; Januar–November 1989*. Berlin, Basis Druck.

Neubert, E. 1990. 'Die Revolution der Protestanten', in R. Schulze, ed., *Nach der Wende*. Berlin, Wichern-Verlag, pp.23–50.

Noack, A. 1990. 'Dauerregen auf das Kirchendach', in J. Hildenbrandt and G. Thomas, eds., *Unser Glaube mischt sich ein:*, Berlin, Evangelische Verlaganstalt, pp.12–21.

Nowak, K. 1992. At the Colloquium, Kirche-Staat-Gesellschaft-Opposition in der DDR, University of Leipzig, 14 June 1992.

Pollack, D. 1990. 'Die Ursachen des gesellschaftlichen Umbruchs in der DDR aus systemtheoretischer Perspektive', in W.J. Grabner et al., *Leipzig im Oktober*, Leipzig, Wichern-Verlag, pp.12–25.

Punge, M. 1990. 'Die Auflösung der real existierenden Denkfiguren', in R. Schulze, ed., *Nach der Wende*, Berlin, Wichern-Verlag, pp.51–68.

Richter, Johannes. 1993. Interview with Superintendent Richter of the West Leipzig diocese, 23 April 1993.

Schorlemmer, F. 1992. *Worte öffnen Fäuste*. München, Kindler Verlag.

Schulze, R., ed. 1990. *Nach der Wende*, Berlin, Wichern-Verlag.

Sievers, H.J. 1991. *Stundenbuch einer deutschen Revolution*. Göttingen, Vandenhoeck & Ruprecht.

——. 1993. 'Kirche des Volkes bleiben', interview with pastor Hans-Jurgen Sievers of the Reformed Church in Leipzig, 12 November 1993, .

Der Sonntag, 29 January 1996.

Der Sonntag, 14 April 1996.

Der Sonntag, 21 April 1996.

Stadt Leipzig.1995. *Statistisches Jahrbuch 1995*. Leipzig.

Tismaneanu, V. 1989. 'Nascent Civil Society in the German Democratic Republic'. *Problems of Communism*, March/June, pp.90–111.

Die Zeit, 19 April 1996.

CHAPTER 3

The Fortunes of GDR Civil Rights Groups and Opposition Movements since the *Wende*

Detlef Pollack

I. Preliminary Remarks

Members of the civil rights groups in former East Germany have often been characterised as the whining losers of the *Wende*: losers who, let down by the dramatic disintegration of their movement, have withdrawn to sulk in their corner, disheartened and still dreaming of an illusionary 'third way' between socialism and capitalism. The truth is not as simple as that. Indeed, significant transformations have taken place within the civil rights and other alternative groups in eastern Germany since unification, and these changes have resulted in sharp differences in the political standpoints of their members. Of course, many of them still cling to their past ideals, to the notion of a fair and egalitarian society, and when they appear in public they do not miss the opportunity to proclaim their dissatisfaction with the constitutional state, with parliamentary democracy or with society's way of dealing with the GDR past. But the majority of civil rights advocates, who are not heard often in public, have long since decided to give their support to parliamentary democracy, even though they may not have abandoned their old ideals and believe that many aspects of this democracy may be in need of improvement. Others even criticise the moralising political stance taken by some of their former fellow activists and have become militant advocates of party democracy.

There is no denying the fact that members of the civil rights and alternative groups found adjustment to the new social system probably more difficult than any other group of GDR citizens, with the possible exception of the hard-line regime supporters. There are two main reasons for this. First of all, unification removed the very object of the civil rights activists' political activity: the GDR itself. What they wanted was to reform the GDR, not to get rid of it. Much like the hard-core supporters of the system, they had made the GDR the central focus of their lives, and after the country had ceased to exist they too had to adjust to its disappearance. The political aims they had pursued for years were suddenly fulfilled, robbing them not only of their political function, but also of their exceptional political status. And secondly, the fall of the Berlin Wall, and the unification process thus set in motion, brought about a restriction in the range of possibilities for action previously open to East German activists. In view of the claim to self-determination which civil rights activists had maintained for themselves over the years in defiance of the patronising bent of the GDR system, they were particularly affected by the fact that the unification process soon gained a momentum of its own. Many of them were upset that this process was taking place outside their control and following a direction which was not the one they had intended.

In spite of these problems of adjustment, civil rights groups and citizens' action committees have now undergone such major changes that the image of a small, desperate herd of '*Wende* losers' publicised by the media can no longer be sustained. In this chapter I shall describe these transformations. I will start with a discussion of the 'objective' transformations within citizens' action committees and opposition groups: changes in their organisational structures, their programmes, their ability to mobilise (part II). I will then look at the 'subjective' transformations, changes in the attitudes of the members of citizens' committees and opposition groups (part III). The empirical basis for my observations is a survey of thirty one former leading representatives of politically alternative groups in East Berlin and Leipzig, which I carried out early in

1990 with the help of a group of students,[1] and which I repeated after two and five years with the same interview partners. The first two meetings were fixed-question-open-response interviews lasting between 45 and 90 minutes, while the last consisted of shorter questioning lasting from 10 to 20 minutes. I have also based my research on a number of interviews with experts in administration carried out between late 1993 and mid-1995 in Leipzig.[2]

II. 'Objective' changes

In order to describe the 'objective' transformations which took place amongst activist groups, it would seem a good idea to look at the various phases involved.[3]

1. The Informality Phase

Up to the summer of 1989, politically alternative peace groups, environmental groups and human rights groups in the GDR were operating on an informal level, outside the official system. As they were stigmatised as enemies of socialism, an important condition for their political survival was to ensure that the degree of their organisational structure was kept to a minimum. Another was the legal protection and the public forum provided by the Lutheran Church. Even though the groups were kept as loosely structured as possible, their organisation still involved a certain amount of division of tasks, hierarchies, networks, et cetera. There were spokespersons, there were leaders, even leading groups – for instance the 'Umweltbibliothek' (Environmental Library) or the 'Initiative Frieden und Menschenrechte' (Initiative for Peace and Human Rights). Many of the groups were regional (in Leipzig, for instance, in the Regional Lutheran Synod Committee), others supraregional but topic-based (arche, INKOTA). During the 1980s, delegates from such groups throughout the country met yearly for the 'Frieden konkret' (Peace in Practice) seminar; but when a suggestion was made at one such meeting in February 1989 to create a GDR-wide umbrella association, the delegates baulked at this. Not only did they want to remain below the confrontation threshold *vis-à-vis* state authorities: they also wanted to retain their autonomy from each other. It was important for them that the way they handled their inter-group relationship now should reflect their aspirations for society as a whole: an autonomous, egalitarian way of life based on mutual understanding, with solidarity between all. From this point of view it could be said that their political commitment was fed on a pre-political, strongly community-based philosophy.

Although the groups were constantly concerned with winning the attention of the general public, their ability to mobilise was extremely slight. Contact with them meant certain social exclusion. As a result, the general public's opinion of the groups was characterised by defensiveness, fear and insecurity. The distance between them was based more on sociocultural than on political factors: in a society where behaviour was dictated by the positive value placed on inconspicuousness and compliance with petty bourgeois standards of normality, the groups were rejected in part because of their eccentric style of self-representation. But then it was paradoxically this very tendency to spectacular behaviour that made them better-known. Indeed, in the homogeneous official political culture of the GDR, it was easy for them to draw public attention to their actions. To mobilise both the police and the interest of Western media, all they had to do was to stand in front of a church holding candles or to unfurl a poster.

2. The Formative Phase

When the border between Hungary and Austria was opened in early September 1989, allowing a freer flow of emigrants, the civil rights activists left the protective cover of the church and re-grouped into official civil rights organisations such as 'Neues Forum' (New Forum), 'Demokratie Jetzt' (Democracy Now) and 'Demokratischer Aufbruch' (Democratic Departure). Hundreds and thousands rushed to join 'Neues Forum', the first of the new opposition groups. As Lothar Probst so vividly demonstrated for Rostock (Unterberg 1991: fn. 3, 117ff.), and Peter Unterberg for Leipzig (Unterberg 1991: 85ff.), the sudden mass popularity of 'Neues Forum' was too much for the organisational capabilities of the movement's initiators. They called for the creation of district, work- and issue-based groups, but were unable to coordinate their activities. In fact, the groups were rather left to themselves in their various initiatives.

What the citizens' groups felt was imperative in the autumn of 1989 was to create openness, democracy and pluralism.

They defined their programme as democratic, ecological and social. Economic considerations played no more than a minor role in their considerations, if they were heeded at all. The only exception in this respect was the SPD: from the start, it acknowledged its endorsement of the principles of a social market economy. This underestimation of the economic aspects of the process of social transformation carried the seeds of a preconditioned conflict which would eventually have a lasting influence on the fate of the citizens' rights movements: the conflict with the economic interests of the majority of the population.

In the autumn of 1989, however, the rift between civil rights activists and the general public was not yet openly visible. The activists were viewed as the leaders of the mass movement. It must be remembered, however, that the politically alternative groups and the civil rights movements that grew out of them neither organised the mass demonstrations nor called for participation in them. In fact, some of them explicitly refused to shoulder responsibility for them (Unterberg 1991: fn. 4, 89). It was not the civil rights groups who were the initiators of the mass protest movement, but the other way round: the civil rights groups, first and foremost 'Neues Forum', were pushed by the masses to the front lines of the movement and made into the symbol of resistance. The movement itself developed spontaneously (Opp and Voss 1993: 77ff.). What really fuelled its growth was the fact that the mass exodus via Hungary had exposed the crisis within the system for everyone to see, and that in view of the one-sidedness of the distribution of political power, no one else but the leaders of the system could be made responsible for this crisis. This clear accountability had a consolidating effect between the groups and the masses. But the distinction must be made between the mass protest movement and the civil rights movement: although the mass movement associated itself with the opposition groups because these were known as critics of the system, the groups, necessary as their catalytic function may have been for the mass protest movement, did not give birth to it. For this reason, Karl-Werner Brand's question as to how 'a torrential flow of democratic mass movements could grow out of the thin trickle of spied upon, harassed and repressed opposition groups in such a short time' (Brand 1990: 10), is wrongly formulated. It was not a thin trickle becoming a torrential flow, but the torrential flow which, because of the mounting pressure within the system and the sudden exit option, brought down the dam put up by the Party, the state security apparatus and the police, swept the thin trickle along with it and parted from it again when it became obvious that the currents were flowing in different directions.[4]

3. The Differentiation and Marginalisation Phase

This phase began after the fall of the Berlin Wall and continued until the elections to the East German Parliament in March 1990. In the face of open borders between East and West and the approaching prospect of German unification, the civil rights groups, after November 1989, began developing separate identities in terms of their organisational structures and programmes. Some of the differences in programmes and personalities, it must be said, had already existed prior to the onset of this phase. 'Demokratischer Aufbruch', the SDP, the Green Party and the Forum Party became political parties, while large segments of 'Neues Forum', 'Initiative Frieden und Menschenrechte', 'Demokratie Jetzt' and other groups avoided party-political structures. This process of organisational and structural differentiation led to an enormous decrease in membership and to shifts of allegiances between the groups. Gains were made by the SDP, the CDU and the FDP, while 'Neues Forum' suffered considerable losses. In spite of diminished membership and the loss of public sympathy for the civil rights groups which set in during the weeks following the opening of the Wall, the activists scored their most significant political victory *vis-à-vis* the SED with the establishment of the Round Table at the beginning of December 1989. The Round Table itself soon became a controlling body for the government. Nevertheless, the civil rights activists were not ready to take over the government: irrespective of whether or not they would have been in a concrete position to do so, they were hampered by their inability to come to terms with the concept of political power.

Discussions within the civil rights groups between November 1989 and March 1990 involved two sets of problems: the organisational and structural issues linked to the adoption of party structures, and the question of German unity. Many supporters of 'Neues Forum' were in favour of a grass-roots form of politics, shaped by the direct participation of the people involved, bypassing political parties and associations and acting as a direct link between the individual and society. The advocates of this type of politics from below promoted a harmonistic political concept and viewed politics primarily as a form of discussion aimed at achieving a broad consensus. They based their concept of politics, dispensing with intermediary organisations and functional divisions, on the experiences they had had at the time of the *Wende* (Wielgohs 1993: fn. 2, 429). Thus politics for them continued to be something to be shaped by committed citizens and not by political parties who – in their opinion – were concerned primarily with the assertion of their own interests. Others considered this view of politics to be unrealistic, were opposed to any experiments and in favour of adopting the concept of parliamentary democracy which had proved its worth until then in the Western part of Germany.

As to the question of national unity, statements made by a number of prominent civil rights activists, in particular Bärbel Bohley, gave rise to the impression that a majority within the civil rights movements were in favour of retaining two states within Germany. The opponents of unification criticised in particular the market economy, which they described as 'dog-eat-dog', and the consumer society. They feared that people would only be interested in improving their standard of living and that they would repress the need to confront political and social problems. Gradually, however, supporters of unity gained the upper hand,[5] arguing that it would have been wrong for the activists to discredit the will of the people and place themselves above the people.

The civil rights groups did agree on one aim: the need to refute the ever re-emerging claims to power of the SED-PDS (Socialist Unity Party of Germany / Party of Democratic Socialism). This common enemy functioned as a uniting force for the civil rights groups and led to the formation, on 3 January 1990, of 'Wahlbündnis 90', an electoral alliance of political interests with the aim of replacing the political forces which had been in power until then.

In spite of falling numbers and loss of public support, the civil rights groups were still able to mobilise the masses up to the spring of 1990. 'Neues Forum' organised citizens' meetings, so-called 'dialogue evenings' and issue-based forum discussions, and thousands came. In early 1990, pressure from citizens' action committees put a moratorium on the demolition of old buildings and on the construction of new ones in the inner city of Leipzig. In March 1990, the mayor of Rostock resigned after a protest demonstration of 10,000 citizens called by 'Neues Forum'. At this time, protests, round tables and other forms of direct democracy were still effective instruments of political activity. In actual fact, however, the civil rights groups were already marginalised to a considerable extent. On the one hand, this marginalisation was the result of the groups' hesitation *vis-à-vis* the prospect of a rapid unification of Germany, but it was also due to their lack of interest in economic issues. The situation was exacerbated by internal dissent within the civil rights groups and by the activists' moralising political style. After forty years of Communist Party domination, GDR citizens had lost patience with all forms of politics based on ideology. And besides, the civil rights groups' programmes, which had been aimed at reforming socialism in the GDR, had become obsolete after the fall of the Wall. From this point onwards, in the opinion of the interviewees, the civil rights groups could do no more than lag behind the development of events.

4. The Fourth Phase: Institutionalisation, Specialisation and Demobilisation

The development of the civil rights groups between the GDR parliamentary elections in March 1990 and today can be summarised under the headings 'institutionalisation', 'specialisation' and 'demobilisation'. Within this period, the accession of the GDR into the Federal Republic in October 1990 marked one particularly clear division, and significant restructuring processes have been at work since 1993; however, it can also be argued that the three general tendencies span both of these turning-points.

The first democratic elections in East Germany in March 1990 accelerated the existing trend towards institutionalisation within the citizens' committees and civil rights movements. Round Tables and protest demonstrations as political models were running out of steam: it was becoming less and less possible to exert direct influence on political decision making with these instruments. The various political options were now represented by democratically elected institutions in proportion to their electoral success. 'Bündnis 90' (Alliance 90) held seats in the East German 'Volkskammer' (People's Chamber); after unification in October 1990, an exception was made to normal parliamentary law to enable it to be represented in the 'Bundestag' (Federal Parliament). Up until 1994, it was also represented in all East German state parliaments, with the exception of Mecklenburg-Western Pomerania, where the electoral alliance between 'Neues Forum', 'Bündnis 90' and the Greens did not get off the ground. And, of course, it was active on a municipal level, for instance in the municipal councils of Rostock, Potsdam and Leipzig.[6] In Leipzig, a considerable number of positions in the municipal administration are still held by people having political roots in the civil rights movement. Due to the continuing drop in membership throughout 1990, the parliamentarisation of the civil rights groups resulted in a diminution at grass-roots level. But whilst the mass basis of the civil rights movement was being eroded, a wave of small project groups and citizens' committees, involving the most diverse topics, started to build up.

In consequence of the introduction of West German law in the autumn of 1990, these project groups soon found it advantageous to become official associations: once a group was set up as a registered association, the law now gave it the right to participate in job-creation programmes. As mounting unemployment made these programmes critically necessary, and because the Federal Employment Agency was generous in granting funds for these jobs, new associations sprouted like mushrooms in the course of 1990/91. Consequently, the people involved in the citizens' committees and associations were no longer just the politically motivated representatives of the civil rights movements: many were paid employees who had had relatively little to do with the civil rights movement until then. Moreover, the mass of jobs created by the job programmes meant a shift from mostly volunteer participation in the committees and associations to paid employment within the same groups. State subsidies are tied to the condition that an association must have an official statute and be defined as non-profit-making. Furthermore, an association can survive only if its officers are familiar with the way subsidies are structured and with qualified accountancy. These conditions, with the introduction of West German law, have forced the various associations to become more institutionalised, more professional and more mindful of economic factors.

With increasing institutionalisation, the citizens' action committees and associations clearly streamlined the issues they dealt with. While, in the spring of 1990, the dominant issues still tended to be those of educational reform, demilitarisation of society or the drafting of a new constitution, efforts soon centred only on the realisation of concrete projects. Since then, the various groups have been dealing with a great variety of issues: there are environmental groups, women's groups, borough initiatives, associations for social work, educational associations, cultural projects, initiatives for the unemployed, et cetera. Just about every conceivable social problem is dealt with somewhere. The citizens' action committees therefore fulfil a compensatory function and deal with deficiencies in the political, economic and social structures. Give or take a few exceptions, they are not involved in opposition politics; toppling the political system is the last thing on their minds. In fact, most of the groups see their work as complementary to the services offered by the political and economic system.

The adoption of the legal system of the Federal Republic in eastern Germany also affected the party-political development of 'Bündnis 90'. The evolution of the group into a party was accelerated by the fact that legal stipulations made party status a prerequisite for financial subsidies. 'Bündnis 90' was founded as a political party in September 1991. Fusion with West Germany's Green Party was also primarily the consequence of external factors: first and foremost it was an electoral strategy, similarity in programmes being no more than a secondary factor. 'Bündnis 90' and the Greens shared the opinion that their only chance of getting past the 5 per cent hurdle was by joining forces. 'Electoral mathematics are the primary motive, and also the most compelling'.[7]

By the end of this institutionalisation process, several organisational forms had emerged in the East German civil rights movements. Now there is, first of all, the 'Bündnis 90' / Green Party and countless local project groups, initiatives and associations. Then, pockets of 'leftover' members of 'Neues Forum', of 'Initiative Frieden und Menschenrechte' and of the United Left group, who had, politically, 'missed the boat' and have almost no influence on social events. Yet another set of groups are supraregional associations such as the Green League and the

Independent Women's Union, which are recognised as official organisations across Germany and work on a professional basis.

And finally, there are still a few church-based, grass-roots groups. Most of the alternative groups from 'pre-*Wende*' times have now disbanded, and those that are still in existence have only a few members and work sporadically. The interviews showed that even in the last three years a number of them have folded. Many former members of the church-based, grass-roots groups are now involved in political parties and associations, and some have withdrawn completely from political activity to concentrate on their own careers.[8] Religion and politics occupy separate functional niches in the new Germany. In the GDR, their connection was a reflection of the overpoliticisation of society. It is thus hardly surprising that the separation of religion and politics should have transformed and in some cases totally dissolved the phenomenon of church-based, politically alternative, grass-roots groups. Nevertheless, our interviews have shown that several former civil rights activists continue to meet on a private basis. Politically and in their careers they have for the most part gone in different directions, but on an informal level the old sub-cultural alternative milieu seems to have loosely survived. Many of the people involved still tend to live in the same areas.

Since 1993, a process of quantitative reduction and of stabilisation seems to have set in within citizens' action committees and associations. The number of new groups being formed has declined, some of the associations which had had excessively large numbers of full-time employees have folded, others have slimmed their staff numbers, and several have even returned to being volunteer-based. The main reason for this re-structuring has been that jobs created under the stipulations of the job-creation programmes run out after two years if they cannot be continued independently of the programme, and subsidies from the Federal Employment Agency for new jobs have dropped considerably.

The ability of civil rights groups and citizens' action committees to mobilise public interest has declined steadily since 1990. The only issues still likely to draw broad participation are questions dealing with the past, particularly with the consequences of the machinations of the former state security apparatus. The activists have lost their monopoly on other issues – democratisation, human rights, the environment.

When the Monday demonstrations were brought back to life for a short time in the spring of 1991, it soon became clear to all participants that this was no longer a way of exerting political influence: the protest cycle broke down after three weeks. The Monday protest demonstration called by 'Bündnis 90' in the spring of 1993, under the motto 'We've had enough', was just as unsuccessful. Issues that tend to stir citizens of the eastern German states nowadays are ones of direct personal interest: the patch of grass in front of their building, the renovation of their district, or local infrastructure. Most eastern Germans now focus on their own private existence: aims transcending the individual level are not their prime concern.

5. Summary

All the stages in the development of the civil rights groups and citizens' action committees were the result of external influences. The mass mobilisation in the autumn of 1989, which would not have come about without the open 'side-door', enabling people to leave the country; the process of differentiation and marginalisation after November 1989, which was the direct consequence of the open East–West border; the process of institutionalisation after March 1990, which was the result of the parliamentarisation of the civil rights movements: at each stage, an external factor set the next phase in the development of the civil rights groups in motion. The restructuring of the committees into official associations was just as much for reasons of legalities as was the formation of 'Bündnis 90' into a political party. The mass mobilisation in the autumn of 1989 started without having been initiated by the grass-roots groups, and it ebbed after the Wall had fallen without the civil rights groups being able to do a thing about it. It would seem reasonable to conclude that shifts in social movements are to a very large extent dependent on legal, political and economic contextual conditions.

III. Changes in Attitude

I will be investigating changes in attitudes among members of politically alternative groups by comparing characteristic political attitudes prior to the *Wende* with 'post-*Wende*' attitudes. My claims are based on comparative interviews made in 1990,

1992 and 1995, where interviewees were asked, among other things, about the motives, aims and forms of their political involvement in the GDR.

1. The Change in Aims: Collective or Private Orientation

Prior to the *Wende*, the aims mentioned by group members for their actions were unmistakably collective in nature. All interviewees stated the need to change society as the motive for their involvement. Collective aims and individual aims were not in any way contradictory. In fact, it was characteristic for group members to adapt their individual actions to their political aims. For some, political involvement was so extreme that their entire private lives served their commitment to social change. K.W., who before the *Wende* was a member of the Leipzig 'Arbeitskreis Gerechtigkeit' (Working Group for Justice), referred to her political work in the group as 'completely fulfilling': 'At the time I lived for it, in actual fact'.

After the *Wende*, private and collective orientations began to diverge. Most of the social problems that had motivated political commitment had disappeared. As a result, fairly soon after the *Wende* many group members began focusing more on their private lives, but without totally giving up their collective orientation and the possibility of a return to political activity at a later date.

E.D., one of the co-founders of 'Neues Forum' in Leipzig, described the focus of his activities in 1992 with the words: 'I have now, quite definitely and for the first time, withdrawn to my professional and family context. I am writing my doctoral thesis and trying to look at the past for myself by writing about a GDR history topic'. He added that after his dissertation he would like to return to active grass-roots politics. J.F., a former member of the Leipzig 'Arbeitsgruppe Menschenrechte' (Working Group for Human Rights), gave the following answer to the same question in 1992: 'At the moment, I'm more concerned with myself, what I'll be doing in the future, whether I should continue nursing or start a university course or whatever'. He was no longer politically active, he said. He felt he should see an activity through, 'do it properly': 'I simply don't want to do things half-heartedly again'.

This articulates clearly what the real problem is: politics is a serious business, something that takes time and practice. It has to be a real career. Some people went into politics with this attitude. They were able to make their career goals and their political orientation mesh together, and derive a great deal of personal satisfaction from this. For those who chose not to become career politicians, however, bringing together individual and social interests is quite often a problem. K.W. finds it unfortunate that she can no longer combine her life and her politics in the way that she could in the past. She said she was disappointed because in her current social position she was not able to achieve much on a political level. It used to be the case that every one of her actions had a political dimension, but now anything an individual could do, she thought, had become socially irrelevant.

H.W., formerly a leading member of the 'Arbeitsgruppe Solidarische Kirche' (Working Group for a Solidarity Church), later a member of 'Demokratie Jetzt' (Democracy Now), has a guilty conscience because his political activity is so slight. He knows that he cannot keep emotions out of politics, and therefore he is glad he did not become a politician. But he adds: 'I'm not happy about it, I must say. If you want to know my political feeling now, I don't feel happy at all about what's going on here and my position in it, because I know I should be doing a lot more'. But then he goes on to describe his professional activity as a pastor as being political in nature. In other words, he solves the problem by redefining his professional activity. To the question of the importance of his political commitment for him at the moment, he replies: 'As I see myself as a political person in every respect, I wouldn't want to do without it. I know that everything I do is political in a way'.

We find a similar redefinition in the words of a former member of 'Umweltbibliothek Berlin' (Berlin Environmental Library), M.S., who was working as a salesman in a computer shop in 1992, but also put political magazines on display in the shop and described this activity as 'politics'. E.D. solved the problem, as we have seen, by shifting the time frame: although he may not be politically involved at the moment, he would return to working for the civil rights groups after finishing his dissertation. Withdrawing from politics, it would seem, creates an internal conflict which must be dealt with somehow. W.F., a representative of 'Initiative Frieden und Menschenrechte' (Initiative for Peace and Human Rights), saw very clearly 'the fantastic opportunities' open to holders of political office when he was interviewed in 1992. He also expressed 'admiration for the way in which quite a few people who were already really good got involved as parliamentarians, as regional ministers for "Bündnis 90"'. Yet he himself is not even a member of 'Bündnis 90': 'I haven't even managed to send back the application form yet'.

The main thing is the decision as to whether to go into politics or to concentrate on something else. The dilettantism of the early days, where it was enough to take an alternative stand and insist on high moral integrity, is gone. 'We are no longer in the days when politics was defined by particular moral attitudes' (L.M. from the 'Initiativkreis Absage an Prinzip und Praxis der Abgrenzung' [Initiative Group on Rejection of the Principle and Practice of Political Polarization], Berlin). Modern society, where one's position in the employment market determines one's individual living standards, exerts strong pressure in the direction of professionalisation. Modern society has no place for political prophets, even though it may, from time to time, honour them with impressive prizes.

By 1995, five years after unification, most of the former activists have made their decision. Politics still fascinates them, but most have chosen private careers over political involvement. After having – in several cases – completed further training or a course of study, most of them are so involved in their careers that they have little time left for politics. They still define themselves as political: whether they are professors or pastors, education officers or social workers, they view their professional activity as a kind of political commitment. It is noticeable how many former civil rights activists indeed work in professions where this type of assessment is possible: in social fields, within the Lutheran Church, in education. Only a few want to have nothing more to do with their political involvement. It would seem that these are people who have experienced political powerlessness. No matter whether they were politically active or not, and no matter what they thought of politics, all interviewees complained – without specifically being asked – about the lack of political interest in the population. The civil rights groups may have gone through significant changes in the last few years, but in one respect they remain at one: their self-image as being distinct from the indifferent mass of the population.

2. The Change in Motives: Optimistic or Pessimistic Perspectives

The scope of action for politically alternative groups in the GDR was extremely limited. Of course, they could use the church as a medium to propagate their demands, arouse public interest through provocative actions and bring their collective dissatisfaction to public attention. Changing society, however, was more or less impossible. For many group members, this experience led to a profound resignation, to a withdrawal into a private niche world or to emigration to the West; for others, it provoked an attitude of defiant self-assertion and a feeling of social superiority which was then boosted by the attention which their activities got from the state security apparatus and, as a consequence, also from the Western media. Even though the alternative groups were hardly in a position to exert an influence on the social realities of the GDR, the amount of public notice taken of their activities gave their political commitment a valid raison d'être.

After the *Wende*, the group members' prospects for action changed significantly. Most of them appreciated the new opportunities for action and self-realisation which the new society offered them, even though for many the disappearance of the GDR meant the loss of a homeland. K.W. reports: 'I have a much better feeling about my life now than I used to have. ... Now I can simply decide what I want to do. As strange as it may sound, this word "freedom", or whatever, that I used to find so idiotic: what is it supposed to mean? – ... Somehow, I feel freer. I think it's because there are now thousands of ways and paths I can take, and before they used to be rather limited'.

Increased scope of activity does not necessarily mean increased effect. 'Now', says G.H., who before the *Wende* was a member of the group 'Frauen für den Frieden' (Women for Peace)] in Leipzig, 'of course there are any numbers of offers, a lot of opportunities to get involved. ... Of course this is better, but I think that now you have to prove your commitment, show that you can do it, so to speak'. She clearly feels the pressure to produce results in the new Germany: 'I also think that it's difficult to steer clear of the pressure to be successful. In western society I have to be successful all the time. In the GDR what was actually important was to suffer, to be aware, but it didn't matter if you were successful or not. Nobody was successful anyway'.

Whether the politically alternative groups can still make a mark on society under the new efficiency-orientated social conditions is something the interviewees viewed with a good deal of scepticism. The political and economic system of Western society, in their opinion, is so stable and integrated that it is almost impossible, or at least very difficult, to make one's mark on it. The kind of changes demanded by the civil rights groups would require the support of at least part of the population. But in view of the economic prosperity and overall satisfaction of the general public, members of politically alternative groups view mass mobilisation as scarcely possible.

Group members see the pluralism of Western political culture as another factor limiting their social effectiveness. In a competitive climate it is clearly more difficult to be heard than in a culturally and politically more homogeneous society, where nonconformity alone is sufficient to attract attention.

And, finally, many civil rights activists believe that the pre-political, community-based attitude inherited from GDR days is another important reason for their relatively slight role in shaping social conditions. The high value placed upon noninstitutional communication and the scepticism *vis-à-vis* all social institutions and organisations which were typical in the GDR can be explained by the limited possibilities for political participation in the East German system. In a system in which the most important task of institutions was to prevent social change and to consolidate existing power structures, the anti-institutional attitude of groups pushing for change made sense. Now, however, if group members still hang on to their anti-institutional convictions and try to achieve attention on the basis of their alternative quality, they suddenly find themselves in a grey area in political terms. Nowadays there are even alternatives to the politically alternative groups, so that the groups have ceased representing a true alternative and become political groups like any others. The conflict lines now run inside the political system. It is within the political system that battles have to be fought. In other words, the laws and the logic of politics now also apply to the civil rights groups.

Right from the start, there was resistance within the groups when it came to recognising these laws and mechanisms of politics. As B.B., founding member of 'Initiative Frieden und Menschenrechte' (Initiative for Peace and Human Rights) and co-founder of 'Neues Forum', Berlin, put it: 'A civil rights group is somehow totally different from a party. It has something to do with "coming from inside". Let's say, what I see as the content and the aim of the civil rights movement can't be achieved according to a plan, so to speak, it has to develop from inside. I mean, each member has to really want it, and if that's not what each member really wants, then there won't be a civil rights movement'. G.H. commented: 'Society shows us the path to power. And I don't believe that a civil rights movement which sees itself as a civil rights movement can follow that path. A civil rights movement is a grass-roots movement, a movement without "power effect". The human aspect, the aspects of truth, goodness and beauty, these are things that grow from below. Whatever comes from above is corrupt and evil'.

This emotional notion of community, however, was disputed within the groups themselves right from the early days of the civil rights movement. Following the experience gathered in the early days, W.F. said in the 1992 interview, that the civil rights groups should adjust to the laws of society and to the social 'conditions which this Federal Republic of Germany creates, or learn to deal with them'.[9] This also includes paying more attention to effectiveness. He explained that, earlier on, he had taken more fundamentalist positions. Now, on the basis of his experience with the participation of 'Bündnis 90' in the Brandenburg government, he believed that

> you can do something there. Of course you have to change your way of thinking in certain respects, you have to understand that this is 'Realpolitik'. That means I have to be willing to compromise. I can't be a bulldozer and simply push my fundamentalist positions through. I know from the start that it won't work. But if you play the game by the rules, then – and you can really see it in the two ministries we have in Brandenburg, environment and education – you can achieve fantastic things.

The question is, then, whether the groups want to influence society or not. If they do, they have to learn to work with the new institutionalised interest groups and conflict-regulating mechanisms and accept them. Most group members have therefore accepted working within the institutions and view this work as a good way of representing their political objectives. J.L., a former member of the Leipzig-based 'Initiativgruppe Leben' (Initiative Group for Life) and now a member of the Leipzig city council, even defends party democracy against its current bad image:

> The feeling these days is that parties are something filthy, where people want to satisfy their own selfish needs. – That's totally the wrong view. But that's the way people think, and because of that, a whole lot of people, those who don't want this, who want to do something good, don't get involved in political parties. It's a disastrous situation. We have to break this vicious circle. ... I think the democratic system, even with a CDU government, is still a great deal better than a non-democratic system.

He sees work in grass-roots groups as 'totally fruitless'.

Others are disappointed by the squabbling that goes on between the various parties in a parliamentary democracy. They don't see that there were also power struggles in 'Neues Forum', in 'Bündnis 90' / the Greens or in any of the many Round Tables, and that power-hungry tacticians could have their way against honestly committed activists. Five years after the introduction of the Western democratic system, they have lost confidence in politics and believe that the 'real changes' happen on a lower level, when people 'get together in small groups ... and get involved' (M. F.). Self-realisation is possible on a community level, they think, while real politicians are controlled by the structures and corrupted by the system. Of course, most of those who hold this opinion are the ones who have remained outside political institutions, while those who have joined in insist that they have learned to respect political processes and business procedures. But even if those who are integrated in the political institutions accept the political system as a whole, they stress that they have their own special opinion about it. And although some of them have attained high positions in the system, they tend to show a certain casualness and indifference towards political institutions. This coolness of attitude appears to be fashionable and typical of those who have 'arrived' in society.

It would seem, therefore, that a significant change of attitude has taken place among the members of civil rights groups in the past few years. Many a critic of institutions and despiser of politics as nothing more than a power struggle has become critical of the grass-roots democratic approach based on discussion and consensus, on spontaneity and self-determination; some have even become career politicians. Most of them, it is true, continue to believe in grass-roots democratic elements, in extending the possibilities for direct political participation or in involving grass-roots groups to complement parliamentary democracy, and they see new opportunities for the work of citizens' action committees, particularly in the future. But the focal point of political work – that is quite clear for them, even though their heart still belongs to the grassroots groups – will remain in parliamentary work. Only a minority of civil rights activists still reject political institutions as a means of influencing society.

3. The Change in Levels of Expectation: Rational or Expressive Types of Behaviour

In GDR days, alternative groups dealt with their frequent experience of state-imposed restrictions and with their limited scope for activity by crediting themselves with a social significance which went beyond their actual effect. They saw themselves as being 'at the focal point of GDR history' (Rüddenklau 1992: 12), as the avant-garde of society, as a 'wisp of flame in the darkness' (B.B.), and they believed it was their task to light up this darkness, in other words, to inform, to sensitise and to mobilise society. The extremely high evaluation of group action which they achieved by setting themselves off against society was a way of coping with the unsolvable contradiction between their claim to action and their powerlessness, between ideal and reality, and a way of reacting to their exclusion by the official system. The groups, their argument went, were the seed of the future new society. In terms of social development, they saw themselves as being 'something like an early form of political self-organisation' (Poppe 1990: 79). At this point, the groups broke a taboo: they crossed the marked and universally accepted boundary and entered the realm of politics, which the system had reserved for itself. With their activities, the groups violated the accepted rules of proper behaviour; they transcended GDR reality which was held together by conformity, obedience, unimaginativeness and habit, and they allowed themselves to dream the dream of a just and democratic society.

After the *Wende*, this level of emotional tension could not be kept up. The groups had to reduce the moral import of their work, relativise its significance and scale down their aims. Democracy – until then an unachievably high goal – became something concrete, which now had to be shaped. No longer a counter-image in a totalitarian society, it became a technical problem: what was to be done with it? The political world lost its magical attraction and became an arena where a person could prove himself or herself, much like a career or a family. Looking through the interviews, one sees that this is exactly the way the process of political normalisation evolved in most of the cases. The most successful were those whose careers gave them the opportunity – at least partially – to implement their political aims and who chose to participate in political institutions.

This development is clearly visible in the case of U.P., who had already realised the need to correct her political ideas at the time of the central Round Table in Berlin in 1990, and who now hopes to develop them even further in her work as an educational officer at the Berlin-Brandenburg Lutheran Academy. In early 1990, she said that a lot of the hypotheses proposed by 'Demokratie Jetzt' were already outdated at this point and

> had to be changed, because of course we also had to change from the position we had held up until then, when what we had formulated was a vision, to our position today, one in which we are forced, much more pragmatically and realistically, to assess the situation and describe future development, because now – and this is one of the results of the Round Tables – we are involved in the responsibilities, and because what we would like to see as social change must always be viewed in terms of feasibility. Until now we could afford to dream, because this dream never touched reality. Now, however, the demands made on us are totally different, namely, to formulate steps that are as practicable as possible.

Two years later, U.P. described her work at the Lutheran Academy in a similar manner, in a job where she saw 'very practical possibilities' of contributing to the raising of political awareness, but also where she herself 'could learn a lot and realise a good deal of what had at one time been my goals. In contrast to the time before the *Wende*, I now have the opportunity in my job, for the first time in my life, to do the things that are really important to me. What I could only do on the side before I can now do as a full-time profession and I even get paid for it. I find that very nice'.

The interesting cases are those where this transformation is not successful, or has not been successful yet. The attitude of K.W. is one example. On the one hand, she feels liberated and sees the new social possibilities as individual opportunities for self-realisation, but she now feels 'smaller' than before. 'The proportions have totally changed. I'm not involved in big things any more and I no longer have the feeling that I can change the world'. The world – that used to be the GDR. In the GDR, which did not offer much in the way of opportunities for self-realisation, one could feel superior to society because of its inefficiency and immobility. At the time, her political work, which had 'fulfilled her completely', had had direct social relevance. Modern society, however, is highly complex, dynamic and effective. Many of the interviewees see this as the root cause of their feelings of inferiority.[10] It reduces their hopes of exerting individual influence. 'I think that big changes are something we can't achieve any more. In any case, I've given up, at least as far as myself is concerned. I don't know, for myself it's very difficult to say, because I feel so frustrated at not doing anything any more. I'm not involved in any of the groups any longer'. To the question as to what the aims of the groups should be today, she gave the following answer: 'To properly prepare and carry out a new revolution. That's what's important for me in the end. The rest, all these little steps, that's all very nice. But it doesn't achieve big changes'.

What is missing in K.W.'s views is a link between her ideals and what is achievable. From her enthusiasm for big changes, she sinks into a feeling of depression as soon as she realises that they cannot be implemented. In GDR days, it was possible to close this gap between political expectations and social reality by what can be called an expressive type of political behaviour, by a way of living that set one's own entire existence against the totality of the state, but now this needs to be followed by a change to a more rationally calculated type of behaviour which uses society's institutionalised possibilities for self-realisation. The institutions have the task of mediating between individuals and society. Those who do not follow this path give the impression of wanting to revolutionise the whole of society and of hanging on unwaveringly to their holistic ideals. The condition on the ability to act is limitation. Those able to submit to this will best succeed in keeping their sights on ideals and goals which extend beyond the possible.

Conclusion

Since 1989, a profound transformation has taken place in the political attitudes of the members of politically alternative groups in the GDR. This process involved strong inner con-

flicts between acquired patterns of behaviour and new requirements for behaviour. Some of the group members refused to
go along with these new requirements and held to their old
behaviour and convictions. Most of them, however, have
adjusted to the new social framework, even if their attitude is
often highly ambivalent, and have found a new political and
professional place within this framework. It would seem that
modern, functionally differentiated society is able to accommodate emancipatory and critical tendencies and integrate
them into the broad range of its structures.

Notes

1. The English translation is by Nicole Gentz, Berlin. Special thanks for their pro-
   ductive cooperation also go to Catherine Gory (Paris), Wolfgang Elvers (Leipzig),
   Manuel Schilling (Bochum), and particularly to Hagen Findeis (Leipzig). All quotations from the statements of group members are based upon interviews which
   I conducted, together with the above collaborators. The original version of the
   interviews differs in some respects from the version published in Findeis, Pollack
   and Schilling (1994). I quote in accordance with the original version which is not
   yet published. D.P., 14.4.98.
2. Findeis, Pollack and Schilling (1994) includes a comprehensive documentation of
   some of the interviews which form the basis of this chapter.
3. The stages postulated here can be contrasted with the divergent distinctions made
   by Wielgohs and Schulz (1991: 385ff.) and Probst (1993: 128f.).
4. Offe's view of the upheaval in the GDR as a mere exit revolution is undoubtedly
   oversimplified (Offe 1993: 293). A better explanation is that the close interrela-
   tion between exit and voice was a characteristic of the upheaval. Compare with
   Pollack (1990: 292–307), Hirschmann (1992: 330–58) and Torpay (1992: 21–42).
5. Joachim Gauck, at the official foundation ceremony for 'Neues Forum' in Berlin
   in January 1990, argued in favour of deleting the programme point concerning
   the existence of two German states. Cf. Probst (Unterberg 1991: fn. 3, 114f.).
6. Since the 1994 elections, 'Bündnis 90' / the Greens are still represented in a number of municipal councils – Schwerin, Rostock, Halle, Magdeburg, Leipzig and
   Weimar, for instance – whereas, on a state level, they managed to hold their position in the Saxony-Anhalt state parliament only.
7. The quotation is from:. 'Die Grünen und Bündnis 90. Perspektiven und Proble-
   men einer Annäherung'. Memorandum of the 'Bundesvorstand zur parteiinter-
   nen Diskussion', 10 December 1991.
8. There is no unbroken continuum between the citizens' action committees and
   associations of today and the civil rights groups as they were at the time of the
   Wende. Although there is evidence that some of the citizens' action committees
   have grown out of the church-based grass-roots groups as they existed prior to the
   Wende – particularly in the area of environmental involvement – many of the
   groups recruit their members from totally different segments of the population,
   even from amongst people who supported the former regime. The claim that the

political participants in the citizens' action committees are for the most part the same people who were involved in the grass-roots groups before the *Wende* is therefore false. What is in fact true is that in the grass-roots scene, there is a clear distinction between 'drop-outs' and those who stayed on, and the citizens' action committees and groups are made up of both 'old' and 'new' participants.

9. 'It took the Greens a long time', said W.F., 'to gain acceptance in the 'old' states of the Federal Republic, because people found it quite outlandish to see them knitting in Parliament and wearing their 60s-style clothes and so on. ... I saw the same thing happen at the Round Table. Its work was followed by a great number of people at the time, and our two people Wolfgang Templin and Gerd Poppe, were both really clever people, and what they said was totally right. But I (saw what happened) in my parents' circle of friends: "And the way they look ...', and Templin keeps scratching his beard". When I heard that I said to him: "When the red light goes on, then the camera is on you, so hold your hands still. And then, maybe you could cut your hair a bit at the back". That's important, the man-in-the-street is watching. For him those are important things on election day, when he puts his x on the ballot. ... I know that nobody's interested in good arguments about real issues. ... Now you have to think about – and now I'm talking like a journalist – how to best sell your ideas'.

10. This reversal of the relationship between the individual and society is perceived very clearly by some of the interviewees. A number of them see the economic and political power of Western society as an overwhelming force which controls all areas of life. W.H. told us that in his first contact with Western society, he 'physically felt the economic power ... of this highly-industrialised Western society'.

References

(There is as yet very little secondary literature on the development of East German civil rights groups and citizens' action committees since the *Wende*).

Blattert, Barbara, Rink, Dieter and Rucht, Dieter. 1994. 'Von den Oppositionsgruppen der DDR zu den neuen sozialen Bewegungen in Ostdeutschland?'.*Discussion Paper* FS III 94–101. Berlin, Wissenschaftszentrum.

Brand, Karl-Werner. 1990. 'Massendemokratischer Aufbruch im Osten. Eine Herausforderung für die NSB-Forschung'. *Forschungsjournal Neue Soziale Bewegungen*, vol. 3, no. 2, p. 10.

Findeis, Hagen, Pollack, Detlef and Schilling, Manuel, eds. 1994. *Die Entzauberung des Politischen: Was ist aus den politisch alternativen Gruppen der DDR geworden?*. Leipzig, Berliner Debatte und Evangelische Verlagsanstalt.

Haufe, Gerda and Karl Bruckmeier, eds. 1993. *Die Bürgerbewegung in der DDR und in den ostdeutschen Bundesländern*, Opladen, Westdeutscher Verlag.

Hirschmann, Albert O. 1992. 'Abwanderung und Widerspruch und das Schicksal der Deutschen Demokratischen Republik. Ein Essay zur konzeptuellen Geschichte', in *Leviathan*, 20, pp. 330–58.

Offe, Claus. 1993. 'Wohlstand, Nation, Republik. Aspekte des deutschen Sonderwegs vom Sozialismus zum Kapitalismus', in Hans Joas and Martin Kohli, eds., *Der Zusammenbruch der DDR. Soziologische Analysen*, Frankfurt am Main, Suhrkamp, p. 293ff.

Opp, Karl-Dieter and Voss, Peter. 1993. *Die volkseigene Revolution.* Stuttgart, Klett & Cotta.

Pollack, Detlef. 1990. 'Das Ende einer Organisationsgesellschaft. Systemtheoretische Überlegungen zum gesellschaftlichen Umbruch in der DDR'. *Zeitschrift für Soziologie*, 19, pp. 292–307.

Poppe, Ulrike. 1990. 'Das kritische Potential der Gruppen in Kirche und Gesellschaft', in Detlef Pollack, ed., *Die Legitimität der Freiheit. Politisch alternative Gruppen in der DDR unter dem Dach der Kirche*, Frankfurt am Main, Lang, p. 79ff.

Probst, Lothar. 1993. *Ostdeutsche Bürgerbewegungen und Perspektiven der Demokratie. Entstehung, Bedeutung und Zukunft.* Cologne, Bund Verlag.

Rink, Dieter. 1995. 'Das Leipziger Alternativmilieu zwischen alten und neuen Eliten', in Michael Vester, Michael Hofmann and Irene Zierke, eds., 1995, *Soziale Milieus in Ostdeutschland. Gesellschaftliche Strukturen zwischen Zerfall und Neubildung.* Cologne, pp. 193–229.

Rüddenklau, Wolfgang. 1992. *Störenfried. DDR-Opposition 1986–1989.* Berlin, Basis-Druck.

Torpay, John. 1992. 'Two Movements, Not a Revolution. Exodus and Opposition in the East German Transformation, 1989–1990'. *German Politics and Society*, 26, pp. 21–42.

Unterberg, Peter. 1991. *'Wir sind erwachsen, Vater Staat!', Background, foundation and effect of Neues Forum in Leipzig.* Diploma Thesis for the Faculty of Social Sciences, Bochum Ruhr University.

Wielgohs, Jan. 1993. 'Auflösung und Transformation der ostdeutschen Bürgerbewegung'. *Deutschland Archiv*, 26 , pp. 426–434.

—— and Schulz, Marianne. 1991. 'Von der illegalen Opposition in die legale Marginalität. Zur Entwicklung der Binnenstruktur der ostdeutschen Bürgerbewegung'. *Berliner Journal für Soziologie*, 1, p. 385ff.

CHAPTER 4

Friedrich Schorlemmer: Speaking Out for the Individual

Roger Jones

Friedrich Schorlemmer, the son of a Lutheran pastor, was born on 16 May 1944, in Wittenberg on the Elbe. His intellectual independence ensured that he was kept under official observation from a relatively early age and as a pacifist he refused to undergo military service. In a television interview with Günter Gaus in 1990 he recounts how, when only fourteen, he was aware that an older fellow-pupil had been given the task of keeping an official eye upon him. To Gaus's question as to how he felt when he became aware of this, he replied: 'A degree of contempt, I have to admit. But at the same time some sympathy for him, when a political system has to resort to such measures' (Gaus 1990: 18).[1] An early letter from Schorlemmer to a friend in Hamburg (which, as he was later to discover, found its way into Stasi files in 1963) is a clear statement of his role as a socially committed Christian – a role to which he was to remain steadfastly true: 'We are not political opponents of our state; rather we see ourselves as Christians who may not sell ourselves to an earthly power, who have to follow their conscience and not to weaken and must speak out as representatives for others' (Schorlemmer 1995: 98).[2]

He studied Evangelical Theology at the University of Halle from 1962–1967 and was appointed to his first post, that of 'Studentenpfarrer' (students' pastor), in Merseburg in 1970 where he remained until 1978. Throughout the 1970s he was active in the environmental and peace movements in the GDR.

In 1978 he was appointed to a lectureship at the 'Evangelisches Priesterseminar' (Protestant seminary) in Wittenberg, at the same time becoming a regular preacher at the 'Schloßkirche' (castle church), on the door of which Luther had nailed his ninety-five theses in October 1517. Throughout the 1980s he gave eloquent expression of his belief that the socialist system, as it had developed within the GDR, was in desperate need of reform. As both an intellectual and a pastor, his view that he was being stifled by the system created a sense of common cause with some of the major writers of the GDR, such as Christa Wolf and Günter de Bruyn. In his sermons he gave voice to an actively political Christianity and, typically for someone with a sense of occasion, often chose a particularly appropriate Sunday in the church calendar. A sermon given on Reformation Day in 1980 on the text 'Eine feste Burg ist unser Gott' (A safe stronghold is our God) expresses the view that security should not be dependent upon ramparts and walls but on trust: 'Security policy is not built upon trust. … It is built upon political power. And political power is distrust' (Schorlemmer 1994: 398).[3] And this distrust creates GDR citizens lacking in confidence and candour. Indefatigably and consistently critical of the regime, he continued to be under constant surveillance by the Stasi, particularly when he became the centre of a group of like-minded reformers whose opposition to the regime eventually became explicit and public. Taking their text from Luther ('The time for silence is past and the time to speak has come') they presented the Evangelischer Kirchentag meeting in Halle, on 24 June 1988, with the '20 Wittenberger Thesen' (Wittenberg theses). Placing the need for change in the GDR in the context of the global threat to the environment and world peace, they demanded not the end of socialism, but its reform, particularly where the involvement of the individual citizen in the political process, the freedom of information, the reduction of bureaucracy and the revision of the legal system were concerned. Central to the theses is a desire to facilitate the proper use of the earth's resources and a concern with the role which the GDR could play in this if only it allowed its citizens a proper democratic input. In this the theses are typical of Schorlemmer's consistent concerns, as was, in November 1989, his signature to the document 'Für unser Land' (For our Country) which appealed to citizens in the GDR to stay in the East and help bring about the necessary reforms.

Schorlemmer was co-founder of the citizens' movement 'Demokratischer Aufbruch' (New Democratic Departures) in September 1989, but in the wake of the tension which ultimately developed between those who continued to call for the GDR to reform from within and those who had come to the conclusion that the only feasible solution lay in unification, Schorlemmer joined the East German SPD (founded on 1 October 1989) early in 1990 and was elected leader of the party within the Wittenberg City Council in May 1990. Since unification he has continued to voice his concern that East Germans should not forget the basic aspirations of socialism, and has also argued for consigning the evils of the Stasi to the past and drawing a line under the investigation of its activities. In 1992 he was appointed Director of Studies at the Evangelische Akademie (Protestant Academy) Sachsen-Anhalt in Wittenberg. Amongst the honours he has received are the Carl von Ossietsky Medal of the International League for Human Rights (1989) and the Peace Prize of the German Book Trade (1993).

In a radio interview in 1990 Schorlemmer was asked why he had not considered becoming a full-time politician in view of the strength of his political commitment and his avowed intention to work for peace and democracy in a united Germany. When one considers the consistency of his contribution to the public debate on the future of socialism and the future of the GDR prior to unification and, following unification, his concern about the nature of the new republic, the question seems a natural one. It is difficult to envisage a pastor who could be more socially involved than Schorlemmer, and the vast range of his pronouncements on the state of his country and his unwavering belief in democratic socialism can sometimes obscure the spiritual aspects of his calling and even lead one to assume that the political kingdom is the focus of his greater concern. His answer to the question was, however, a clear indication that the kind of socialism which he espouses is one which builds upon the integrity of the individual and the individual's capacity for renewal in a spiritual sense: 'Very early on I decided to remain within my profession since this country needs priests who stress the connection between inner renewal and external liberation, that is, priests who know that the liberation of humanity in general can only be realised if we are, as individuals, renewed and liberated' (Schorlemmer 1993a: 316).[4]

For Schorlemmer there is no discrepancy or conflict between the individual's Christian standpoint and his relationship to his fellow human beings in a social context. Luther's exhortation to the Christian to examine his or her capacity for good or for evil, to assess the potential to help one's neighbour and particularly the poor, is regarded by Schorlemmer as the test of one's awareness of the Kingdom of God. And this Kingdom is partially but clearly understood as a community which brings people together. The central teaching of Christ is not focused, according to Schorlemmer, on the individual's spiritual salvation or even on his or her moral integrity but on a concept of justice and love which binds and overcomes division. This interpretation of the duty of the Christian can be seen as the underlying theme in all the social and political issues which he addresses, ranging from his concern with what being German means at the end of the twentieth century to his views on literature and the inspiration he acquires from reading the Book of Isaiah.

Indeed it is axiomatic for Schorlemmer that the supplication 'Thy Kingdom come' implies a concern with the oppressed and the underprivileged, wherever they are and regardless of their persecutors. Schorlemmer, who never flinches from speaking the truth even when it means stepping on toes and causing offence, is often concerned to make his fellow-Germans aware of their particular responsibility in this area, in order to establish a view of Germany as a nation concerned with democracy and human rights. This is the 'other Germany' in support of which, in his view, too few were willing to speak up during the Nazi period: 'During the war there were only a few who through their opposition represented the other Germany, a Germany in the middle of a civilised Europe' (Schorlemmer 1995: 129).[5] A concern with the moral state and the image of his country is expressed in regular references throughout his writings to the need to rediscover and to nurture the qualities of tolerance, enlightenment and justice, and to place what are perceived to be traditional German virtues at the service of a continual search for peace and justice. He is often quite specific in what this should *not* involve: for instance, he criticised those who advocated sending German troops to the Balkans, a step which in his view could only have caused escalation of the conflict, in view of the Serbs' memories of the Second World War. He is not afraid to remind his fellow-Germans of the fear which they have often evoked in other nations; nor does he fail to remind his fellow-Christians that in praying for the Kingdom of God they are implicitly rejecting nationalism and racism.

Schorlemmer has not been afraid to point to the greater potential for racism and nationalism in the former East Germany than in the Western part of the Federal Republic. Part of the catching-up process which he sees his fellow-citizens engaged in includes assimilation into a more multicultural society in the West, despite the limits to this multiculturalism and despite whatever reservations he may have about its material orientation. He can be scathing in his criticism of the much-vaunted internationalism of the GDR in relation to the Third World: 'The apprentices, workers and students from the Third World who, under the slogan of "Solidarity", were taken in by the GDR, lived almost exclusively in ghettos. They were, and were to remain, strangers' (Schorlemmer 1993a: 220).[6]

The picture he paints of East German society is of one which was separated not only from the influence of the West, but also from any sense of what life was like for anyone beyond the borders of the GDR. The GDR citizen, according to Schorlemmer, was deliberately excluded from confrontation with the world beyond its borders, rather like a child who is shielded from what might harm him by overprotective parents. The frequency with which Schorlemmer uses the noun 'Bevormundung' – the act of making up someone else's mind for them – to describe the attitude of the GDR regime towards its citizens is indicative of his belief that the overwhelming influence of the state deprived its citizens of the ability to make any meaningful political and social decisions for themselves and, when unification came, made them incapable of resisting the material blandishments of the West and standing up for those genuine achievements of socialism which were now under threat. The extreme sense in which the state acted as guardian and provider – of employment and comprehensive social care – also rendered East German citizens prey to base reactions when these provisions were suddenly no longer available to them in the cold climate of market forces.

Not that he argues that there is overwhelming evidence of multiculturalism in West German society – it is only in comparison to the East that it appears to be somewhat more enlightened. He is sensitive to the fact that 'Volksdeutsche' (ethnic Germans) whose families have lived outside German borders for, in some cases, up to 250 years now enjoy far greater rights of integration and citizenship than a third-generation Turkish family in the former Federal Republic or a Vietnamese worker who has lived in East Germany for twenty years. This lends weight to his argument for a new definition of German citizenship, based not on ethnic characteristics, but on basic human rights which derive from domicile and employment.

At the beginning of 1992 he warned of a regression into fundamentalism and nationalism: 'We stand at a critical moment in human history; we are witnessing a chaotic regression into the seductive shelter of fundamentalist and nationalist viewpoints' (Schorlemmer 1993a: 124).[7] A year later he saw his prognosis confirmed by a survey which had shown that one in two young Germans in Brandenburg supported the slogan 'Germany for the Germans – foreigners out'.[8] To point, as he does, to the social reasons for such an attitude – to the loss of social cohesion and national prestige, economic uncertainty, an ignorance of what democracy demands of its citizens – underlines his belief in the causal connection between social conditions and social, or antisocial, behaviour. He does not remove the obligation on the individual to take responsibility for his or her actions; there is no doubt, however, that one of his constant themes is the overriding need to address the social problems attendant upon unification and the crisis of unemployment – and this includes a more transparent, effective and speedy asylum procedure – and that the constant denial of the opportunity to earn one's living, while the investors in east Germany make a killing, will lead eventually to social unrest on a massive scale. Allied to this conviction is the suspicion that many West Germans are either unsympathetic to or ignorant of the plight of their fellow- citizens in the East: 'It was to be expected that the West Germans, who were not asked if they wanted to be given us, are now no longer prepared to shell out for the East. After all the West Germans' desire for unification had not been as strong' (Schorlemmer 1993a: 76).[9]

The fact that West Germans were not ready for unification, either politically or economically, is held by Schorlemmer to be just as damaging to social cohesion as the political immaturity of the citizens of the former GDR. Once the initial euphoria was over, West Germans were confronted with the unpalatable truth of the economic costs of unification. In a phrase which reflects Schorlemmer's characteristic fondness for word-play, the swiftness of the transition is well conveyed: 'There were plans in place in the event of attack but not in the event of unification' (Schorlemmer 1993a: 67).[10] Secure in their material prosperity, West Germans had not urgently desired unification and had even, according to Schorlemmer, resented the manner in which East Germans now seemed to be demanding an instant share in what had been painstakingly achieved by others over a period of forty years. He even observes among West Germans criticism of the perceived greed of the East Germans who, far from being entitled to immediate economic parity with their Western neighbours, ought to be glad that they are at least better off than the Poles or the Russians. As a Christian he deplores the failure of both sides to see that the only real and morally justifiable comparisons are those between the West (in the universal sense and including the former GDR) and the Third World. Whether this appeal is convincing to the unemployed in West Germany who blame the costs of unification for their predicament is a matter for conjecture.

It might seem that the differences between East and West Germany, arising from forty years of politically diverse experience and a determination on the part of the GDR to keep its citizens from contamination by Western ideas, are so great as to render those who, like Schorlemmer, appeal to a sense of shared history or identity upon which understanding and unity could be based, as voices crying in the wilderness. Furthermore, in adhering to his deeply held socialist principles, Schorlemmer admits to cutting a somewhat naive figure, now without honour in either his old or his new country. Having failed to witness the desired reform of socialism within the boundaries of the GDR and lamenting the rapid and irresistible replacement, at the end of 1989, of this desire by the demand for unity, he refers constantly to a take-over of the GDR by the former Federal Republic of Germany and not to the unification of equals. The subsequent reform of the GDR economy, with the accompanying unemployment (particularly devastating for women) and the effects of market forces have, according to Schorlemmer, replaced one tyranny by another and have encouraged East Germans to adopt the economic philosophy of the West without securing in exchange an acknowledgment that they too had something useful – such as a sense of social cohesion and purpose – to bring to the process of unification. And not only have the positive aspects of life in the former GDR been sidelined and forgotten: the role of the churches, which was so central to the reform movement in the GDR and which provided the only effective voice of protest, has diminished in significance in the wider political context of a united Germany. The church seems now to have nothing of relevance to offer to the young and appeals only to the older generation: 'If the church does not have a more decisive, aggressive and convincing message for the younger generation, it will rapidly become a moribund club for old-age pensioners' (Schorlemmer 1995: 29).[11]

In surveying the course of events since unification there are, therefore, considerable grounds for disillusionment and regret on Schorlemmer's part where his social and religious aspirations are concerned, yet his concern with the state of his country has never been an exclusive one. The principles he believes in – which, in their political dimension, are those of social democracy – inform his view of a united Europe, and he places at the centre of his vision of European unity, not the pursuit of material prosperity but the preservation of cultural differences and traditions:

A Europe without borders will arouse more hopes than fears if each country and region can be allowed to develop. Europe will flourish if each part of it flourishes. We share a common destiny, a tragic history and now a unique common opportunity. Europe represents a richness of diversity and an end to threatening rivalry. No nation or group must raise itself above its neighbour. We have a common destiny (Schorlemmer 1993a: 89).[12]

Concern for our common destiny is for Schorlemmer indivisible from a concern for the environment and the future of the planet. Whether he is talking about the environmental pollution in the GDR, the state of the North Sea or the effects of Chernobyl, there is a constant message that we are all guests on this earth and, in gratitude for such a status and for the sake of future generations, we have a duty to protect and preserve the environment. The vision of a reconciled creation which inspires him when he reads Isaiah clashes with the stark reality of economic growth, especially in the manner of its relentless pursuit by the West. According to Schorlemmer, environmental issues have to be taken into account in economic policy on a worldwide scale – the West has to reform and give a lead, otherwise Second and Third World countries, which have been the main victims of environmental pollution, will eventually be counted amongst the culprits. The symbol of his concern is the tree – anyone who has shared an outing or a walk with him will be aware of his tendency to lament the dead and decaying trees along the roadside. The image of the tree is a recurrent one in his writings and sermons and reflects his belief that concern for the environment is a religious, as well as a moral duty: 'To use an image: the practice of theology must be such as to enable trees to grow' (Schorlemmer 1993a: 252).[13]

Schorlemmer's commitment to environmental issues, which is also reflected in his concern for animal welfare, particularly where it is undermined by intensive farming methods and the unacceptable and unnecessary transportation of animals over long distances, is a practical expression of his belief that we need to find our way back to a proper relationship with nature. Through materialism and the pursuit of economic growth we have become alienated from our natural environment:

> I regard this process of alienation from the ways of nature as alienation from life itself and therefore from religion too – in the sense in which we gaze at life in amazement. This is for me an essential part of my belief and my religiousness. Anyone who sees an animal only in terms of a sausage or a steak can be assumed to have no conception of what happens to these fellow-creatures on a large scale or of what happens when we transport tightly penned-in animals from Portugal to Poland by night. (Drewermann and Schorlemmer 1995: 125/6)[14]

A combination of personal and political experiences seems to have been central to the shaping of Schorlemmer's attitudes and the motivation of his actions. For obviously different reasons the building of the Berlin Wall and the Prague Spring of 1968 made a deep impression on him, the first event intervening directly in his life, since in 1961 he was nurturing the hope of studying in West Berlin while living in East Berlin. The complementary importance of events in his personal life is reflected in the vividness with which he recalls falling twenty metres from a church tower when he was thirteen, and, many years later, saving his baby son from drowning when his pram rolled into the River Saale. It is significant that he has not attempted to rationalise these events, from which he and his son emerged physically unscathed, but draws strength from them in his belief that his life has a purpose.

In pursuing this purpose Schorlemmer has never been afraid to speak his mind; in this he follows in the footsteps of Luther, his great mentor. Although mindful of Melanchthon's dictum that truth can be the victim in heated dispute, Schorlemmer is temperamentally closer to Luther in his willingness to take risks – and to make mistakes – in the pursuit of that truth. He would argue that a failure to make a principled stand would lead only to a diminution of the argument and that the Church should not be so concerned with retaining its followers and maximising its income that it fails to give a moral and spiritual lead. Schorlemmer defines sin as social apathy and a failure to see our individual destiny as intertwined with that of our neighbour in the environment for which we have a shared responsiblity. The concept of 'Gemeinschaft' (community) is central to his beliefs, but that does not mean that he undervalues the need for the individual to maintain also a sacrosanct sphere of independence. Whatever our achievements in the wider sphere of the community, we remain justified by grace and have a personal as well as a social responsibility.

Notes

1. 'Ich muß Ihnen sagen, ein bißchen Verachtung. Gleichzeitig ein bißchen Mitgefühl, daß ein System so etwas nötig hat'.
2. 'Wir sind nicht politische Gegner unseres Staates, sondern fühlen uns als Christen, die sich nicht an eine irdische Macht verkaufen dürfen, die ihrem Gewissen zu folgen, nicht nachzugeben haben and für andere stellvertretend auftreten müssen'.
3. 'Sicherheitspolitik baut nicht auf Vertrauen. ... Sie baut auf Macht. Und die Macht ist das organisierte Mißtrauen'.
4. 'Ich habe mich sehr früh dafür entschieden, in meinem Beruf zu bleiben, weil in diesem Land eben auch Pfarrer nötig sind, die den Versuch machen, die innere Erneuerung zu verbinden mit der äußeren Befreiung, die also wissen, daß Befreiung der Menschheit nur dann geschehen kann, wenn wir selber erneuerte, befreite Individuen sind'.
5. 'Im Krieg gab es nur wenige, die das andere Deutschland durch ihren Widerstand repräsentierten, ein Deutschland in der Mitte eines zivilisierten Europa'.
6. 'Die Lehrlinge, Arbeiter, Studenten aus der Dritten Welt, die die DDR aufnahm, das Wort Solidarität dafür benutzend, lebten fast ausschließlich ghettoisiert. [...] Sie waren Fremde und sollten es bleiben'. In: 'Wir sind alle Gäste auf Erden', a lecture in the Thalia-Theater, Hamburg, 16 April 1992.
7. 'Wir stehen an einem kritischen Punkt der Menschheitsentwicklung; es vollzieht sich ein chaoischer Regreß in den verführerischen Schutzraum von Fundamentalismen und Nationalismen'. In: 'Das riskierte Wesen', a public lecture at Leipzig University in January 1992.

8. 'Deutschland den Deutschen – Ausländer raus' (Schorlemmer 1993a: 157).
9. 'Vorhersehbar war, daß die Westdeutschen, da sie nicht gefragt wurden, ob sie uns geschenkt haben wollten, nun nicht weiter bereit sind, für den Osten abzugeben. ... Schließlich hatten die Westdeutschen sich nicht in vergleichbarer Weise nach der Einheit Deutschlands gesehnt.' In: 'Trümmer des Vergangenen, Bausteine für das Künftige?', *Sächsische Zeitung*, 20 October 1992.
10. 'Es gab Konzepte für den Verteidigungsfall, aber nicht für den Vereinigungsfall.' In: 'Nicht nur Jammer-Ossis', *Stuttgarter Nachrichten*, 24 August 1992.
11. 'Wenn die Kirche nicht entschlossener, offensiver und überzeugender für die heranwachsende Generation da ist, wird sie sehr bald zu einem absterbenden Rentnerverein'.
12. 'Ein Europa ohne Grenzen wird mehr Hoffnungen als Sorgen auslösen, wenn jedes Land und jede Region sich entfalten kann. Europa geht es gut, wenn es jedem Teil gutgeht. Wir haben ein gemeinsames Schicksal, eine tragische Geschichte und nun eine einmalige gemeinsame Chance. Europa, das ist der Reichtum der Vielfalt. Das ist das Ende bedrohlicher Konkurrenzen. Keine Nation oder Gruppe erhebt sich mehr über die andere. Wir haben ein gemeinsames Schicksal' ('Vision Europa '92').
13. 'Im Bilde gesprochen: Theologie ist so zu betreiben, daß Bäume wachsen'. In: 'Liebe den Baum wie dich selbst', a sermon in Wittenberg on 4 September 1978.
14. 'Dieser Entfremdungsprozeß von den natürlichen Vorgängen ist für mich gleichzeitig ein Entfremdungsprozeß vom Leben und damit auch von religiösen Vorgängen – im Sinne eines staunenden Wahrnehmens von Leben. Das ist für mich wesentlicher Teil meines Glaubens oder meiner Religiosität. Wer das Tier nur noch als Wurst wahrnimmt oder als Steak, hat der noch im Blick, was denn eigentlich mit den Geschöpfen in der Großviehhaltung geschieht – was passiert, wenn wir eingepferchte Tiere von Portugal bis nach Polen transportieren über Nacht?'

References

Drewermann, Eugen and Schorlemmer, Friedrich. 1995. *Tod oder Leben: Vom Sinn und Unsinn des Gottesglaubens*, ed. Michael Albus, Freiburg im Breisgau, Herder.
Ebert, Andreas, ed. 1989. *Räumt die Steine hinweg – DDR Herbst 1989 – Geistliche Reden im politischen Aufbruch*, (with a preface by Heinrich Albertz). Munich, Claudius-Verlag.
Gaus, Günter. 1990. *Zur Person Friedrich Schorlemmer, Lothar de Maizière, Gregor Gysi, Ingrid Köppe, Christoph Hein, Hans Modrow: Sechs Porträts in Frage und Antwort*. Berlin, Verlag Volk und Welt.
Schorlemmer, Friedrich. 1993a. *Freiheit als Einsicht: Bausteine für die Einheit*. Munich, Knaur.
——. 1993b. *Es ist nicht umsonst: Predigten und Reden 1983–1993*. Leipzig, Gustav Kiepenheuer.
——. 1994. *Zu seinem Wort stehen*. Munich, Kindler.
——. 1995. *Was ich denke*. Munich, Goldmann.

CHAPTER 5

A Dissident Life

Friedrich Schorlemmer in conversation with David Rock and Roger Jones [1]

DR: Herr Schorlemmer, your problems with the Stasi began when you were only fourteen years of age. Could you tell us how it all started?

FS: It was in 1958. One evening, a man stood at the door, offered me his hand which was shaking and told me he was being followed. He asked if we could help him as the state security was after him. He wanted to go over to the West – his wife had already gone. He was from Wittenberg, about twenty kilometres from us, and had walked over to us along the banks of the river Elbe. He asked us for somewhere to stay and whether we knew of any way to get to the West. At that I got scared but took pity on the poor fellow and led him to my father's office where my little brothers and sisters were playing, sat him down beside the desk and raced off to get my father who was at a funeral. He didn't want to leave straight away and tried to calm me down, telling me to just hang on for a while. I had to almost drag him home! When he did get back, he spoke to the man and sent him on his way again. The man then got a lift with our stove-fitter and headed off with him on his motor-bike in the direction of the district town, but got off after five kilometres (as we learnt later). That evening I severely reproached my parents, accusing them of treating this man the way the Jews were treated when they asked for help, and of being afraid of taking him in because of what might happen to them. I, a fourteen-year-old, expressed my scorn for them and told them they were cowards. A few weeks later it turned out that this gentleman had called on several priests' houses to test whether they were prepared to smuggle people to the West. This was one of the nastiest experiences of my childhood – manipulating my father, manipulating my feelings too, leading me into conflict with my parents. It shook me deeply. I still wonder just what the man's dealings with the Stasi were: what had they done to him, how had they got him to do this, was he himself a victim of blackmail? Was he testing us to save himself?

The second time was in the spring of 1958. I was not supposed to get into the upper school (Oberschule) – I was to leave school after the eighth class. Yet the solitary decision of one teacher (a lady from the Baltic) changed all that: without telling anyone, she sent me the admission form for the high school (Mittelschule), the one going up to class ten, so that I wouldn't have to stop at the eighth grade. Things like that happened in those days. But my name was not on any of the lists or registers. Now, I turned up at six o'clock in the evening on my bike with all my things, even my duvet, expecting to be taken into the school boarding-house. 'What!' they said, 'No way! You are not enrolled here, there's no place allocated to you, go on to another school, perhaps your name is down on their list!' I went to the other school, straight to the headmaster who sent me to yet another school! 'Sorry, we've not got your name down here. Go on back home, or else maybe go to that colleague of your father's, stay the night with him, he'll explain it all to you!' These were pretty bitter experiences for a fourteen-year-old, my first trip away from home: my mother had sent me on my way with the ritual farewell ceremony with the handbrush, I had cycled twenty kilometres and then been told 'Nope!' But then, in the end, the wife of the headmaster did finally take me in, she must have taken pity on me – it was by now already dark. But hardly had I made my bed when someone came in and bellowed – just like in a military barracks: 'Schorlemmer, out! Get out! You're in a different room.' So I went out and into the next room, and the boy who was in there said: 'Just to put you in the picture: I've had to leave my own room because of you. The headmaster has put me next to you to make sure you don't start any religious propaganda here.' I was fourteen and had no intention whatsoever of making any political or religious propaganda! He climbed into his old iron-framed bunk next to me and started grilling me. 'What do you have to do when you're a pastor's son? Do you have to find reasons to justify the crusades et cetera, et cetera?' He went on and on, even asking me what sort of things I did with other young people in the holidays. Very early on they considered me to be a potential effective enemy of the state. In a way they actually produced one. Maybe I didn't want to be one at all.

RJ: What sort of difficulties did this create for your father and your family?

FS: It wasn't quite like that. My father was one of those who refused utterly and completely to have anything to do with the state. I had seven brothers and sisters and none of us joined any kind of organisation. I was the only one at my school not to go through the 'Jugendweihe'-initiation.[2] In 1956, when I was twelve, there was a lot of very fierce anti-church propaganda in schools. It amounted to a confrontation between unscientific belief and a scientific view of the world. To put it pointedly, it was the dispute about whether man is descended from the apes or from Adam and Eve. They devised this story that we were descended from the apes, from a primeval horde. Their entire social theory was this myth that we were now somehow or other standing at the apex of the history of mankind and were actually reverting to prototype as liberated peaceful human beings, to a primal horde as it were. Most people believed it at the time. I must admit, we were in the minority. When confirmands pointed out that the church was saying one thing and the school another, my father would join in the dispute with the following memorable words: 'Listen lads, you've got to bear in mind that the teachers are poor bastards: they always have to say what the government tells them to. Their opinions are like a reed in the wind'. Next day, when the teacher started to polemicise against the church again, one of them, Willi Stürmer was his name, put his hand up and said that the Pastor had told them that teachers were poor bastards. The teacher reported it immediately.

After that, there were depressing things at home too: occasionally, my father was only saved from prison through the fact that the local party, when it was trying to attract support, refused to give the required consent to my father being taken away. Despite all the things being said retrospectively about communists, one has to say that communists in our town knew what being 'taken away' for some political remark meant, and they were for me nobler communists – yes, there were nobler communists too! They may also have had their hopelessly romantic notions of revolution, but I experienced their human side too: they had retained some warm-heartedness precisely because they had had some terrible experiences themselves! It was them that really saved my father at that time.

Perhaps one more little anecdote: I had some friends who travelled, illegally of course, to West Berlin in 1961 to have a look at the city. In my darkroom I developed the photos of their trip and I was found out. I was going to be prosecuted for it – it was in October 1962, when I began studying theology at the University of Halle Wittenberg.

DR: Wasn't it difficult for sons of the clergy to get into university?

FS: It certainly was. I hadn't been able to do my Abitur, the school leaving examination which you needed for university entrance. I did it in the Volkshochschule (adult education centre) and with this exam – this is one of the peculiar things about the GDR – I could have studied anything, because pupils from the Volkshochschule, doing their courses through night school, received preferential treatment.

What was I about to say? Yes, when I arrived at university, there was the autumn ball at the theological faculty. One of the postgraduate students whom I did not know came up to me, addressed me by name and said: 'Listen, watch out, watch out!' That was all he said. When he finished at university in '67 or '68, he explained to me that they had put him on my tail and that he had wanted to warn me. In 1990 I discovered the name of this student, later to become a priest, through his Stasi records. I now know how he got drawn into it, he told me everything. It was because he had the misfortune to be a passenger in the worst train-crash ever in the GDR. They exploited people in extreme situations. I know of three people blackmailed by the Stasi because they happened to be sitting in the train which crashed near Leipzig in 1961/2. Such was the perfidious nature of the system. And hence my difficulty when suddenly I discovered from his records that he had been an IM (unofficial collaborator). I can't tell you anything about his work for the Stasi, except that he warned me. So even though I had as yet not even been to Halle, they already knew who to watch out for. And you know, this State Security really did accompany our lives in a way which the majority of GDR citizens did not notice at all because they were all nice and upright! During our time at university, we found out through a similar sort of story that in my year, three out of twenty-three students were working for the Stasi. Now we know that there were six – out of a total of twenty-three! One of my best friends was involved, someone I had lots of conversations with. And yet again and again I have to reiterate that we did not live in South Africa, we did not live under Idi Amin, indeed, to make a comparison, we did not even live in the Soviet Union where it was much worse, nor in Czechoslovakia either. One mustn't build it up too much after the event to make it appear especially heroic. The system of Stasi informers was extremely unpleasant, but unlike the present view of things, the Stasi was never the main issue for us at this time in the GDR. Now, of course it is *the* main issue to do with the former GDR. That's absurd!

DR: When did you refuse to do military service? Wasn't it after you went to university?

FS: The law about military service only came after the Wall was built. And I objected straight away when I had my medical at the start of 1964. There were only three others in my year at university who objected, and one of them was very ill anyway and felt he had to refuse to join up to avoid losing his self-respect by being invalided out. And at that time, I must say, we were very much on our own, even my parents were very much against it. My mother said to me (and from that point in time stems my problem with mothers and war): 'Son, how can you do this to us, your parents', because she knew that I could be taken off to the clink at any time and they would not be able to get me out; and in jail I would be broken and she and my father would then suffer too. So my mother said: 'Son, how can you do this to us?' And afterwards I thought about this a lot. And I also read my grandmother's letters to my father during the Russian campaign. My grandmother was really terribly worried about her son and painstakingly darned his socks. That was the way German mothers reacted to the war. I'm not chiding them, I'm just saying that that's the way it was. After all, my grandmother lost her husband in the first week of August 1914 – because he was reported missing, she hoped he would return. So I refused to do military service, pointing out that I was ready to do community service at any time, but under no circumstances would I fight with a weapon.

DR: And the actual consequences?

FS: At the time, we didn't know whether we'd be sent down from university or not, or whether we'd be arrested, as there were no actual specific laws pertaining to it. But during the medical we were immediately taken to a special room where I sat opposite twelve gentlemen who interrogated me for two hours. Looking back, I admit I was incredibly scared. I was no hero. I was afraid of what might happen. But at the same time, I had the feeling I had to do it, I couldn't join an army which bound people to absolute obedience after what has happened in German history – and in view of the Wall where people were shot when they tried to get to their friends or parents, or because they were fed up to the back teeth with this system, or because they were farmers who had been ruined and had not been able to get out at the right time – they were shot! Yes, and people were called up for border duty on the Wall, into an army which thought it represented the progress of humanity per se, and so the goal was just – as were the weapons and the war! Yes, and somewhere along the line I had learnt that the worse the practices are, the more noble the goal is!

RJ: Perhaps a quotation from an article about Martin Niemöller fits well into this context: 'How to give concrete expression to the content of Christian faith in terms of political witness and commitment, most forcibly of all in the face of the challenges of totalitarianism, has been without doubt the most contentious issue in the life of the German Protestant Church in the twentieth century. Virtually all accounts of the German resistance to Nazism have drawn attention to the contribution of individual churchmen.' I'm thinking here of what you have just been explaining to us. 'But I have also noted the church's institutional failure to mount any effective opposition to the monstrous crimes of the Nazi regime. The true story of the German churches in this period can be seen as a sad tale of betrayal, timidity and unbelief.' In the present context I have two questions: Would it be going too far to make any comparison between these two periods, i.e., the Nazi regime and conditions in the GDR? And was there and is there any difference between the actions of individual clergymen like you and the general views of the church as an institution?

FS: Any answer to your question which took less than half-an-hour would give a distorted picture. It's such a complicated subject to which unfortunately people today give too hasty and too simplified answers and so help to create new myths and legends.

First: Whoever tries to compare the GDR system with National Socialism in such a way as to suggest they are basically the same, is guilty of trivialising National Socialism and its victims and of simultaneously demonising a system which deserves to be criticised in the most lucid way possible. But I think too that, unlike the case of National Socialists, one must try to do justice to the people who were Gorbachev-communists, particularly when they had previously been victims of National Socialism. There are specific structural features which are comparable and which in extreme cases, as under Stalin, led not only to comparable but perhaps even to worse things. Camus formulated it pointedly in a sentence. I read it in a book smuggled through to me by a friend, namely *The Rebel*, a work which was important for my whole way of political thinking. It reduced the distinction between Stalinism and National Socialism to a simple formula: fascism/National Socialism is the extolling of the executioner by the executioner, whereby the executioners mutually confirm one another as to how good they are and how necessary what they are doing is. And Stalinism is the extolling of the executioner by the victim, whereby the victim is good too: I may not understand it, but the fact that I am now a victim will probably make good sense in terms of history. I read, too, Solzhenitsyn's *One Day in the Life of Ivan Denisovich*. And other things as well, conversations which I had with people whose parents were murdered, communists like Werner Eberlein or even, one must admit it, Markus Wolf. His father went off to the Spanish Civil War for one simple reason: he wanted at least to die for something meaningful instead of perishing in one of Stalin's camps. He left Russia for Spain not only because he was a fervent internationalist, but because he wanted to die for something meaningful. This is a profound aberration or seduction of a person's way of thinking. And with all this criticism of communists today we should take into account this notion of seducing people's thinking, because Socialism in its various shades tried to achieve its goal with methods which were diametrically opposed to this goal. But that does not mean that the goal itself is reprehensible: in my view it is not wrong, it is unreal, yet the paths towards it were also criminal. Whereas National Socialism had a goal which was in itself completely reprehensible and the paths towards it corresponded entirely to that goal: because the goal was reprehensible, the ways were too.

Second: Even in the GDR there were things that did succeed which people saw as worth achieving, as the fulfilment of human yearnings. Of course, with their belief that everything would get better came a partial clouding over of their view of reality. As the idiom puts it so nicely, they had blind faith. But this blind faith had a good aspect to it, too. And not all the people were involved in a crime. Many did not want to know what was going on. I can give you an example. People who had been communists and socialists in the GDR read one of my books in which I tried to write down a few biographical things, and they commented: 'We had no idea that this GDR about which you write actually existed. We had absolutely no experience of it'. OK, this sometimes makes me laugh, but I also do have to accept it and not dismiss them as idiots or something. That's the way it was, that's what they were capable of. Let me give you a few more examples: according to Marx, man is a being who achieves self-realisation in his social existence through working with others and who is aware of himself in the products of his labour and in his coexistence with others. Only now do some people realise that unemployment is a scourge, even when it is taken care of in material terms in the still neatly functioning Federal Republic. Work was something in the GDR which enabled everyone to participate in the riches of society – indeed, they had to: working was not only a right but also a duty. So nearly everyone was occupied doing something. It may not have been efficient, but it was work. And this is not to be despised.

Third: the sharp divide between the very poor and the very rich was nowhere near as great as the one now opening up in eastern Germany.

Fourth: They made sure that everyone had a roof over their head, that accommodation was affordable and that the basic necessities were at a giveaway price. Experience taught us, though, that this does not work economically: it doesn't work as far as housing is concerned, nor for energy either when you make things so cheap. Nor for water. OK, but at any rate they did provide these things, they even provided people coming out of the clink with a roof over their heads, even when the mood of the people was against it. Access to education was guaranteed for all sections of the population. And I say that as someone who did not have such access. But to some extent I belonged to a section of society which always had educational privileges, whereas my wife comes from a background where she could never have even contemplated studying medicine. I can see that. Then there was the old 'Einheitsschule' (comprehensive school) which had a lot of ideological baggage, OK, but it did offer a very thorough, almost ideologically excessive encouragement of weak pupils without any real corresponding equivalent encouragement of the bright ones. But there was something along the lines of: 'We won't leave anyone out!' That's what I remember about the GDR now that I've been living for five years in the Federal Republic or at least in the area annexed to it: there was something akin to an equivalence of all forms of work. And it was really celebrated as a principle, on the first of May too: working men and women were at the centre of things; and a professor was in this sense also an intellectual worker, but in principle by no means less in value than the woman who cleans the floor or the man who paints houses. That is the reason, too, why the wage differentials were actually not a serious problem. OK, the professor wasn't well paid, and that's why many professors went over to the West: because they wanted wage-freedom – sorry, they said they wanted freedom! I'm not reproaching them, but I have to tell the truth about the way things were. These issues are always ambivalent. The health system too: of course, 60 Marks per month for everyone, that was the most anyone paid. And naturally a modern health system could not be financed in this way in the long term. Of course there were some people who could get private treatment. But taken as a whole, it wasn't so bad. True, my wife's wage was considerably higher than mine, but if I compare today what a notary rakes in and what a shop assistant earns or a receptionist. What we have is the reinstallation of the class society pure and simple. The problem with socialist society was the fact that, in the way it constructed itself, it lost sight of reality and thought it could whitewash over economic criteria with ideological glamour. It actually foundered on its own lies about itself. But I have to add: it was in the majority of cases a well-meaning lie. And a well-meaning lie has bad consequences. But it was not a case of an army of vicious men telling lies, there was ultimately something well-meaning about it all.

RJ: That was a very convincing answer to my first question about possible comparisons between the Nazi regime and the GDR. But what about my second question as to the difference between the actions of individuals and the church as an institution? You rebelled against this lie, but what did the church do?

FS: I will give you an answer from my personal point of view. I cannot imagine my life in the GDR at all without this Protestant church in which I grew up. Without this source of strength, I could not have found the direction which I have followed in my life. That's why I can understand, too, how many people who did not have this were not able to be as resistant as I could afford to be. So I find it self-righteous to question why others did not do what I did. OK, true, I was often completely alone, at school I was completely alone, except for one friend who was the only one interested in what I was interested in, namely German literature. I got that from my father. I was able to talk to my friend about Kleist. The others would have dismissed me as a bit of a nutcase for actually wanting to discuss Kleist. Because his parents were teachers, my friend was forbidden to talk to me at break as this could have been an obstacle to his future advancement. And my friend Uwe said to me: 'Hey, we can't get together at break any more, we'll have to meet in the evenings'. So we two pupils met secretly in the evenings to have our talks. And that's what school was like. Later, though, I was lucky: I found people in the student religious society who thought in a similar way to me, even people who studied physics. This student religious society was the greatest haven of strength in a society which for the most part not only cooperated but also joined in the howling and even in the cheering! We were really isolated. Every year in autumn there was a conference held by an international scientific society, the so-called Leopoldiner, and for us this had to suffice for a whole year. One evening Herr Weizsäcker[3] came to the student religious society and gave a lecture. I mention this for two reasons: first, for his great speech in '63 after he had received the Peace Prize of the German Book Trade. You can perhaps imagine how proud I felt when I received this prize thirty years later. Weizsäcker's speech was something fundamental to a whole generation and was also printed in the GDR. He encouraged us by simply following thoughts consistent with Christian belief, philosphically tenable, accountable ideas, not going beyond the bounds of reasonable human thinking. Secondly, he unfolded and expounded the close connection between science and philosophy, between knowledge and ethics. We found that really great.

The last point I wanted to make in anwer to your question: in the church of which I was part there were always people who I knew would speak up for me if I was taken away. And right up to the end I never lost this feeling. But I know that there were also others in the church who thought that we should not overstep the mark as we were also dependent on the state. Yet I was never muzzled by my superiors in the church. And there was also a third group, not so much in the Magdeburg Church but in other regional churches, who tried to learn their lessons from the disastrous history of the church: when the monarchists and nationalists had been in power they had held themselves in check, so their view was that they could not offer very great resistance now simply because the communists were in power. In their opinion, what was really needed was modesty and contrition. Precisely because the church had betrayed the working class and peace, they could not insinuate that the communists were evil from the outset for at bottom the communists wanted something very similar to what they wanted. Rather they should seek not what separates them but what unites them and so support the policy of peace and proclaim that the GDR was the more just society because it removed the individual's right of disposal of property, the individual's economic power. Is that not an attempt to construct a more just society?

I have a certain sympathy for all three positions. But I have no sympathy with the fact that there were also people who violated their pastoral duty by passing on to the Stasi things that were confided to them, or passed on information which could damage others. What I do regard as acceptable was what Manfred Stolpe, the Consistorial President of the Evangelical Church, did.

RJ: The Protestant church in the GDR was certainly not a state church, but would it be fair to view the position of the church positively and say that it also stood for a social conscience?

FS: Yes, but there were certain things which we were never allowed to mention. There were taboos. I believe that communism is finished for the foreseeable future. But I think it more than likely that capitalism as an economic system will put paid to us too in the foreseeable future. I am unable to rejoice at the demise of communism. However, I do severely reproach the communists for the fact that they criminalised one of Marx's own highest principles, for when he was asked as an eighteen-year-old what was the most important thing, he answered that it was Doubt. The communists replaced Doubt with the Party, which removed all doubt. My second reproach is their negation of another of the young Marx's ideas when he said that they were not setting up a new principle and proclaiming it to be the truth but advocating free discussion. But the later Marx himself contributed a great deal to this with his critique of the Gotha Programme and his dictatorship of the proletariat. I consider all that to be complete political adventurism which others then converted into political practice. The much more serious point is the fact that Marxism did not develop a realistic anthropology and simply allowed this crude form of Marxism to become practice: the idea that Man is in principle good and we simple have to make the conditions and circumstances such that he is able to become what he actually is. That's why Freud, the interpretation of Shakespeare and the Bible were bourgeois defeatism. Ultimately all economic theory will be of no avail to anyone who fails to confront the central importance of evil and of dealing with it. We have this, though, before our very eyes now in this bourgeois society which is not a democracy but a mediocracy which, in the form of private television stations and their related viewing figures, simply exploits the evil within us: pleasure in destruction which for hundreds of thousands of people, even for children and young people too, is quite normal and no longer distinguishes between reality and fiction. I am more afraid of this society than of communism.

RJ: Comparison has often been made between you and Luther. What is your view of this?

FS: I live in a very small town which was very small in those days too but which has had an enormous influence. Every time I visit a proper city and then return to my small town, I'm amazed: from this town emanated all Europe's disasters, not only the renewal but also the division. So one thing that Luther signifies for me is the fact that he believed in the word, the power of the word and not the words of the powers that be. In other words, he countered the words of the powers that be with the power of the word and declared that to be his task, for there was no other way. This was the idea which I, which we faced up to during the whole process of radical change in 1989. We said that we didn't want the new society to start with new injustice, that we would rather take suffering upon ourselves than inflict suffering on others, very much in the spirit of Bonhoeffer who was shot by the Nazis in 1945.

DR: You have often spoken of the importance of the part played by writers in the GDR. What is your view of the role and status of writers and literature in the present situation?

FS: Let me exaggerate a little and put it like this. Fast Food literature is taking over the market and the market is taking over literature. But there are fortunately still a few niches for people who want something different, and there still are such people! A second point: there is a turn to the right by left-wingers which goes under the name of 'the capacity to learn' and as far as I'm concerned, they are thereby simply giving expression to the fact that they are trendsetters, nothing more. People whose greatness, or so they think, now consists in insulting themselves and considering everything they believed in to be rubbish now, including any literature which intends something beyond itself. I come from a country where literature was always supposed to have a specific intention but also to have value in itself. Yet even at the end of the '70s, former communists like Erich Arendt were pulling me to pieces, attacking the appellative character of literature. But I don't want to have to give up the direct message of an Erich Fried whose intentions go beyond merely producing a nice line of verse, or a Volker Braun. Or like Brecht, conceal the imperative in the indicative. Is literature not a little bit like secularised prayer: laments, hopes, grief, anger, deception, depression, protest – all brought together and given shape? I share the view that the significance of literature should not simply rest within itself, with formal concerns. Today a clique of intellectuals in Germany is fostering this postmodern cynicism, adopting an incredibly clever, know-all stance. And then along comes someone whose literary intentions go beyond the actual lines he writes, and his contribution shows that some things about us do change. It fills me with grief that even someone like Günter Kunert now belongs to this category: he wrote great poems which were meat and drink to us, an aid with which each one of us was then able to exert his own small changing influence on the world around us once we had found a more precise image of ourselves in his writing – yes, the good old Marxist combination of self-knowledge and knowledge of the world, of changing yourself and changing the world. This is the sense in which I see myself as a theologian. We must never again have the dull roll call, the dull imperative. God preserve us from Weinert, from revolutionary lyric poetry, from ideology written in verse. But there are just as many off-putting examples in religion too.

Volker Braun is someone who refuses to conform today just as he refused to conform in the past, but the current victor-mentality wants to eliminate all such unruly spirits. The process of emancipation in the GDR was one which really was carried out via the written page, whereby people who read the written page took seriously what they read – and the dictators took it seriously too: Kunze, Biermann, Kunert, Brasch, Christa Wolf, de Bruyn, Hein; but they also took seriously the things we did ourselves, for instance, the 'twenty propositions for the social renewal of the GDR' in 1987, or the texts of the Ecumenical Assembly (in which tens of thousands participated, taking up questions relevant to the future such as peace, disarmament, conscription, justice and human rights, seeking to answer them from world- , GDR- and personal viewpoints) or the ideas we smuggled in from Poland and Czechoslovakia.

The greatest reversal in the revolutionary movement in the GDR in the late '80s was the disappointment at the fact that the democratic movement was bought off so quickly. The people who had been spokesmen and spokeswomen for something which had broader horizons became completely geared up for possession of the DM. I have no desire to chide them for this, but it became the sole subject of discussion: 'We'll elect anyone who gives us the DM!' And now they're paying for it. When money becomes scarcer, democracy will go for a burton if people don't realise that democracy is more important than our financial prosperity and that it has to prove itself under conditions where we no longer have so much to distribute but where everyone will have something to eat and be able to live if we distribute it properly. And my concern is that in the long run, the question of currency will be more important to people than proving how democratic we are.

Notes

1. Translated by David Rock.
2. A GDR ceremony to replace religious confirmation.
3. The Weizsäcker referred to here is the physicist Carl Friedrich von Weizsäcker, not former Bundespräsident Richard von Weizsäcker.

CHAPTER 6

Intellectuals, Citizens and Writers in East Germany – Before and After the *Wende*[1]

Friedrich Schorlemmer *

In October 1985, Mikhail Sergeyevich Gorbachev gave a sensational lecture before the National Assembly in Paris. The Western press wondered whether this was all just new rhetorical tones in the same old garb. They were not prepared to accept that a new age, soon to be known as the age of *Glasnost* and *Perestroika*, really had begun, one which would lead to the end of the Cold War and to extensive disarmament. Temporarily, it would appear.

Ten years on we have been pushed out of the stuffy waiting-room of history and into the draughty express-train, a fast train which no longer has a timetable. The system of Western democracies which, by dint of market forces, just about functions effectively even if not very humanely, has been at the mercy of its own devices since the collapse of communism. At least it no longer needs to prove itself by its counter-image. The 'signs of the time' in which capitalism is again able to do what it wants, are unmistakable. It started ten years ago. We saw the resurrection of hopes which we believed we had been forced to bury in 1968. Though I don't want to insist on the term 'resurrection' in its theological sense, I confess that I was amongst those who saw in Gorbachev almost something messianic because it was something which we had no longer reck-

*The original German text is reproduced at the end of this chapter

oned with, and we were amazed at the vision and skill with which he made things progress. And you can imagine how someone feels when, after being threatened with being immured for a hundred years to come, a few months later the monstrosity, this lethal wall of concrete, suddenly comes down one night in November. A hope which had flared up briefly in the shape of the 'Prague Spring' started to burn again. Intellectuals in Germany, particularly East Germany, were again spurred on to keep the struggle going for the alliance of social justice and freedom, despite the failure of 1968. Or perhaps it was because Prague did not fail but was crushed by tanks without being able to prove whether socialism, freedom and economic prosperity can go together. I might also say that in 1968 we experienced the 'draught' of history. In this 'draught', Kurt Bartsch, one of our most amiable satirists, wrote a small volume of poems with the title 'Zugluft' (Draught). Later he was drawn to the West, as many others were. Yet he is not one of those who have come back to settle accounts. I'll quote two poems from 1968 which reflect the way things were. One is called 'Sozialistischer Biedermeier' (Socialist Biedermeier), an example of the continuous reproducibility of the petty bourgeois in all possible social orders:

Zwischen Wand und Widersprüchen
machen sie es sich bequem.
Links ein Sofa, rechts ein Sofa,
in der Mitte ein Emblem.

Brüder, seht, die rote Fahne
hängt bei uns zur Küche raus.
Außen Sonne, innen Sahne,
so sieht Marx wie Moritz aus.

(Between walls and contradictions/ they make themselves at home./ On the left a sofa, on the right a sofa, / in the middle an emblem. /Brothers, look, the red flag / is hanging out of our kitchen. / Outside sun, inside cream, / makes Marx look like Moritz [Simple Simon].)[2]

Now, when the superiority of communism fails to actually materialise and someone comes along talking about 'flourishing landscapes',[3] then such people say: 'Wonderful' and chant: 'Helmut, Helmut, help us', in Karl-Marx-Stadt of all places.

The same Kurt Bartsch also wrote of the courage of German intellectuals :

> Wenn ich einmal meine eigene Meinung darf,
> begann er ungewöhnlich kraß,
> so hat schon Karl Marx gesagt, daß...

(If I may express my own opinion for once, /he began, not mincing matters for a change, /even Karl Marx said that...')

Socialism is over and done with. Why? Because when it comes down to it, what is 'between their teeth' is more important to people than what is 'on the tip of their tongue'. In this respect, capitalism and socialist bureaucracy are one. The contest was essentially an economic one, in so far as affirmation of a particular political system depends essentially on the material situation. Reiner Kunze composed the following verse along these lines:

> 'Prag '68'
> Eine Lehre liegt mir auf der Zunge,
> aber der Zoll sucht zwischen den Zähnen.

('Prague '68': A doctrine is on the tip of my tongue, but the customs search between my teeth).

Doctrine alone is not enough to fill people's stomachs. The customs officers are afraid and make people afraid of the doctrine but can only search between the teeth. The majority of the people, too, seek the things that get stuck between the teeth. Should those that have enough to eat mock this?

Almost six years ago today, on 28 October 1989, I was in the 'Erlöserkirche' (Church of the Redeemer) in Berlin-Rummelsburg. People had to be there three hours early to be sure of a seat. The so-called GDR-intellectuals came along to speak about the brutal police intervention which had taken place on 7 October. and to some extent too, to express their aesthetic and political credos. They were all there together, at least those from Berlin.

The Berliners had anyway always regarded themselves as the real front runners until they later had to hand on the baton of courage to Leipzig. For a short while. From Leipzig came the *Wende* within the *Wende* (change within the change) which the East Berliners at first did not want at all: 'One people'.

In Rummelsburg was the police prison where the young people who had demonstrated on 7 October had been brought and treated badly, indeed brutally, by the police. The 'Chinese solution'[4] seemed to be looming. And in the

Erlöserkirche in Rummelsburg, there was the meeting of what we called 'Kunstschaffenden' ('creative artists') 'Wider den Schlaf der Vernunft'[5] ('Against the Sleep of Reason'). The creative artists came together and 'unanimously', as we always used to say, demanded *Perestroika* for the GDR. Daniela Dahn and Jürgen Rennert ran the meeting. The writers nailed their colours to the mast, demanded 'Rechtsstaatlichkeit' (the rule of law), siding with the people, not the powers that be. Many of them still belonged to the SED (the Socialist Unity Party).

In view of the promise of 'flourishing landscapes' in 1990 on the one hand and the 1995 lament about the gaping financial hole which has opened up behind the now demolished Wall on the other, we might recall the words of the first Federal President, Theodor Heuss, who impressed upon us in 1946: 'Democracy is not a promise of happiness but the result of political education and a democratic way of thinking.' We have reached this point in Germany again: is democracy important to us as the result of political education and a democratic way of thinking and will democracy remain stable in our country if the promise of material happiness is absent? This is becoming a very serious question for our united republic.

I will now attempt in the first part of my exposition to give a 'time-check' on the unified Republic following on from a provocative proposition of Heiner Müller's. Peaceful unification on a democratic basis is a stroke of luck in German and European history, but this lucky chance can be gambled away again through 'Siegermentalität' ('victor mentality').

Secondly, I will go into the question: 'Was bleibt?'[6](What remains?) The role of the writers in the GDR. My thesis is that books and not files will remain.

First, the 'time-check' of the united Republic in connection with the late Heiner Müller's dictum: 'Both parts are disappearing in the unification which is taking place. At first it looked as if this GDR bit would simply be incorporated. But this doesn't seem to be working. Now both parts are disappearing and an indescribable vacuum is emerging which is held together by the Deutschmark'. Is unification leaving behind a vacuum, as Heiner Müller says, a vacuum which is only being filled by the Deutschmark, and thus far only in the pockets of the eastern 'Zweidrittelgesellschaft'[7] (two-thirds society)? For the great majority, Germany is virtually identical with the *hard* Deutschmark and it would therefore be the utmost sacrilege to abandon it in favour of a Euro-currency. How many people are there in East and West Germany who are really concerned about the *soft* 'd' of democracy and who give voice to it in the daily efforts of democratic processes and institutions? Nothing is yet decided. At any rate if a vacuum is not to emerge, then Germany has to be re-founded after two independent part-states were founded from what was left of the Reich in 1945, both dependent upon the grace and favour of their respective occupying powers. This 'grace and favour' was fundamentally different in the two parts. The one state was nourished with the Marshall Plan and equipped with a constitution based on the principle of liberty, the other was economically drained and nursed back to health with ideology. (After my recent visit to Wales, I thought to myself: 'That's what Morgenthau[8] imagined Germany would be like. It looks so nice!'). Both German states integrated themselves (into their respective blocs) and were kept under control[9] by the victors. I would even maintain that we Germans needed these forty years of political quarantine in order to retain our sanity. Both parts of Germany recommended themselves to the former adversaries on their territory as loyal allies and as imitators who were extremely quick to learn until they were able, as indispensable partners, to feel almost victors themselves. Thus we East Germans were at least the Victors of History,[10] along with the victorious Soviet army. The price for freedom through integration into Western Europe was the sacrifice of German unity. Adenauer, of course, only wanted an extended Rhine province, no more, something we need to discuss more openly today. For years, the Federal Republic developed a self-confidence which found satisfaction in itself. After being able to travel through the Federal Republic, I was able to understand this too: such a rich, varied, beautiful land – why does it need the wild east? There are perhaps 10 to 20 percent of West Germans who felt the division to be a real deficiency and for whom unity, with all its consequences, will always remain something positive. No more than that. I can understand this too. But we must get clear in our minds why we now have internal problems with unification. If real populists came along, they could direct all the anger at East Germany. A few sentences from Edmund Stoiber[11] about the bottomless financial pit in the East have already had their effect, on both sides, incidentally.

'Deutsche an einen Tisch' (Let all Germans sit at one table) was the slogan on all the banners in the East[12] too from the 1950s onwards. My own childhood is plastered with watchwords, with the long noses of Western politicians, caricatures on every telegraph pole, in every village.

From the outset, each part of Germany called for unity, but on its own conditions. It proved exactly the same with unification in 1990: the Federal Republic produced unity on its own conditions, with the East Germans agreeing to Deutschmark-unification. The communists would have done likewise too. It's good that it turned out this way round! To avoid giving any false impressions, let me say that I do not mourn the GDR of Ulbricht and Honecker for a single minute. But life there was more than today's sound-bites of condemnation are able to express. One hardly has to mention it to be suspected of 'Ostalgie' (nostalgia for the GDR). But there were other things which are hardly mentioned today.

The demarcation line between East and West soon became a lethal border, and East and West became politically loaded terms. Just as the words 'Westsender' (West German radio stations), 'Westkaugummi' (Western chewing-gum) and 'Westmark' (the West German Deutschmark) had a mysterious ring to them, so too the words 'Westzeitung' (West German newspaper), 'Westfernsehen' (West German television), and 'Westkontakte' (contacts in the West) became politically notorious. There were times when the act of chewing gum was a declaration of political belief. (Once when I was thirteen and we were leaving West Berlin by the 'S-Bahn', my father warned me to spit out my chewing-gum). On the other hand, anyone who had connections or even relatives in West Germany could rejoice. Can you imagine what an incredible difference there was between 'Besuch' and 'Westbesuch' (ordinary visitors and visitors from West Germany)? When visitors from West Germany were coming, then things were literally turned on their heads. People would manage to get hold of cheese which just wasn't available anywhere. At any rate, more often than not West Germans felt at home with us and we gave them a very cordial reception. The children, though, would be quite open about it all and would ask straight away: 'What have you brought with you?' Grandma too, returning from a trip to the West, would be able to enjoy the special attention paid to her. Old-age pensioners in the GDR had one great privilege: they were allowed to travel to West Germany and would, of course, even if they came back at night, be picked up from the station by the whole family. Now grandma can take a taxi. And grandma can now travel to where she wants as well. That is now entirely up to her. The radical change has also completely altered family relationships. Up to 1989, GDR functionaries had to openly break off all family contacts in West Germany and deny or even disown relatives. In the West, on the other hand, people were able to feel confirmed in things every day by gratefully reminding themselves that they did not have to live in the communist East. Having the wicked East just over there was good for the West, and the East was held together by words giving stable images of the enemy: anti-imperialism, anti-fascism and anti-capitalism. The 'Bau-auf-Bau-auf-Pathos'[13] sustained many in their convictions until, in August 1961, it culminated in the huge admission of failure when they had to build the Wall because the GDR was not capable of surviving without a wall. The GDR, threatened with being bled white, immured itself – no, its inhabitants – and lied its way through history about the reasons for cementing itself in. Whilst the one part, economically successful and politically 'mature', soon felt itself to be Germany, with its solemn 'Einheitsgebot' (moral obligation to seek German unity) its 'Grundgesetz' (Basic Law) and its 'Provisoriumsvorbehalt' (the conditional/provisional character of the Basic Law), the other part remained the 'Ostzone' (Eastern Zone), the GDR in inverted commas, until the policy of *détente* brought some easing of the situation. Ten years after the building of the Wall, Willy Brandt's appearance at the window of the 'Erfurter Hof' showed that the Wall had achieved nothing. Those brief scenes of joy as Willy Brandt came up to the window in Erfurt in 1970 and the people, whom the Stasi had not been able to disperse, shouted and cheered, they were the real shock for the leaders of the GDR who now realised that the Wall had not been worth while. 'Willy, Willy!' He was the all-German hero with his step-by-step approach to the greater goal of peaceful unity.

From now on, what Germans from both sides were discussing together under the cloak of diplomacy was for both Eastern and Western secret services highly suspect but also well known. Even in 1987, with Hans-Dietrich Genscher's Davos speech, people in the West, in Great Britain too, were rather concerned about a new version of Rapallo[14] when Genscher said to the West: 'Let us take Gorbachev seriously and seize the chance that he offers'. That helped the Germans more than anyone else. Only a year before, in 1986, the German Federal Chancellor had described the Soviet General Secretary Gorbachev as a master of rhetoric 'like Goebbels'. How quickly such things are forgotten!

Each part of Germany kept on declaring its loyalty to its respective bloc, but for quite some time, Schalck-Golodkowski[15] had been setting up unity by means of the Deutschmark before Strauß once more saved the GDR six years before its demise with a Deutschmark-loan[16] and then afterwards went with Honecker to his hunting lodge. – They lorded it together! From now on Strauß would fly to the GDR by private plane and land wherever he wanted. And then the people who wanted to get out came along and shouted 'Strauß, we want to get out!' Whoever managed to get close to him and slip him a note would soon be in the golden West. The disputed money, along with the pork-export deals with the agricultural entrepreneur März, were forms of euthanasia. (März was a big pig-breeder who had personal connections to the Bavarian state-leadership.) As an East German I must point out that the real problem for us East Germans was not the pigs which we had to produce for the West but the liquid manure which we were left with.

But as a cultural nation, Germany did come together time after time: in the form of Heine editions and in Caspar David Friedrich exhibitions. Curiously enough, even if somewhat delayed, we have changed our tastes in East and West. In the sixties, I could not have imagined going voluntarily to a Caspar David-Friedrich exhibition, yet later, when the big exhibition was in Dresden, I too like everyone else stood there with mouth agape. The reciprocal licences of contemporary writers from East and West Germany became bridges; literature became *the* bridge during these forty years of separation, and of course the 'Westpakete' (parcels from West Germany) too. Just as we East Germans craved for Heinrich Böll, West Germans wanted to read Christa Wolf. Even in East–West renaissances we came to resemble each other: we both became Luther's heirs; in 1983 we celebrated Luther's 500th birthday together. Frederick the Great was erected in East Berlin again. Bismarck got a biography which almost made people forget the fact that it was he who had brought in the anti-socialist laws. Each part of Germany claimed all these as their heritage, yet had to admit too that it was a common heritage. When we had the 'first German in space' (the title-page of *Neues Deutschland*), the people of the state of the GDR became confused. So were we proud Germans too, after all? What was there deep down inside the people I experienced in Poland in 1980 during the workers' revolts: German feelings of superiority can be reactivated, even after these forty years of socialist-internationalist upbringing. Moreover, discussions are said to have taken place at that time between Russian and German top brass, clearly involving conditions with regard to certain Polish territories.

'We' were Germans as well, but better ones on account of the social system with education, work, housing for everyone, and a bulwark of peace. Only this prime political specimen had to be protected without and within with every means at its disposal and its citizens had to fall into line. That was the tiny blemish. The Republic itself was quite OK, only the small flaw was that it had to be protected in such a martial way. Officially they lied their way around the reasons for it. Protection without first required imprisonment within. From the outset, the pull of economic prosperity in the West became mingled with longings for freedom. Now the sequence of this fascination is clear and understandable. Around four million Germans streamed towards the West, even though Ulbricht built the Wall for his survival and Honecker was 'perfecting' dog-leads and automatic shooting devices, whilst the newspapers spoke of the developed socialist society becoming more and more 'perfected'. We never improved anything in the GDR anyway, we only ever 'perfected' things. It was always a case of just that little bit missing to make everything complete. And when I as an East German hear, as I have been hearing for the last five years, people in the German 'Bundestag' (German Parliament) saying that 'German unity is now being completed', it again appears to be just a question of the last small stone to capture the the perfect mosaic. What sort of metaphysical language is it that people have to use all the time? Is there anything in human affairs that is 'complete'?

Each part-state had its Hallstein doctrine.[17] The one was able to put it into effect politically because it was politically bound into the West and had a flourishing economy; the other postulated in a positively teleological fashion[18] that it was 'the only legitimate German state'. In practice, it could just about afford the red paint and the protection for the slogans that were written in it. For example: when Walter Ulbricht's nose was torn from a public poster in 1958, the sleuths and the tracker dogs came from the main district town. When my father went to cut asparagus in the morning, he saw the security people trying to get their dogs to sniff out the right trail. It could only have been me that tore away comrade Ulbricht's nose. What was that story about the fly-droppings on the portrait of the Kaiser in *Schwejk*?[19]

What was proclaimed as imminent victory governed by the laws of History – and there were many who were convinced of the rightness of the ideology – imploded on its fortieth birthday under an eighty-year-old FDJ functionary.[20] And many from the start but not so many at the finish had believed that they had believed the slogans. And nearly everyone had obeyed, voted, waved and chanted. Life in a dictatorship does not offer alternatives. Now that we are united, we are starting increasingly to fear each other as strangers. Paradoxically, it was precisely the division of Germany which created a sense of unity full of contradictions, and only since we have been united are we aware of what divides us. The disgrace of being born in the East[21] will continue to be experienced as long as the East has to justify itself to the West, but also as long as fellow travellers deny to themselves how much they bowed and scraped during all those years.

Previously, there was a consciousness of being a West German just as there was also very much a GDR consciousness, whether positive or negative. Those who had lived divided from their fellow-Germans for more than a generation allowed themselves to be happily joined together for a few emotional moments. The memory of our common history and so too of our historical responsibility, the memory of our culture and also of our cultural barbarity, and the memory of our great achievements and also of our perverse achievements created and do still create 'WE-feelings' in Germany, feelings of togetherness, of belonging together as Germans in East and West, which will only stabilise when the two now formally unified parts of Germany rediscover each other and themselves, and the smaller, economically needier part, grown unaccustomed to freedom, is not compelled, as in a time-lapse film, to catch up on everything and at the same time, both individually and collectively, to answer grudgingly for its history.

There will be no unity as long as one part of Germany holds the other's very existence against it. There will only be unity if we discuss honestly with one another what we have experienced together in forty years. And the intellectuals have some important things to say here, though with the current West–East PEN[22] disputes, they are demonstrating that they too are only human and occasionally even more backward than the general public. As I see it, intellectuals and writers in particular should at least be trying to show that any attempt to finish the GDR off juridically is a blind alley.

What Remains are Books

The wholesale defamation of GDR intellectuals is also a case of envious trampling underfoot. Many in the West would have liked for themselves the role which GDR writers played in their society. And some of those who left are taking their revenge not least because they are finding it difficult to forgive themselves for their own disappointment after fleeing the GDR.

Upright literature in the GDR always was always difficult to get hold of.[23] Conflicts in the GDR were always conflicts also conveyed in literature. Literature propelled the country forward and opened up spaces which appeared to be completely closed off. Literature both addressed and expressed taboos and even ventured into the realms of utopia. GDR writers now have to find a completely different way of coping in the new situation with its market forces, and also with criticism which is very much politically slanted and now and then devastating, even belatedly so. In the new conditions, literature has a different function. Writers have to (and want to) come to terms with the fact that they are no longer the preceptors, the gurus, the revered personalities before whom everyone bows down. They were a substitute public sphere and substitute critics of public ills. This substitute public sphere ceased to exist when the *BILD-Zeitung*[24] became available. And it is no longer enough simply to voice criticism, what writers say has to be good as literature as well. The criteria for this are now, however, being defined by West Germans.

The history of the GDR is most accurately depicted through its literature. In the future, too, literature will depict most accurately the way things were. This statement appears banal, but it is precisely what is being negated in current practice. I could describe the make-up of the GDR with three quotations.

Reiner Kunze wrote about both the GDR constitution and the reality of things. Much of what he said has not become outdated. Taking up a quotation from the constitution, Kunze writes:

> 'Ethik'
> Im Mittelpunkt steht der Mensch
> nicht
> der einzelne.

('Ethics'. At the focal point stands Man/ not/ the individual).

That was the point. At the focal point stands 'Man'; not you, though, but everyone, not the individual. That is in a way the political and anthropological basis because 'Man' is 'das Ensemble der gesellschaftlichen Verhältnisse' ('the totality of social relationships'). Is he not, though, much more than that? The GDR, indeed the entire soviet-socialist system, was constructed on the basis of a false citation of the Communist Manifesto. I shall return to this later.

The second 'dialectical' text comes from Bert Brecht's poem 'Lob des Zweifels' ('In Praise of Doubt/Scepticism') and describes the political psychology of the SED-autocrats:

> Da sind die Unbedenklichen, die niemals zweifeln.
> Ihre Verdauung ist glänzend, ihr Urteil ist unfehlbar.
> Sie glauben nicht den Fakten, sie glauben nur an sich.
> Im Notfall müssen die Fakten dran glauben.
> Ihre Geduld mit sich selber ist unbegrenzt.
> Auf Argumente hören sie nur mit dem Ohr des Spitzels.

(There are the harmless, unthinking ones who never doubt./ Their digestion is splendid, their judgement is infallible./ They don't believe the facts, they only believe in themselves./ If needs be, the facts must be made to fit./ Their patience with themselves is boundless./ They only listen to arguments with the ears of informers).

Ultimately, books had the effect of breaking taboos. Thus Christa Wolf writes in her novel *Kindheitsmuster* (Patterns of Childhood): 'What one cannot speak about, one must gradually cease to be silent about'.[25]

Since its demise, I miss the GDR because I miss its literature and the role which it played. As a citizen and as a reader, I am now involved in all kinds of things, but hardly at all with literature any longer. You will forgive me if I come to the paradoxical conclusion that dictatorships even have something beneficial about them in so far as they make the essential things essential to us and they make literature important, for whoever is under threat writes differently and also reads differently. And 'prose in particular breaks down deadly simplifications. ... It supports the process by which human beings emancipate themselves. ... It is revolutionary and realistic, it entices and encourages us to achieve the impossible' (Christa Wolf).[26] The direct relationship of literature to reality under oppressive conditions is inevitable, its inner task can be clearly designated in so far as it stands in constant opposition to external taskmasters.

The process of political, legal and economic transformation since 1990 is without historical precedent. It has also shaken the very substance of culture and cult, cultural life and the churches. In a society with a market economy, everything is measured and evaluated according to its price. Values become immaterial.[27] The outcome of existential and politico-economic irritations is uncertain, in all areas of life. It would seem that the Western system was relatively stable as long as the one in the East existed. Now its own viability is under discussion, as well as its ability to prosper in its links with the rest of the world. I believe that there will either be a worldwide *perestroika*, or else capitalism will implode the same way that socialism did. Just as those in the West, almost triumphally after the 'victory', proclaimed the end of history, so the intellectuals in the East were still talking of a surplus, despite the restricted and depressing reality. A life without utopia is no life at all, for 'those who no longer have time to dream, haven't any strength left either for the fight' (Christa Wolf).

What remains of the GDR? Books that have been opened. People who have grown up with literature will also find their way back to (their) literature again. Writers in the GDR helped many of us to carry on living in the GDR and to persist in our attempts to live our lives truthfully. Very early on, the emancipatory groups found allies in the writers. Young people carried lines by Reiner Kunze, Thomas Brasch and Wolf Biermann in their inside breast pockets. (And this included apprentices in the chemical industries and trainee bakers which I, as a vicar with special responsibility for young people, found particularly pleasing.) Christa Wolf's *Kindheitsmuster* (Patterns of Childhood), Stephan Hermlin's *Abendlicht* (Evening Light) and Franz Fühmann's *Vor Feuerschlünden* (Before the Jaws of Fire) helped us to be honest in the present on account of their honesty about our past. Just how closely peace and truth are inter-

connected was made clear by Franz Fühmann in a short
speech to the Peace Symposium in 1981:[28]

> The basis of all trust is truthfulness. It always starts out as truthfulness
> towards oneself. Untruthfulness can never be a means to an end, how-
> ever good the latter may be. It undermines this end and discredits it. Ulti-
> mately it simply undermines trust, whose resources are exhaustible, in all
> areas and in every respect, I might add. Trust which has dwindled away
> or been undermined is like feet which have grown numb – very difficult
> to regenerate. I have always agreed with Immanuel Kant for whom 'lies
> are the true blight in human nature'. Lies should be proscribed just as war
> should be. They both spring up from one root and both lead to destruc-
> tion. It is essential to declare war on lies in whatever one does.

Christa Wolf expressed a similar sentiment too in 1981: 'To
avoid war people also have to criticise the ills in their own
respective countries. The role of taboos in preparations for
war: the number of shameful secrets grows incessantly,
immeasurably.[29] How insignificant all the censors' taboos and
the consequences of breaking them become through the threat
to life'. These and other sentences by Christa Wolf were cut by
the censor. We got hold of them via Western editions and saw
what it took to goad the lion, though it must be admittted that
now and again the censors were very clever in so far as they
allowed quite specific and much more important sentences to
get through. I suspect that occasionally, the censors threw
some fodder in the direction of their superiors and thus
allowed other things through. Even censors, professionally
preoccupied with good literature, do not remain uninfluenced
by their reading of such works. This is the artfulness of truth,
its subcutaneous effect. Anyone wishing to make judgements
on lyric poetry has to understand it first. And anyone understanding it is moved by it too. Otherwise their judgements
lead to completely comical evaluations such as those evidenced in Kunze's Stasi files.

I shall now give a few more selected examples of the effects
of people's critical involvement in the GDR. In 1965, the infa-
mous 11th Plenum of the SED took place at which Honecker
gave the report. The focal point of the Party's criticism was a
film by a man who had once made the most effective film of
all in terms of political agitation, namely *Ernst Thälmann, Sohn
seiner Klasse* (Ernst Thälmann, Son of his Class), by Kurt Maetzig. His latest film had the title *Das Kaninchen bin ich*[30] (I am the
Rabbit). None of us had ever seen this film or knew what it

was about. But 'Das Kaninchen bin ich' nevertheless became a standard quotation. And there was no question as to who was the snake. Anyone could become a rabbit, or even a snake too! There was not much distance between them in 'actually existing socialism', and that is why trying to clearly distinguish victim from perpetrator without blurring anything is today so agonisingly difficult. I saw the film in 1990 together with Kurt Maetzig – a wonderful film which cracks open the GDR political penal system and shows the emancipation of a young woman. It still fills young women from the GDR with courage even today when they see this film. It was not supposed to be like that: encouragement through truth!

Biermann, Heym and Bieler were massacred by Honecker. But part of the complicated 'historical truth' is the fact that Biermann was allowed to travel to West Berlin in 1965 to put on a programme together with Wolfgang Neuss, one of the great cabaret artists, when the GDR chiefs knew precisely that we would all be sitting by the radio with our tape-recorders, recording and writing down everything. Who helped you to get to West Berlin at that time then, my dear Wolf Biermann? Who had to give his permission? I am not in any way reproaching you for this because we all profited from it. But it was a privilege, you know it was. The best lines about everyday life in the GDR are to be found in the 1965 ballad 'Buckower Kleinstadtsonntag' (Small-town sunday in Buckow): 'Ist hier was los? Nein hier ist nichts los!' ('Is there anything going on here? No, there's nothing going on here!') Or in the song about the state prosecutor who brought a case against Fredi Rohsmeisl because he danced a wild dance[31] and now the discharged prisoner has to watch the state prosecutor dancing the same wild dance. And then we have these wonderfully thought-out lines of Wolf Biermann's: 'I have seen people changing, sometimes it was no longer very nice. But does it help us?' One answer to this is a very hesitant 'Yes'. Wonderful, yes it does help us when people change. But isn't that still just as valid today?

Stefan Heym's books were absolutely devoured. One needs only to recall his *Schmähschrift* (Defamatory Piece) or the story *Ein sehr guter zweiter Mann* (A Very Good Second Man). With meticulous, historically exegetic and sociopsychological precision, Heym investigates the family history of the royal house of Saul, David and Solomon, demonstrates in an alarming and entertaining way the functional mechanisms of power, and tells of a chronicler's art of survival in a dictatorship. Remain true to yourself and survive in this world of Joabs and Jehudas,[32] every Tom, Dick and Harry, Jagoda, Beria and Mielke.[33] With Stefan Heym, it was always – and still is – socialist criticism of socialism; he was for emancipation, for freedom of the word, for more justice. Stefan Heym made full use of the scope which his life-history gave him and the degree of inviolability which he enjoyed, accepted his expulsion from the GDR Writers' Union in 1979 along with other authors, and spoke openly, indeed almost prophetically, but he remained in the GDR and maintained his domicile and his area of influence there.

In 1978, exactly ten years after Prague, Rudolf Bahro published his 'Alternative', a blueprint for an emancipatory form of socialism, and was convicted – the system functioned in absurd ways like this – of an offence under the GDR equivalent of the Official Secrets Act, imprisoned[34] and deported to the West. In 1979, pointing to the symptoms of sickness and decline in our society, *Sinn und Form*[35] published for the first time a story which touched upon the most taboo of all themes: leaving the country, and worse still, those leaving were the children of functionaries. The problem of leaving the country was one which preoccupied many writers, as is now again emerging from the correspondence between Christa Wolf and Franz Fühmann. The latter had already given full expression to his views on this in essays and discussions and had decided to bring his criticism to bear in the country itself in order to change the country. He was particularly anxious about several talented but pressurised younger writers.

In 1979, the slender volume *Abendlicht* by Stephan Hermlin appeared, which began with a meditiation on Bach's Easter Cantata for the second sunday after Easter, the Walk to Emmaus: '... for it is toward evening'.[36] The entire book results from the shock and joy of discovering a far-reaching error, life at second hand in Stalinist socialism. GDR society had been constructed according to the proposition that the new society was an association 'in which the free development of all is the condition for the free development of each individual'. But in the Communist Manifesto of Marx and Engels, it actually says: 'In place of the old bourgeois society with its classes and class-differences comes an association, in which the free development of each individual is the condition for the free development of all.' How far did this blindness go if nobody noticed that one of the fundamental scriptures of the GDR had, in a fundamental way, been quoted wrongly. In 1981, Stephan Hermlin organised the Berlin Meeting for Peace where the principle of a dichotomous world-view of good and evil, and correspondingly of good and evil weapons, was breached for the first time. There, Franz Fühmann spoke his great words on truthfulness which he had presented in his autobiographical book *Vor Feuerschlünden* (Before the Jaws of Fire) with his inter-pretation of poems by Trakl.[37]

When Christa Wolf published her story *Kassandra* together with the *Frankfurt Lectures* in 1983, it considerably reinforced the peace movement in East and West. As I see it, nowhere have the machinations of Eumelos (the typical, unscrupulous scaremonger of power with a hidden face) been more clearly portrayed. And in this story, Christa Wolf makes clear in a really convincing way that the noble goal of war does not exist at all, but that the result of war would be the destruction of everyone. And she nevertheless offers us a tiny ray of hope when, in the midst of the threatening apocalypse, we read: 'We were frail; as our time was limited, we were not able to waste it with trivialities. And so, with consummate ease, as if we had been given all the time in the world, we got straight down to the thing that was important – us'.

With all his defiant sadness, Günter Kunert became one of the seismographs of our time through his poems and essays. In his *English Diary*, for instance, he makes it clear in a very sim-ple way that socialism cannot succeed as long as it denies us access to vegetables. And he stands up most clearly against the exploitation of literature for ideological purposes and insists that literature is a positive surplus in a world which is merely utilitarian. Literature becomes the individual's search for meaning whereby the individual seeks and needs others.

> Ich bin der Sucher
> eines Weges
> für mehr als mich.

(I am the seeker/ of a way/ for more than me).

He remains 'Unterwegs nach Utopia' (on the way to utopia). The small volume of poems with this title appeared whilst he was on the way to the West. Most of those leaving the country left along with their horses, their cats and all their household goods and got a 'Doppelpaß' (dual German passport). In a way writers who left, such as Monika Maron, anticipated German unity in their various private, privileged ways. Was Kunert's poem 'Auf der Flucht' (Escaping) meant to apply to those leaving the country as well?

> Vor dem Beton
> geht es zu
> wie im Märchen:
> Wo du
> auch ankommst,
> er erwartet dich
> grau und gründlich.

(On this side of the concrete wall, things happen as in a fairy-story: Wherever you turn up it awaits you, grey and thorough).

Erich Loest's novel *Es geht seinen Gang* (Things Run their Course, 1978) begins with the sentence: 'Sure, there is Hemus'.[38] Anybody who did not live in the GDR cannot understand this. You have to explain it by recounting it. Only when you have understood this can you understand what life in the GDR was really like. In the novel, the 'man in the street' has an imaginary nocturnal conversation with the First Secretary in Leipzig in which he says everything which the First Secretary, in his superior aloofness, neither can nor wants to hear. The fateful irony is that it takes place in Leipzig. Erich Loest then describes the effect of a ban on going to Leuschner Square to hear a concert which has been banned. The concert does not take place at all, but many of the people who are warned off going actually do go because it has been banned. And one young man, like everybody else too, goes out of curiosity but is bitten by one of the many police dogs. So he lives with the political consequences of the 'dog bite at Leuschner Square'. Anyone who at any time protested in the GDR has been left with his 'dog bite'.[39]

This choice of examples is, of course, a random one. Naturally, one ought also to refer to Joachim Walther's novel *Bewerbung bei Hofe* (Applying for a Post at Court), a brilliant story about the secret service and lyric poets which shows that it is impossible for a writer to remain true both to the 'court' and to his vocation. Or another example: Volker Braun waited twenty years before his play *Lenins Tod* (Lenin's Death) could be performed. Dieter Schubert wrote satires about a high-ranking dignitary's visit to the country. Here laughter becomes a form of resistance.

Uwe Grüning published a cycle of Jeremiah poems about the prophet who wrote 'gegen die Wahrheit' ('against the truth') and was cast into the well[40] but still spoke out because he had to.

Hanns Cibulka, in his Baltic diaries and in poems, trained his sights on the threat to the environment. Gabriele Eckart, in her own particular way, did reverence to 'Socialist Realism' by writing both what the people working in the 'Havelobst'[41] were saying and the way in which they were saying it. And the documentary collection of women's statements *Guten Morgen, du Schöne* (Good Morning Pretty Woman) by Maxi Wander were read in theatres and offer a history of women's emancipation *à la* GDR. This led to discussion of these issues throughout the whole of society, making it clear that the emancipation movement in the GDR was a movement towards the liberation of man – men as well as women. There were, indeed, quite some differences to feminism in the West.

All these examples are chosen at random. A history of the GDR via the history of its literature is still to be written. It could be a rewarding interdisciplinary task. Only by so doing would one get away from the insidious demonisation of and fixation with the Stasi files and get close to the phenomenon of the failure of an idea. On the other hand, only by doing so can one counteract any false transfiguration of things. Also, one will be able to follow the inner struggles of the intellectuals, the way in which they contributed towards the attempt to make an emancipatory idea of justice and freedom take shape in society. We have not yet even begun to see what lessons we can draw from this failure.

Conclusion

Volker Braun called the resilience of the individual and the courage to be moral 'walking upright': 'But during this time, a new, tougher stage began in the painful and wonderful process of learning to walk upright' (Volker Braun).[42] The ideological pressure is gone, economic pressure has taken its place. And yet one cannot overlook the fact that the cities were and still are being saved – just. In many places, the environment has recovered. Flowers, vegetables, fruit and the everyday things of life are 'in stock'. Restaurants are there for the customers. The armour of fear has been smashed. The involvement of everyone in the democratic process is possible. Information is accessible to all. But there is a small or a large snag to everything. For the 'haves', it is easy to get everything. The process of transformation is without historical precedent and has led to long-term condemnations which are going to be with us for some time. The East is becoming silent and being silenced: with the cudgel of the Stasi, the PDS[43] and nostalgia. Anyone asking questions or reminding people that this or that in the GDR was not so bad, is immediately informed: 'I suppose you want the GDR back again!' They now demand that everyone should conform and adapt to the successful West German way, following their recipe for success over forty years. For four years already, 150 billion have been invested in the dilapidated East. And now West Germans are looking anxiously into the gaping hole in their finances and exhorting the East Germans to show more gratitude. This is not an entirely unfair attitude towards people who, finding themselves suddenly part of a 'culture of entitlement', are actually claiming their entitlement, especially by pointing to forty ostensibly 'lost years'. There is without doubt a discernible mood of grousing and carping amongst many East Germans who have almost forgotten what was politically, materially and spiritually ruinous about the GDR, but prefer to remember the good sides to the GDR, comparing these with the great promises of 1990. But what will happen when the overstretched public budgets start to cut back in the areas of life which are crucial to developing and sustaining us as human beings, the areas of education, culture and social matters? Economic growth in the form we have known hitherto is a dead end if the lives of future generations really do matter to us. Spiritual-cultural 'growth' is not. Or will that be taken over by the 'modern media' in a manipulative, banal, brutal way dictated by viewing figures? Will men and women defend what makes them human and rediscover the riches of their creativity? The answer remains open. Literature is again in demand as a catalyst for the coming-together of past and present, East and West.

Notes

1. This contribution, translated by David Rock, is based on a German transcription of the speech which Friedrich Schorlemmer gave at the Keele Symposium and which he kindly reworked for this volume. Thanks are also due to Stefan Wolff for his helpful suggestions.

2. A reference to Wilhelm Busch's satirical story in verse, *Max und Moritz* (1865).

3. During his political and election campaign in East Germany in1990, Helmut Kohl used the phrase 'blühende Landschaften' to presage economic revival.

4. The GDR was the only socialist state to broadcast the Chinese version of what happened at Tiananmen Square.

5. The title of one of Goya's etchings from the cycle *Los desastros de la guerra.*

6. The title of Christa Wolf's controversial novella, published in 1990 in Berlin.

7. 'Zweidrittelgesellschaft' is a term describing the division of society into two-thirds which are better off and one-third which is not. It does not refer exclusively to a division between employed and unemployed but also to issues such as access by any group or individual to a general level of affluence and opportunities in life.

8. The plan advanced in 1944 by Henry Morgenthau, U.S. Secretary of the Treasury under Roosevelt, advocated the 'pastoralisation' (removal of all industry) from Germany in order to strip it of economic power

9. The original German is a pun: 'Beide deutsche Staaten banden sich ein und blieben gebändigt'.

10. The notion 'Sieger der Geschichte' was a significant element of GDR-identity. It lay at the heart of the anti-fascist myth of the foundation of the state and implied a rejection of all responsibility for the Nazi past.

11. Edmund Stoiber, Prime Minister of Bavaria,in the 1990s.

12. Such slogans appeared in the GDR in the 1950s because there were some signs that Stalin was willing to accept German unification, but only on condition that it remained demilitarised.

13. An emotionally loaded phrase from a popular FDJ-song (Honecker's favourite) which reminded people of the achievements after the war, specifically the attempt to rebuild a new society.

14. In 1923, this Italian town near Genoa was the scene of the first diplomatic treaty between the Soviet Union and the Weimar Republic, signalling economic and (to some extent) military cooperation between Germany and the Soviet Union, two internationally outlawed and hence isolated states.

15. Details of Schalck-Golodkowski's dealings started to emerge after 1989. The former Stasi colonel had been involved in shady foreign-currency deals in order to keep the GDR solvent.

16. Franz Josef Strauß, the then Bavarian Premier, visited the GDR in 1983 and shocked his CSU supporters by arranging a government-backed loan of DM 1 billion, part of a long-term strategy to draw the insolvent GDR irreversibly into the financial orbit of the West.

17. Hallstein was a state secretary in the the foreign ministry under Adenauer. According to the Hallstein doctrine of 1955, the Federal Republic regarded any other state's establishment of diplomatic relations with the GDR as a hostile act.

18. 'geschichtsteleologisch' is a Hegelian/Marxist concept describing the definite, determined course of history which is beyond human influence.

19. In Jaroslav Hasek's *Die Abenteuer des braven Soladten Schwejk während des Weltkriegs* (1921-23), the flies have to avoid leaving their droppings on the portrait for fear of 'Majestätsbeleidigung' (*lèse-majesté*)!

20. FDJ – Freie Deutsche Jugend (Free German Youth). Honecker was for many years in charge of the FDJ as its First Secretary.

21. The phrase used here, 'die Ungnade östlicher Geburt', is an allusion to Helmuth Kohl's reference to his and his generation's having escaped any implication in

Nazism because of their age when he spoke of 'die Gnade der späten Geburt' (the grace of being born late).

22. PEN – Pen-Club (Writers' Club). The German PEN-Zentrum, founded in 1947, split in 1951 into West and East German centres. For details of the disputes which arose after unification see: Dieckmann, 'Deutsche PEN-Geschichte', in the supplement to the weekly *Das Parlament. Aus Politik und Zeitgeschichte*, vols. 13–14, 22 March, 1996.

23. 'Aufrechte Literatur war in der DDR immer Bückware': The word 'Bückware' was a common GDR term – certain items were not on the shelf in GDR shops but under the counter, hence the need to 'stoop' ('bücken') to get them in order to sell them to 'special customers'.

24. The *BILD-Zeitung* is a low-quality popular German newspaper.

25. This quotation from *Kindheitsmuster* is a rewording of Wittgenstein's famous last words in the *Tractatus Logico-Philosophicus* (Leipzig, 1921).

26. This is the last sentence of Wolf's *Lesen und Schreiben* written in 1968 (Darmstadt, 1980, p.48).

27. It is not possible to render the true force of the original 'gleich-gültig', spelt as it is with a hyphen.

28. Stephan Hermlin organised the 'Berliner Begegnung zur Friedensförderung' (Berlin Meeting for Peace) for German writers in December 1981, providing a forum for some remarkably critical speeches by eminent East German writers at the time when rearmament was being discussed, with Nato threatening to install Pershing missiles in West Germany unless the Soviet Union withdrew its missiles from the East. This was the first time that writers from East and West Germany had come together under the auspices of official East German bodies without any attempt to 'doctor' the list, which included 'uncomfortable' figures such as Stefan Heym (who had just been expelled from the Writers' Union and prevented from publishing in the East) and writers making their first visit 'home' again after going into exile in the West. Hermlin himself was widely respected at the time as one of the more independent spirits amongst GDR intellectuals; he was also a personal friend of Honecker and 'a doer of many careful good deeds in private' (*Guardian*, 29 May 1982). See John Sandford, *Swords and Ploughshares*, London, 1983, pp. 52–57.

29. The phrase 'die Zahl der unwürdigen Geheimnisse' is a citation from Ingeborg Bachmann's anti-war poem 'Alle Tage'.

30. After the novel of the same title by Manfred Bieler.

31. 'auseinandergetanzt': literally 'not dancing together physically'. The GDR authorities were initially against any form of modern, American-style dancing. Cf. Dorothee Wierling, 'Die Jugend als innere Feind. Konflikte in der Erziehungsdiktatur der sechsziger Jahre', in: Hartmut Kaelble, Jürgen Kocka and Hartmut Zwahr, eds., *Sozialgeschichte der DDR*, Stuttgart, 1994, pp. 410–11.

32. Joab and Jehuda are Biblical characters who appear in Heym's novel *König David Bericht*, Berlin, 1973.

33. Jagoda and Beria were consecutive heads of the Soviet secret police under Stalin, Mielke was Minister for State Security (Stasi) in the GDR.

34. Sentenced to eight years, Bahro served one year in Bautzen.

35. *Sinn und Form* was the leading literary journal in the GDR.

36. St Luke 24: 13.

37. Franz Fühmann, *Vor Feuerschlünden. Erfahrungen mit Georg Trakls Gedicht*, Halle, 1982.

38. 'Hemus' was a GDR wine of typically poor quality but also low, affordable price.

39. Despite what was in effect a police ban (licence to perform had been withdrawn from the rock bands), 2,500 rock fans turned up at Leuschner Square on 31 October 1965. They were driven off by the police who also arrested 267 of them cf. Wierling, *Sozialgeschichte der DDR*: 408.
40. A reference to Joseph, who was cast into the well by his brothers.
41. A fruit-growing region on the River Havel and name of the company.
42. From the volume of poems entitled *Training des aufrechten Gangs* (Learning to Walk Upright), Halle, 1979.
43. In late 1989 , the SED, the state party of the GDR, changed its name to SED-PDS and then finally in February 1990 to PDS (*Partei des Demokratischen Sozialismus*).

Intellektuelle, Bürger und Schriftsteller in Ostdeutschland – vor und seit der 'Wende'[1]

Im Oktober 1985 hielt Michail Sergejewitsch Gorbatschow vor der Nationalversammlung in Paris einen sensationellen Vortrag und die westlichen Zeitungen machten sich darüber Gedanken, ob das nur neue rhetorische Töne im alten Gewand seien. Sie wollten nicht sehen und erkennen, daß wirklich ein neues Zeitalter begonnen hatte, das man bald mit den beiden Worten Glasnost und Perestroika bezeichnete und zum Ende des Kalten Krieges und umfassender Abrüstung führen sollte. Vorläufig, wie sich zeigt.

Zehn Jahre später sind wir aus dem stickigen Warteraum der Geschichte in den zugigen D-Zug gestoßen, einen Schnellzug, der keinen Fahrplan mehr hat. Das System der westlichen Demokratien, das mittels Marktwirtschaft notdürftig effektiv, wenn auch nicht sehr menschlich funktioniert, ist seit dem Zusammenbruch des Kommunismus gnadenlos mit sich selbst allein. Es braucht sich jedenfalls nicht mehr an seinem Gegenbild zu beweisen. Die 'Zeichen der Zeit', in der der Kapitalismus wieder machen kann, was er will, sind unübersehbar. Vor zehn Jahren begann das. Wir sahen die Hoffnung, die wir 1968 meinten, begraben zu müssen, wieder aufstehen. Ich will nicht gleich theologisch sagen: 'wiederauferstehen'. Jedenfalls bekenne ich, daß ich zu denen gehörte, die in Gorbatschow beinahe etwas Messianisches sahen, weil wir damit nicht mehr gerechnet hatten und staunten, mit welcher Vision und mit welchem Geschick er die Dinge voranbrachte. Und Sie mögen sich bitte vorstellen,

wie es einem geht, dem angedroht wird, daß er noch hundert
Jahre eingemauert bleibt und ein paar Monate später fällt das
Monstrum, diese tödliche Betonmauer in einer Novembernacht.
Eine Hoffnung, die 1968 als 'Prager Frühling' aufgeflackert war,
lernte wieder gehen. Die Intellektuellen in Deutschland, in Ostdeutschland zumal, wurden erneut beflügelt, an dem Kampf für
die Verbindung zwischen sozialer Gerechtigkeit und Freiheit
festzuhalten, trotz des Scheiterns 1968. Vielleicht, weil Prag nicht
gescheitert war, sondern weil Prag durch Panzer niedergewalzt
wurde, ohne erweisen zu können, ob Sozialismus, Freiheit und
wirtschaftliches Gedeihen zusammengehen. Ich könnte auch
sagen: 1968 erlebten wir die Zugluft der Geschichte. In dieser
Zugluft machte einer unserer liebenswürdigen Spötter, Kurt
Bartsch, einen kleinen Gedichtband mit dem Thema 'Zugluft'.
Später zog es ihn in den Westen, wie viele andere auch. Doch er
gehört nicht zu den rückkehrenden Abrechnern. Ich zitiere zwei
Gedichte von 1968, die widerspiegeln, was gewesen ist. Das eine
heißt 'Sozialistischer Biedermeier', ein Beispiel für die stetige
Reproduzierbarkeit des Kleinbürgers unter allen möglichen
Gesellschaftsordnungen.

> Zwischen Wand und Widersprüchen
> machen sie es sich bequem.
> Links ein Sofa, rechts ein Sofa,
> in der Mitte ein Emblem. ...
>
> Brüder, seht, die rote Fahne
> hängt bei uns zur Küche raus.
> Außen Sonne, innen Sahne,
> so sieht Marx wie Moritz aus.

Ja, wenn sich dann die Überlegenheit des Sozialismus nicht so
richtig einstellt und es kommt jemand und sagt: 'Blühende
Landschaften', dann sagen diese Leute: 'Wunderbar' und
rufen im Chor: 'Helmut, Helmut hilf', ausgerechnet in Karl-
Marx-Stadt.
      Derselbe Kurt Bartsch schrieb über den Mut der deutschen
Intellektuellen:

> Wenn ich einmal meine eigene Meinung sagen darf,
> begann er ungewöhnlich kraß,
> so hat schon Karl Marx gesagt, daß...

Mit dem Sozialismus ist es vorbei. Warum? Weil das, was
'zwischen den Zähnen ist', wenns drauf ankommt, den Leuten
wichtiger ist als das 'auf der Zunge'. Darin sind sich Kapitalis-

mus und sozialistische Bürokratie eins. Der Wettkampf war wesentlich ein ökonomischer Wettkampf, wie die Zustimmung zu einem politischen System wesentlich von der materiellen Lage abhängt. Reiner Kunze hat sich darauf diesen Vers gemacht:

> 'Prag '68'
> Eine Lehre liegt mir auf der Zunge,
> aber der Zoll sucht zwischen den Zähnen.

Von der Lehre allein wird man nicht satt. Der Zoll hat Angst und macht Angst vor der Lehre, aber suchen kann er nur zwischen den Zähnen. Das Volk sucht auch, mehrheitlich das, was zwischen den Zähnen hängenbleibt. Soll der, der satt ist, darüber spotten?

Heute vor sechs Jahren, am 28. Oktober 1989, war ich in der Erlöserkirche in Berlin-Rummelsburg. Da mußte man die Plätze drei Stunden vorher besetzen, um in die Veranstaltung zu kommen. Dort kamen die sogenannten Intellektuellen der DDR zusammen, um über die Übergriffe am 7. Oktober zu reden und gewissermaßen ihr ästhetisches und politisches Credo zugleich auszusprechen. Da waren sie alle zusammen, jedenfalls die Berliner.

Die Berliner hielten sich sowieso schon immer für die eigentlich Maßgeblichen, bis sie nachher die Stafette des Mutes an Leipzig abgeben mußten. Kurzzeitig. Aus Leipzig kam die Wende in der Wende, was die Ostberliner zunächst gar nicht wollten: 'Ein Volk'.

In Rummelsburg war das Polizeigefängnis gewesen, in das die jungen Leute, die am 7. Oktober demonstriert hatten, eingeliefert und drangsaliert, ja brutal behandelt worden waren. Die 'chinesische Lösung' schien nahe. Und in der 'Erlöserkirche' in Rummelsburg war jene Versammlung der – wie das damals hieß – Kunstschaffenden 'Wider den Schlaf der Vernunft'. Die Kunstschaffenden kamen zusammen und haben die Perestroika für die DDR 'einmütig' – so hieß das bei uns immer – eingefordert. Moderatoren waren Daniela Dahn und Jürgen Rennert. Die Schriftsteller zeigten Flagge, forderten Rechtsstaatlichkeit und waren beim Volk, nicht bei den Machthabern. Viele von ihnen gehörten noch der SED an.

Angesichts des Versprechens blühender Landschaften im Jahre '90 einerseits und des Lamentos im Jahre '95 über das Milliardenloch, das sich hinter der abgerissenen Mauer auftut, ist an den ersten Bundespräsidenten, Theodor Heuss, zu erinnern, der 1946 einschärfte: 'Demokratie ist keine Glücksversprechung, sondern das Ergebnis politischer Bildung und demokratischer Gesinnung.' An diesem Punkt sind wir in Deutschland wieder: Ist uns die Demokratie wichtig als Ergebnis politischer Bildung und demokratischer Gesinnung und bleibt Demokratie bei uns stabil, wenn materielle Glücksversprechungen sich rarer machen? Das wird eine sehr ernste Frage für unsere vereinte Republik.

Ich versuche nun im ersten Teil meiner Ausführungen eine Zeitansage der vereinigten Republik, im Anschluß an einen provozierenden Satz Heiner Müllers zu geben. Die friedliche Vereinigung auf demokratischer Grundlage ist ein Glücksfall deutscher und europäischer Geschichte, ein Glücksfall, der durch Siegermentalität verspielt werden kann.

Zweitens werde ich auf die Frage eingehen: Was bleibt? Die Rolle der Schriftsteller in der DDR. Meine These ist, daß Bücher und nicht Akten bleiben werden.

Zunächst die Zeitansage der vereinigten Republik im Anschluß an das Diktum von Heiner Müller: 'Die Vereinigung findet als Verschwinden beider Teile statt. Zuerst sah es so aus, als ob dieses Stück DDR einfach einverleibt würde. Das scheint aber nicht zu funktionieren. Jetzt verschwinden beide Teile und es entsteht ein unbenennbares Vakuum, das von der D-Mark zusammengehalten wird.' Hinterläßt die Vereinigung, wie Heiner Müller sagt, ein Vakuum, das allein durch die D-Mark gefüllt wird, soweit in den Taschen der östlichen Zweidrittelgesellschaft vorhanden? Für die große Mehrheit ist Deutschland mit der harten D-Mark geradezu identisch, die an eine Eurowährung aufzugeben deshalb das Sakrileg schlechthin wäre. Wieviele sind es in Ost und West, denen das weiche D der Demokratie am Herzen liegt und die ihm Stimme in der täglichen Mühe demokratischer Prozesse und Institutionen geben? Es ist noch nichts entschieden. Deutschland ist jedenfalls, wenn kein Vakuum entstehen soll, neu zu begründen, nachdem 1945 zwei unabhängige Teilstaaten aus dem zusammenschrumpften Reich begründet wurden, beide von Gunst und Gnaden ihrer Besatzungsmächte. Gunst und Gnade unterschieden sich grundsätzlich. Der eine wurde mit dem Marshallplan gefüttert und mit einer freiheitlichen Verfassung ausgestattet, der andere wirtschaftlich ausgesaugt und ideologisch aufgepäppelt. (Nachdem ich hier in Wales war, habe ich gedacht: 'So hat sich das Morgenthau für Deutschland vorgestellt. Es sieht doch ganz schön aus.') Beide deutsche Staaten banden sich ein und blieben gebändigt, banden sich selbst ein und blieben gebändigt durch die Sieger. Ich behaupte sogar, wir Deutschen brauchten diese vierzig Jahre politischer Quarantäne, um bei Troste zu bleiben. Beide Teile empfahlen sich den einstigen Gegnern auf ihrem Territorium als treue Verbündete und äußerst gelehrige Nachahmer, bis sie sich als unentbehrliche Partner selber beinahe als Sieger fühlen konnten. Also wir Ostdeutschen waren jedenfalls 'die Sieger der Geschichte', zusammen mit der siegreichen Sowjetarmee. Der Preis für die Freiheit in der Westbindung war die Einheit und darüber muß heute offener geredet werden, wie Adenauer selbstverständlich eine erweiterte Rheinprovinz wollte und nicht mehr. Die Bundesrepublik entwickelte jahrelang ein Selbstbewußtsein, das in sich selbst Genüge fand. Nachdem ich die Bundesrepublik bereisen durfte, konnte ich das auch verstehen: Ein so reiches, vielfältiges, schönes Land – was braucht das noch den wilden Osten? Es sind vielleicht 10–20 Prozent der Westdeutschen, die die Teilung als wirklichen Mangel empfunden hatten und die Einheit nachhaltig, mit allen Konsequenzen, nach wie vor bejahen. Mehr sind es nicht. Ich versteh das auch. Aber wir müssen uns nur darüber klarwerden, warum wir jetzt innere Vereinigungsprobleme haben. Wenn richtige Populisten kämen, könnten sie die ganze Wut auf Ostdeutschland lenken. Ein paar Sätze von Herrn Stoiber über das Milliardenloch im Osten haben schon ihre Wirkung getan, auf beiden Seiten übrigens.

'Deutsche an einen Tisch', hatte es auch ostwärts seit den 50-iger Jahren geheißen, transparentlosungsstark überall. Meine Kindheit ist vollgepflastert mit Losungen, mit langen Nasen westlicher Politiker, Karikaturen an allen Telefonmasten, in jedem Dorf.

Jeder Teil Deutschlands beschwor von Anfang an die Einheit, doch zu seinen Konditionen. Das hat sich bei der Vereinigung 1990 genau so gezeigt: Die Bundesrepublik hat die Einheit zu ihren Konditionen hergestellt, mit Zustimmung der Ostdeutschen zur D-Mark-Vereinigung. Das hätten die Kommunisten auch so gemacht. Bloß gut, daß es so herum gekommen ist! Damit kein falscher Eindruck entsteht. Ich trauere der Ulbricht-Honecker-DDR keine Minute nach. Aber das Leben war mehr als heutige Aburteilungskürzel ausdrücken können. Das kommt kaum noch zur Sprache und gerät unter Ostalgie-Verdacht! Doch da gab es noch anderes, das kaum noch zur Sprache kommt. Die Demarkationslinie zwischen Ost und West wurde bald todbringende Grenze, Ost und West zu politisch hochbesetzten Begriffen. Westsender, Westkaugummi und Westmark hatten einen geheimnisvollen Klang, so wie die Worte: Westzeitung, Westfernsehen und Westkontakte politisch anrüchige Worte wurden. Es gab Zeiten, da war das Kauen eines Kaugummis ein politisches Bekenntnis. (Mein Vater mahnte mich, als ich dreizehn war und wir mit der S-Bahn Westberlin verließen, meinen Kaugummi auszuspucken.) Froh konnte im Osten andererseits sein, wer Westbeziehungen hatte oder gar West- verwandschaft. Können Sie sich vorstellen, welch ein unglaublicher Unterschied bestand zwischen 'Besuch' und 'Westbesuch'? Wenn Westbesuch kam, dann wurde alles auf den Kopf gestellt. Dann wurde Käse besorgt, den es überhaupt nicht gab. Jedenfalls haben sich die Westdeutschen bei uns meist sehr wohl gefühlt, und wir waren ziemlich herzlich. Die Kinder indes waren ziemlich offen, die fragten sofort: 'Was hast Du mitgebracht?' Auch die Oma, die von der Westreise zurück- kam, konnte sich besonderer Aufmerksamkeit erfreuen. Die Rentner in der DDR hatten ein großes Privileg: Sie durften in den Westen reisen und wurden natürlich, selbst wenn sie nachts zurückkamen, vom Bahnhof abgeholt, von der ganzen Familie. Jetzt kann Oma ein Taxi nehmen. Oma kann jetzt auch reisen, wohin sie will. Das ist ganz ihre Sache geworden. Der Umbruch hat auch die familiären Beziehungen völlig verändert.

Bis 1989 mußten Funktionsträger auf allen Ebenen famil- iäre Kontakte offen abbrechen, Verwandschaft verleugnen, oder sich gar lossagen. Im Westen dagegen konnte man sich täglich selbst bestätigen, indem man sich dankbar erinnerte, nicht im kommunistischen Osten leben zu müssen. Dem Westen tat es gut, daß es den bösen Osten gab und der Osten wurde zusammengehalten durch seine feindbildstabilen Wörter: Antiimperialismus, Antifaschismus und Antikapitalis- mus. Das Bau-auf-Bau-auf-Pathos trug viele Überzeugte, bis es im August 1961 zum großen Eingeständnis des Scheiterns kam, als man die Mauer bauen mußte, weil die DDR ohne Mauer nicht überlebensfähig war. Die DDR drohte auszubluten, mauerte sich ein – nein, ihre Bewohner – und log sich für die Gründe ihrer Einbetonierung durch die Geschichte. Während sich der eine Teil wirtschaftlich erfolgreich und politisch

'nachgereift' schon bald als Deutschland empfand, mit feier-
lichem Einheitsgebot, mit Grundgesetz und Provisoriumsvorbehalt, blieb der andere Teil die Ostzone, die
Gänsefüßchen-DDR, bis die Entspannungspolitik Entkramp-
fung einleitete. Zehn Jahre nach dem Mauerbau zeigte sich bei
Willy Brandt am Fenster des Erfurter Hofes, daß der Mauerbau
nichts gebracht hatte. Diese kurzen Szenen, als Willy Brandt
1970 in Erfurt an das Fenster kam und die Leute, die die Stasi
nicht hat abwimmeln können, jubelten, das war der Schock für
die DDR-Führung überhaupt, daß die Mauer sich nicht
gelohnt hatte. Willy, Willy! Er war der gesamtdeutsche Held
der kleinen Schritte zum größeren Ziel der Einheit im Frieden.

Was die Deutschen fortan unter der diplomatischen Decke
miteinander beredeten, war den östlichen wie westlichen
Geheimdiensten höchst verdächtig, doch wohlbekannt. Noch
1987 hatte man bei Hans-Dietrich Genschers Davos-Rede im
Westen, auch in Großbritannien, ziemliche Sorgen vor einer
Neuauflage von Rapallo, weil Genscher dem Westen sagte:
'Nehmen wir Gorbatschow ernst und nehmen wir die Chance
wahr.' Das nützte vor allem den Deutschen. Noch 1986 hatte
der deutsche Bundeskanzler den sowjetischen Generalsekretär
Gorbatschow als Rhetoriker 'wie Goebbels' bezeichnet. Wie
schnell wird alles vergessen!

Jeder Teil Deutschlands beteuerte unaufhörlich seine Treue
zu seinem Block und Schalck-Golodkowski konstituierte die
Einheit längst mittels D-Mark, ehe Strauß mit dem D-Mark-
Kredit die DDR sechs Jahre vor deren Ableben noch einmal
rettete und hernach mit Honecker zur Jagd ging. – Fürsten
unter sich. Mit seinem Privatflugzeug flog Strauß fortan in die
DDR und landete, wo es ihm beliebte. Und dann kamen die,
die rauswollten und riefen. 'Strauß, wir wollen raus.' Wer an
ihn herankam und ihm einen Zettel zustecken konnte, der war
dann bald im goldenen Westen. Das umstrittene Geld war
neben den Schweinegeschäften mit dem Agrarunternehmer
März reine Sterbehilfe. (März war ein großer Schweinezüchter,
der persönliche Beziehungen zur bayrischen Staatsführung
hatte.) Als Ostdeutscher muß ich erwähnen, daß das Problem
für uns Ostdeutsche nicht die Schweine waren, die wir für den
Westen produzieren mußten, sondern das Problem war die
Gülle, die bei uns verblieb.

Doch die Kulturnation fand sich auch immer wieder zusammen: in Heine-Ausgaben, in Caspar-David-Friedrich-Ausstel-

lungen. Wir haben merkwürdigerweise, etwas zeitverschoben, in Ost und West unsere Geschmäcker geändert. Ich hätte mir in den sechziger Jahren nicht vorstellen können, daß ich freiwillig zu einer Caspar David Friedrich-Ausstellung gehen würde und habe später, als in Dresden die große Ausstellung lief, genauso den Mund aufgerissen, wie alle anderen. Die gegenseitigen Lizenzen der Gegenwartssschriftsteller aus Ost und West wurden Brücken; die Literatur wurde d i e Brücke in diesen vierzig Trennungsjahren und die Westpakete natürlich. So wie wir Ostler nach Heinrich Böll gegiert haben, haben Westdeutsche Christa Wolf gern gelesen. Auch in ost-westlichen Renaissancen wurden wir uns gleich: Luther wurde beerbt; wir feierten 1983 zusammen Luthers 500. Geburtstag. Friedrich der Große wurde in Ostberlin wieder aufgestellt. Bismarck bekam eine Biografie, die fast vergessen ließ, daß er das Sozialistengesetz durchgesetzt hatte. Jeder Teil reklamierte sie alle als sein Erbe und mußte doch gestehen, daß das Erbe ein gemeinsames ist. Als der 'erste Deutsche im All' war (so titelte das *Neues Deutschland*), verwirrte sich alles im Staatsvolk der DDR. Waren wir also doch auch stolze Deutsche? Was da im Schoß des Volkes lag, habe ich 1980 bei den Arbeiteraufständen in Polen erfahren: Die deutschen Überlegenheitsgefühle sind reaktivierbar, selbst nach diesen vierzig Jahren sozialistisch-internationalistischer Erziehung. Außerdem soll es seinerzeit Gespräche zwischen den Militärs der Russen und Deutschen gegeben haben, die durchaus mit Bedingungen verknüpft waren, was bestimmte polnische Gebiete anlangt.

'Wir' waren auch Deutsche, aber bessere wegen des Gesellschaftssystems mit Bildung, Arbeit, Wohnung für alle und ein Bollwerk des Friedens. Nur, dieses politische Prachtstück mußte mit allen Mitteln nach innen und außen geschützt und die Bürger in Reihe geschaltet werden. Das war der kleine Schönheitsfehler. Die Republik war schon ganz in Ordnung, nur der kleine Fehler war, daß sie so martialisch geschützt werden mußte. Über den Grund log man sich offiziell hinweg. Der Schutz nach außen brauchte zuerst die Einsperrung nach innen.

Von Beginn an vermischte sich der Sog der wirtschaftlichen Prosperität des Westens mit Freiheitssehnsüchten. Indes ist die Reihenfolge der Faszination so klar wie verständlich. Etwa vier Millionen Deutsche strömten gen Westen, obwohl Ulbricht um sein Überleben mauerte und Honecker Hundeleinen und Schußanlagen 'vervollkommnete', während in der Zeitung stand, daß die entwickelte sozialistische Gesellschaft immer weiter vervollkommnet wird. Wir haben in der DDR sowieso nichts verbessert, sondern wir haben immer nur 'vervollkommnet'. Es war immer nur noch das I-Tüpfelchen nötig. Und wenn ich als Ostdeutscher nun schon fünf Jahre höre, wie im Deutschen Bundestag gesagt wird, daß 'die deutsche Einheit jetzt vollendet wird', dann scheint es auch nur noch um das letzte Mosaiksteinchen für etwas Vollkommenes zu gehen. Was ist das bloß immer wieder für eine metaphysische Sprache? Gibt es unter Menschen etwas 'Vollendetes'?

Jeder Teilstaat hatte seine Hallsteindoktrin. Der eine konnte sie politisch durchsetzen, weil er im Westen politisch eingebunden war und wirtschaftlich erblühte, der andere postulierte geradezu geschichtsteleologisch, er wäre 'der einzig rechtmäßige deutsche Staat'. Es reichte gerade mal für die rote Farbe und für die Bewachung der Losung. Ein Beispiel: Als 1958 Walter Ulbricht auf einer Litfaßsäule eine Nase ausgerissen wurde, kamen aus der Kreisstadt die Spürhunde. Mein Vater ging morgens zum Spargelstechen und sah, wie die Sicherheitsleute versuchten, die Hunde auf die richtige Fährte zu bringen. Das konnte ja nur ich gewesen sein, der dem Genossen Ulbricht die Nase ausgerissen hatte. Wie war das mit dem Fliegendreck auf dem Bild des Kaisers im 'Schwejk'?

Was als gesetzmäßig bevorstehender Sieg der Geschichte proklamiert wurde – und nicht wenige waren von der Richtigkeit der Ideologie überzeugt -, implodierte zu seinem vierzigjährigen Geburtstag unter einem achtzigjährigen FDJ-Funktionär. Nicht wenige hatten von Anfang an und nicht viele bis zum Schluß geglaubt, daß sie den Parolen geglaubt hatten. Und fast alle hatten gehorcht, gewählt, gewunken, geschrien. Leben in der Diktatur macht alternativlos. Nun sind wir vereint und fangen immer mehr an zu fremdeln. Paradox: gerade die Trennung schuf eine widerspruchsvolle Einheit, die erst seit der Einheit als Trennung bewußt wird. Die Ungnade östlicher Geburt wird solange weitererlebt, wie sich der Osten vor dem Westen rechtfertigen muß, solange andererseits Mitläufer sich selbst verleugnen, wie krumm ihr Rücken in den langen Jahren geworden ist. Es gab ein Bundesrepublikbewußtsein, so wie es durchaus ein DDR-Bewußtsein gegeben hatte, ob positiv oder negativ. Wer über eine Generation lang getrennt gelebt hatte, ließ sich für Gefühlsmomente glücklich zusammenfügen. Erinnerung an

gemeinsame Geschichte, also auch an unsere Geschichtsver-
antwortung, Erinnerung an unsere Kultur, auch an unsere
Kulturbarbarei, Erinnerung an unsere großen Leistungen,
auch an unsere perversen Leistungen, schafften und schaffen
in Deutschland WIR-Gefühle, die nur dann stabil bleiben,
wenn beide jetzt formal vereinten Teile sich neu finden und
nicht der eine, kleinere, freiheitsentwöhnte und wirtschaftlich
bedürftigere Teil im Zeitraffer genötigt wird, alles nachzu-
holen und gleichzeitig seine Geschichte individuell und
kollektiv nachtragend zu verantworten. Einheit gibt es nicht, solange der eine Teil dem anderen
sein Leben vorwirft. Einheit gibt es dann, wenn wir das, was
wir miteinander erlebt haben in vierzig Jahren, redlich
miteinander besprechen. Dabei haben die Intellektuellen ein
gewichtiges Wort mitzureden. Bei den gegenwärtigen West-
Ost-PEN-Querelen zeigen sie allerdings, daß sie auch nur
Menschen sind, bisweilen gar weiter zurück als das Allge-
meinbewußtsein. Für eines jedenfalls hätten aus meiner Sicht
besonders Intellektuelle und Schriftsteller zu wirken: Die juristische Erledigung der DDR ist eine Sackgasse.

Was bleibt, sind Bücher.

Die pauschale Diffamierung der DDR-Intellektuellen ist auch
ein Niedertreten aus Neid. Solche Rollen wie sie DDR-Schrift-
steller in der Gesellschaft hatten, hätte sich mancher im
Westen wohl gewünscht. Und einige Weggegangene rächen
sich nicht zuletzt, weil sie sich ihre Fluchtenttäuschung schwer
verzeihen können.
    Aufrechte Literatur war in der DDR immer Bückware.
Konflikte der DDR waren stets auch in Literatur vermittelte
Konflikte. Literatur brachte das Land voran und öffnete
Räume, die gänzlich verschlossen schienen. Literatur sprach
Tabus an und aus und wagte sogar so etwas wie Utopie. Die
Schriftsteller in der DDR müssen sich jetzt in den neuen Buch-
Markt-Verhältnissen ganz anders zurechtfinden, auch mit einer
Kritik, die durchaus politisch gefärbt und bisweilen vernicht-
end ist, sogar nachträglich. Literatur hat unter den neuen
Bedingungen eine andere Funktion. Schriftsteller müssen (und
wollen) damit fertig werden, daß sie nicht mehr die Präcep-
toren, die Gurus, die verehrten Persönlichkeiten sind, vor

denen sich jeder verneigt. Sie waren eine Ersatzöffentlichkeit und Ersatzkritik an öffentlichen Mißständen. Diese Ersatzöffentlichkeit gibt es nicht mehr, seit es die BILD-Zeitung gibt. Und es reicht nicht mehr, Kritisches zu sagen – es muß auch literarisch gut sein. Die Meßlatte dafür legen indes Westler. Die Geschichte der DDR läßt sich am zutreffendsten durch ihre Bücher schreiben. Literatur wird auch künftig am zutreffendsten beschreiben, was war. Das zu sagen, scheint banal, aber das wird in der gegenwärtigen Praxis negiert. Was die DDR ausmachte, könnte ich mit drei Zitaten beschreiben. Reiner Kunze schrieb über die Verfassung und Wirklichkeit. Vieles von dem ist nicht veraltet. Kunze nimmt ein Zitat aus der Verfassung auf und schreibt:

'Ethik'
Im Mittelpunkt
steht der Mensch
nicht
der einzelne.

Das war der Punkt. Im Mittelpunkt steht 'der Mensch', aber nicht du, sondern alle, nicht der einzelne. Das ist gewissermaßen die politische und anthropologische Grundlage, weil der Mensch 'das Ensemble der gesellschaftlichen Verhältnisse' ist. Ist er aber nicht viel mehr? Die DDR, überhaupt das ganze sowjetsozialistische System, ist auf einer falschen Zitation des Kommunistischen Manifests aufgebaut worden. Darauf komme ich noch zurück.

Der zweite 'dialektische' Text stammt aus Bert Brechts Gedicht 'Lob des Zweifels' und beschreibt die politische Psychologie der SED-Herrschaften:

Da sind die Unbedenklichen, die niemals zweifeln.
Ihre Verdauung ist glänzend, ihr Urteil ist unfehlbar.
Sie glauben nicht den Fakten, sie glauben nur an sich.
Im Notfall müssen die Fakten dran glauben.
Ihre Geduld mit sich selber ist unbegrenzt.
Auf Argumente hören sie nur mit dem Ohr des Spitzels.

Schließlich wirkten Bücher als Tabubrecher. So schreibt Christa Wolf in *Kindheitsmuster*: 'Wovon man nicht sprechen kann, darüber muß man allmählich zu schweigen aufhören.'

Inzwischen vermisse ich die DDR, weil ich die Literatur und ihre Rolle vermisse. Ich, als Bürger, als Leser, bin mit allem Möglichen beschäftigt jetzt, aber kaum noch mit Liter-

atur. Verzeihen Sie, aber ich komme zu dem paradoxen
Schluß, daß die Diktatur insofern a u c h etwas Förderliches
hat, als sie uns Wesentliches wesentlich macht, als sie Literatur
wichtig macht, denn wer gefährdet ist, schreibt anders und
liest auch anders. Und 'Prosa zumal baut tödliche Verein-
fachungen ab. Sie unterstützt das Subjektwerden des Menschen. Sie ist revolutionär und realistisch, sie verführt und
ermutigt zum Unmöglichen' (Christa Wolf, 1972). Der Bezug
der Literatur zur Realität unter bedrängenden Bedingungen ist
unausweichlich, ihr innerer Auftrag klar benennbar, insofern
er stets im Widerspruch zum äußeren Auftraggeber steht.

Der politische, juristische und ökonomische Transformationsprozeß seit 1990 ist historisch ohne Beispiel. Er hat auch die
Kultur und den Kult, also die Kirchen und das Kulturleben in
ihrer Substanz erschüttert. In der Marktgesellschaft wird alles
nach seinem Preis bemessen und bewertet. Werte werden gleich-
gültig. Der Ausgang der existentiellen und politökonomischen
Irritationen ist ungewiß, in allen Lebensbereichen. Anscheinend
war das westliche System relativ stabil, solange es das östliche
gab. Jetzt steht seine eigene Zukunftsfähigkeit und weltweite
Anschlußfähigkeit zur Debatte. Ich meine, es wird eine
weltweite Perestroika geben, oder der Kapitalismus wird ebenso
implodieren wie der Sozialismus. Hatte man im Westen nach
dem 'Sieg' fast triumphal das Ende der Geschichte proklamiert,
so hatten die Intellektuellen im Osten immer noch von einem
Überschuß gesprochen, trotz eingeengter und deprimierender
Realität. Ein Leben ohne Utopie ist kein Leben, denn 'wer
keine Zeit zum Träumen mehr hat, hat auch keine Kraft mehr
zum Kämpfen' (Christa Wolf).

Was bleibt von der DDR? Aufgeschlagene Bücher. Menschen, die mit Literatur aufgewachsen sind, werden auch wieder
zu (ihrer) Literatur zurückfinden. Die Schriftsteller in der DDR
haben vielen von uns geholfen, in der DDR leben zu bleiben
und beharrlich den Versuch zu machen, in der Wahrheit zu
leben. Die emanzipatorischen Gruppen fanden in den Schriftstellern sehr früh Verbündete. Reiner Kunzes, Thomas Brasch's
und Wolf Biermanns Zeilen trugen Jugendliche in ihrer Brust-
tasche. (Was mich als Jugendpfarrer besonders freute: darunter
waren Lehrlinge in der Chemieindustrie und Bäckergesellen.)
Christa Wolfs *Kindheitsmuster*, Stephan Hermlins *Abendlicht* und
Franz Fühmanns *Vor Feuerschlünden* halfen wegen ihrer
Aufrichtigkeit gegenüber unserer Vergangenheit zur

Aufrichtigkeit in der Gegenwart. Wie eng Frieden und Wahrheit zusammenhängen, machte Franz Fühmann in einer kurzen Rede zum Friedenssymposium 1981 klar:

Die Grundlage allen Vertrauens ist Wahrhaftigkeit. Sie beginnt immer als Wahrhaftigkeit gegenüber sich selbst. Unwahrhaftigkeit kann niemals ein Mittel für einen noch so guten Zweck sein. Sie zersetzt diesen Zweck und diskreditiert ihn. Sie baut letztlich nur Vertrauen ab, dessen Vorräte erschöpfbar sind, übrigens in allen Bereichen und in jeder Beziehung. Geschwundenes oder zersetztes Vertrauen ist wie abgestorbene Füße – nur schwer regenerierbar. Ich halte es immer mit Immanuel Kant, nach dem 'die Lüge der eigentliche faule Fleck in der menschlichen Natur' ist. Wie der Krieg sollte die Lüge geächtet sein. Sie sprießen beide aus einer Wurzel und führen beide zur Zerstörung. Der Lüge da, wo man wirkt, den Krieg anzusagen, das ist das Wesentliche.

In ähnlichem Sinne schrieb Christa Wolf ebenfalls 1981: 'Um Krieg zu verhindern, müssen auch Menschen in ihrem jeweils eigenen Land Kritik an den Mißständen ihres eigenen Landes üben. Rolle der Tabus bei der Kriegsvorbereitung: Unaufhörlich, unermeßlich wächst die Zahl der unwürdigen Geheimnisse. Wie unbedeutend alle Zensurtabus und die Folgen ihrer Übertretung durch die Bedrohung des Lebens werden.' Solche Sätze von Christa Wolf wurden von der Zensur herausgestrichen. Wir besorgten sie uns in den Westausgaben und sahen, mit welchen Sätzen man den Löwen reizen konnte, wobei hin und wieder zuzugestehen ist, daß die Zensoren insofern ganz geschickt waren, als sie ganz bestimmte, viel wichtigere Sätze durchgehen ließen. Ich vermute, manchmal haben Zensoren den Oberzensoren etwas zum Fraß hingeworfen und anderes dadurch durchgehen lassen. Selbst Zensoren, mit guter Literatur beruflich beschäftigt, bleiben nicht unbeeinflußt von solcherart Lektüre. Das sind die Listen der Wahrheit, ihre subkutanen Wirkungen.

Wer Lyrik beurteilen will, muß sie erst einmal verstehen. Wer sie versteht, den rührt sie auch an. Oder das Urteil führt zu gänzlich skurrilen Bewertungen, wie dies etwa in Kunzes Stasiakte sichtbar wird.

Ich gebe nun noch einige ausgewählte Beispiele für die Wirkung der kritischen Einmischung in der DDR. 1965 fand das berüchtigte 11. Plenum der SED statt, auf dem Honecker Berichterstatter war. Im Mittelpunkt der Kritik stand ein Film von einem Mann, der einmal den politisch-agitatorisch wirksamsten Film gedreht hatte, nämlich *Ernst Thälmann, Sohn seiner Klasse,* Kurt Maetzig. Sein neuester Film hatte den Titel *Das Kaninchen bin ich.* Niemand von uns hatte diesen Film je gesehen oder wußte, worum es ging. *Das Kaninchen bin ich* wurde dennoch zum geflügelten Wort. Wer die Schlange war, war auch keine Frage. Jeder konnte Kaninchen werden, auch Schlange! Das lag im 'real existierenden Sozialismus' eng beieinander, weshalb es heute so quälend wird, Opfer und Täter klar zu unterscheiden und bei aller Differenzierung trotzdem nichts zu verwischen. Den Film habe ich 1990 mit Kurt Maetzig zusammen gesehen. Ein wunderbarer Film, der den politischen Strafvollzug der DDR aufknackt und die Emanzipation einer jungen Frau zeigt. Das macht noch heute junge Frauen aus der DDR mutig, wenn sie diesen Film sehen. Das sollte nicht sein: Ermutigung durch Wahrheit!

Biermann, Heym und Bieler wurden von Honecker niedergemacht. Doch zur komplizierten 'historischen Wahrheit' gehört auch, daß Wolf Biermann 1965 nach West-berlin reisen durfte, um mit Wolfgang Neuss, einem der großen Kabarettisten, ein gemeinsames Programm zu machen, wobei die DDR-Oberen genau wußten, daß wir alle mit unseren Tonbändern am Radio sitzen und das alles aufnehmen und abschreiben würden. Mit wessen Hilfe, lieber Wolf Biermann, bist Du denn damals nach Westberlin gekom-men? Wer mußte da seine Zustimmung geben? Ich werfe Dir das keineswegs vor, denn wir alle profitierten davon. Aber ein Privileg für Dich war es schon. Die besten Zeilen über DDR-Alltag finden sich 1965 schon im 'Buckower Kleinstadtson-ntag': 'Ist hier was los? Nein, hier ist nichts los!' Oder der Song vom Staatsanwalt, der den Fredi Rohsmeisl angeklagt hatte, weil er auseinandergetanzt hatte und nun muß der Strafent-lassene zusehen, wie der Staatsanwalt selber auseinander tanzt. Darüber diese wunderbar reflektierten Zeilen Bier-manns: 'Ich hab' Leute sich ändern sehn, das war manchmal nicht mehr schön. Aber nützt uns das?' Darauf ein sehr zöger-liches Jaa. Wunderbar, ja, es nützt uns, wenn Leute sich ändern. Gilt das aber nicht heute noch?

Stefan Heyms Bücher wurden geradezu verschlungen. Man erinnere sich an seine *Schmähschrift* oder die Erzählung *Ein sehr guter zweiter Mann.* Mit historisch exegetischer und sozialpsychologischer Akribie geht Heym der Fami-liengeschichte des Königshauses Saul, David, Salomo nach und zeigt auf bestürzende und unterhaltsame Weise die Funk-

tionsmechanismen der Macht auf und erzählt von der Über-
lebenskunst eines Chronisten in der Diktatur. Sich treu
bleiben und überleben in der Welt der Joabs und Jehudas, der
Krethi und Plethi, der Jagoda, Berija und Mielke. Immer blieb
das bei Stefan Heym – bis heute – sozialistische Kritik am
Sozialismus, für Emanzipation, für Freiheit des Wortes, für
mehr Gerechtigkeit. Stefan Heym schöpfte den ihm durch
seine Lebensgeschichte gegebenen Rahmen und seine gewisse
Unantastbarkeit aus, nahm 1979 den Rausschmiß aus dem
Schriftstellerverband zusammen mit anderen in Kauf und
redete offen, ja fast prophetisch, aber er blieb, behielt seinen
Wohnsitz und Wirkungsort in der DDR.

1978 veröffentlichte Rudolf Bahro die *Alternative*, einen
Entwurf für einen emanzipatorischen Sozialismus, genau zehn
Jahre nach Prag und wurde – so absurd funktionierte das System – wegen Geheimnisverrat verurteilt und in den Westen
abgeschoben. *Sinn und Form* veröffentlichte 1979 zum ersten
Mal eine Geschichte, die das Tabuthema schlechthin berührte:
die Ausreise, sogar die von Kindern von Funktionären und
wies auf das Krankheitssymptom unserer Gesellschaft hin. Das
Problem der Ausreise beschäftigte viele Schriftsteller, wie jetzt
aus den Briefen zwischen Christa Wolf und Franz Fühmann
wieder hervorgeht. Letztere hatte sich dazu in Essays und
Gesprächen schon ausführlich geäußert und sich dafür entschieden, seine Kritik in diesem Lande zur Veränderung dieses
Landes einzubringen. Er fürchtete besonders einige jüngere so
begabte wie bedrängte Schriftsteller.

1979 kam das schmale Bändchen *Abendlicht* von Stephan
Hermlin heraus, beginnend mit einer Meditation zu Bachs
Osterkantate für den zweiten Ostersonntag, der Gang nach
Emmaus: '... denn es will Abend werden.' Das ganze Buch ist
die Folge eines Erschreckens und einer Entdeckerfreude über
einen weitreichenden Irrtum, über ein Leben aus zweiter
Hand im stalinistischen Sozialismus. Man hatte die
Gesellschaft mit dem Satz aufgebaut, daß die neue
Gesellschaft eine Assoziation ist, 'worin die freie Entwicklung
aller die Bedingung für die freie Entwicklung eines jeden ist.'
Im kommunistischen Manifest von Marx und Engels heißt es
aber wirklich: 'An die Stelle der alten bürgerlichen
Gesellschaft mit ihren Klassen und Klassengegensätzen tritt
eine Assoziation, worin die freie Entwicklung eines jeden die
Bedingung für die freie Entwicklung aller ist.' Wie weit ging

die Verblendung, wenn niemandem aufgefallen war, daß eine der Grundschriften grundlegend falsch zitiert worden war? 1981 organisierte Stephan Hermlin die Berliner Begegnung zur Friedensförderung, wo zum ersten Mal das Prinzip eines dichotomischen Weltbildes von Gutem und Bösen und entsprechend von guten und bösen Waffen durchbrochen wurde. Dort sprach Franz Fühmann seine großen Worte über die Wahrhaftigkeit, die er in seinem autobiografischen Buch anhand der Interpretation von Gedichten Trakls vorgelegt hatte: 'Vor Feuerschlünden aufgestellt'.

Als Christa Wolf 1983 ihre Erzählung *Kassandra* samt den Frankfurter Vorlesungen vorlegte, war dies eine kaum beschreibbare Bestärkung der Friedensbewegung in Ost und West. Nirgendwo ist aus meiner Sicht deutlicher die Machenschaft des Eumelos (des typischen skrupellosen Angstmachers der Macht mit verborgenem Gesicht) dargestellt worden. Und Christa Wolf macht in dieser Erzählung auf bestechende Weise deutlich, daß das hehre Kriegsziel gar nicht vorhanden ist, aber das Kriegsergebnis die Zerstörung aller wäre. Und sie läßt dennoch ein Hoffnungstürchen offen, wenn es da mitten unter der Drohung der Apokalypse heißt: 'Wir waren gebrechlich; da unsere Zeit begrenzt war, konnten wir sie nicht vergeuden mit Nebensachen. Also gingen wir, spielerisch, als wär uns alle Zeit der Welt gegeben, auf die Hauptsache zu, auf uns.'

Günter Kunert wurde mit seiner ganzen kämpferischen Traurigkeit durch seine Gedichte und Essays einer der Seismographen unserer Zeit. In seinem *Englischen Tagebuch* zum Beispiel macht er auf sehr einfache Weise klar, daß Sozialismus nicht gelingen kann, solange er uns um das Gemüse betrügt. Und er tritt am deutlichsten an gegen die Benutzbarkeit von Literatur für Ideologien und besteht auf dem Überschuß von Literatur in der Welt des bloßen Utilitarismus. Literatur wird Sinnsuche des Einzelnen, der dabei andere sucht und braucht.

> Ich bin der Sucher
> eines Weges
> für mehr als mich.

Er bleibt *Unterwegs nach Utopia*. Während er in den Westen ging, kam das Gedichtbändchen mit diesem Titel heraus. Die meisten Ausreiser reisten aus, zusammen mit ihren Pferden, Katzen und all ihrem Hausrat und bekamen einen Doppelpaß. Sie nahmen gewissermaßen die Einheit voraus, ganz pri-

vat-privilegiert, so auch Monika Maron. Sollte das Gedicht
'Auf der Flucht' auch für die Ausreise und die Ausreiser Gel-
tung haben?

> Vor dem Beton
> geht es zu
> wie im Märchen:
> Wo du
> auch ankommst,
> er erwartet dich
> grau und gründlich.
> (Günter Kunert)

Der Roman *Es geht seinen Gang* von Erich Loest (1978) beginnt
mit dem Satz 'Bestimmt gibt's Hemus.' Das kann niemand
verstehen, der nicht in der DDR gelebt hat. Das muß man
erzählend erklären. Erst, wenn man das verstanden hat, versteht man, was Leben in der DDR war. Da gibt es ein
nächtliches Selbstgespräch mit dem Ersten Sekretär in Leipzig,
in dem 'der Mann auf der Straße' alles sagt, was der Erste
Sekretär, hoch oben wohnend, weder hören kann, noch hören
will. Ironie des Schicksals: Es spielt in Leipzig. Erich Loest
beschreibt sodann die Wirkung eines Verbotes, auf den
Leuschnerplatz zu gehen, um dort ein verbotenes Konzert zu
hören. Das Konzert findet gar nicht statt, aber viele, die davor
gewarnt werden, dorthin zu gehen, gehen dort hin, weil es
verboten ist. Und ein Jugendlicher geht aus Neugier hin, wie
alle andern auch, aber Hundestaffeln sind da und er wird
gebissen. So lebt er mit den politischen Folgen des 'Hunde-
bisses vom Leuschnerplatz'. Jeder, der einmal in der DDR
aufgemuckt hat, hat seinen 'Hundebiß' abbekommen.

Diese Auswahl von Beispielen ist sicher zufällig. Man
müßte natürlich hinweisen auf Joachim Walthers Roman
Bewerbung bei Hofe, eine glänzende Geheimdienst-Lyriker-
Geschichte über die Unmöglichkeit eines Schriftstellers, dem
Hofe und seinem Berufe treu zu bleiben. Oder Volker Braun
wartete 20 Jahre, bis sein Stück *Lenins Tod* gespielt werden
konnte. Dieter Schubert schrieb Satiren über den Landbesuch
eines hohen Herren. Da wird Lachen zum Widerstand. Uwe
Grüning veröffentlichte einen Jeremia-Gedichtzyklus über
den Propheten, der 'gegen die Wahrheit' schrieb und in die
Zisterne geworfen wurde und dennoch redete, weil er mußte.

Hans Cibulka nahm in Tagebüchern von der Ostsee und in
Gedichten die Umweltbedrohung aufs Korn. Gabriele Eckart

machte dem 'sozialistischen Realismus' auf ihre Weise alle Ehre, indem sie schrieb, was und wie die Leute redeten, die im 'Havelobst' arbeiteten. Und die Frauenprotokolle *Guten Morgen, du Schöne* von Maxi Wander wurden in Theatern gelesen und geben eine Frauenemanzipationsgeschichte a la DDR. Das führte in einen gesamtgesellschaftlichen Diskussionsprozeß und machte deutlich, daß die Emanzipationsbewegung der DDR eine Bewegung zur Befreiung des Menschen und nicht allein der Frau war. Da gab es schon einige Differenzen zum Feminismus im Westen.

Alle diese Beispiele sind zufällig. Eine DDR-Geschichte anhand von Literaturgeschichte steht noch aus. Das könnte eine lohnende interdisziplinäre Aufgabe sein. Nur so würde man von der schleichenden Dämonisierung und Fixierung auf die Stasiakten loskommen und dem Phänomen des Scheiterns einer Idee nahekommen. Andererseits ist nur so einer verlogenen Verklärung entgegenzuwirken. Man wird auch den inneren Kämpfen der Intellektuellen und ihren Versuchen nachgehen, wie sie daran mitwirkten, daß eine emanzipatorische Idee von Gerechtigkeit und Freiheit soziale Gestaltung gewinnt. Welche Lehren aus dem Scheitern zu ziehen sind, ist uns noch überhaupt nicht in den Blick gekommen.

Ich schließe: 'Aber in dieser Zeit begann ein neues, härteres Training des schmerzhaften und wunderbaren aufrechten Gangs.' (Volker Braun)

Der ideologische Druck ist weg; der ökonomische hat seine Stelle besetzt. Und doch ist nicht zu übersehen: Die Städte wurden und werden gerade noch gerettet. Die Umwelt hat sich vielerorts erholt. Blumen, Gemüse, Obst und die täglichen Dinge des Lebens sind 'vorrätig'. Gaststätten sind für Gäste da. Der Angstpanzer ist geplatzt. Demokratische Mitwirkung für alle ist möglich. Die Information ist jedermann zugänglich. Aber alles hat einen großen oder kleinen Haken. Alles ist leicht für die zu haben, die 'haben'. Der Transformationsprozeß ist ohne historisches Beispiel und hat zu Langzeitverwerfungen geführt, an deren Ende wir noch nicht angelangt sind. Der Osten verstummt und wird zum Verstummen gebracht: mit der Stasi-, der PDS- und der Nostalgiekeule. Wer eine Frage stellt oder daran erinnert, daß dieses oder jenes in der DDR nicht so schlecht war, dem wird sofort beschieden: 'Du willst wohl die DDR wiederhaben!' Nun wird die Anpassung aller an den Erfolgsweg der Bundesrepublik nach deren Erfolgsrezept von vierzig Jahren verlangt. Schon vier Jahre lang werden 150 Milliarden in den verkommenen Osten investiert. Und da schauen Westdeutsche ängstlich in das Milliardenloch und mahnen bei den Ostdeutschen mehr Dankbarkeit an. So ganz unberechtigt ist das nicht für die, die plötzlich in eine Anspruchskultur gekommen sind, in der sie ihre Ansprüche erheben, vor allem mit dem Verweis auf angeblich 'vierzig verlorene Jahre'. Richtig ist, daß eine Mecker- und Mäkelstimmung vieler Ostdeutscher zu beobachten ist, die kaum eine Erinnerung mehr haben an das, was an der DDR politisch, materiell und geistig ruinös war, vielmehr aber die guten Seiten der DDR erinnern und sie vergleichen mit den großen Versprechungen von 1990. Was aber wird werden, wenn die angespannten öffentlichen Haushalte zuerst in den Lebensbereichen sparen, in denen sich Menschsein entfaltet und bewährt, also bei Bildung, Kultur und Sozialem? Der ökonomische Wachstumsweg in seiner bisherigen Form ist versperrt, wenn uns am Leben künftiger Generationen gelegen ist. Der geistig-kulturelle 'Wachstums'-Weg ist nicht versperrt. Oder wird das von den 'modernen Medien' manipulativ-banal-brutal-einschaltquotendiktiert besetzt? Wird der Mensch sich wehren und die Reichtümer seiner Kreativität wiederentdecken? Die Antwort ist offen. Literatur ist erneut gefragt als Katalysator des Zusammenkommens von Vergangenheit und Gegenwart, von Ost und West.

Note

1. This piece is based on Friedrich Schorlemmer's contribution to the Symposium in Keele on 28 October 1995.

CHAPTER 7

Stefan Heym and the Transformation of East Germany

Peter Hutchinson

The leadership of the GDR, like that of all totalitarian states, did not encourage the rise of the critical intellectual. On the contrary, it did its best to repress figures like Stefan Heym, who was not only pluralist in his sources of inspiration, but also rich in cross-cultural and general historical awareness. It repeatedly tried hard to intimidate such a dangerous individualist, who was regularly exhorting his audiences never to accept uncritically, but to reflect – not just on such diverse issues as petty bureaucracy, capitalism and Stalinism, but also on the ideals associated with socialism, with the abuse of power by the state, with the question of why certain socialist structures had failed. Despite the countless obstacles put in his way, Heym remained the most outspoken of the GDR's intellectuals, and one of the most successful in challenging the Party line. Ironically, his success in this sphere was undoubtedly achieved in part through his ability never to appear an embittered outsider: he remained a committed member of GDR society who was not prepared to 'desert' to the other German state. In this respect he perfectly fits Ralf Dahrendorf's model of the critical German intellectual who stands on the fringes of society, but nevertheless clearly belongs to it (Dahrendorf 1965: 318).

Yet Heym's life, his reading, his iconoclastic tactics and his lifestyle (which included regular trips to the West), were most untypical of his country, and indeed, of its intellectuals, as a whole. In numerous respects he is an unrepresentative figure through whom to consider the aftermath of the 'gentle revolution', a concept that he used as a title for an anthology (*Die sanfte Revolution*) and about which he himself was to write so much. On the other hand, though, despite Heym's being an intellectual, in so much of his writing he is not *addressing* intellectuals: above all in his journalism, he is trying to write for what he terms 'the little man', he is viewing events through the eyes of that figure, and he is judging developments by *his* standards. In this respect Heym can indeed be a useful figure through which to trace the East German path through euphoria to bewilderment and finally to prolonged unease between 1989 and 1994. For in him we find not simply a sharp, questioning gaze and the desire to write for a wide readership, but also, given his remarkable personal history, an ability to judge events in an international context and with a firm sense of historical development. At some points, though, like numerous other intellectuals, Heym shows himself seriously out of touch. These are moments at which he ceases to campaign for the majority in a way which for many years he had managed to do. But his experience as the oldest dissident of the GDR meant that a change of government did nothing to weaken his critical energy. As he would regularly joke around this time, he had not changed in his role as critic of the regime – it was simply that the regime itself had changed. The question whether his criticism had as much impact on the new Germany as it did on the old must, however, be answered negatively. For all his loud protesting at the transformation of a failed socialist society into a primitive capitalist one, Heym's stature in a state of just under eighty million was obviously lower than that in a state of just under seventeen. The resultant feeling of relative impotence undoubtedly played a role in his decision, early in 1994, to stand as a candidate for Parliament.

Heym, a charismatic bundle of apparent contradictions, began his questioning very young: in 1933, at the age of nineteen, he was Hitler's youngest literary exile; he was effectively exiled again in 1951, at the age of thirty-eight, when, as an obvious Communist sympathiser, he had to leave the United States, the country for which he had fought during the war; at the age of forty, having settled in the GDR, he became one of the most successful critics of that state's bureaucracy and what he saw as misguided policy; and in 1989, at the age of seventy-six and as one of the few nonconformist writers whom the Stasi had failed to drive from the country, he was one of the first to take a symbolic step through the Berlin Wall. Writing both in English and in German, composing fiction as well as pieces for newspapers, writing the occasional light-hearted item alongside soul-searching essays on Germany's future, Heym was an extraordinary mixture of belief in the socialist ideal and unrelenting criticism of the 'actually existing' version of it.

Through his fiction, his journalism and his speeches, Heym had been trying to change East Germany for many years before 1989: his first criticism had been levelled as early as 1952 (when he questioned the current policy of never quoting from anything that had been published in the West), and over the years he was to attack such diverse issues as party bureaucracy, 'Schönfärberei' ('government white-washing'), censorship, socialist realism, GDR news reporting, and particularly Stalinism. Some of these attacks cost him dearly: for many years he could not publish his novels in the GDR; he was expelled from the East German Writers' Union; and he was subject to intense scrutiny by the Stasi. But we must remember that at the same time that he was trying to improve the Eastern state he was also attacking aspects of Western capitalism: exploitation, poverty, anti-Semitism. He was doing precisely this in 1989, a year when he moved closer to other Eastern reformers. For long periods of his life Heym had been something of a loner, and in the mid-eighties he had not been quite as much in touch with other groups as one might have expected: with church groups in particular. I also do not think he was as aware as he might have been of the motives of so many of the refugees for leaving the GDR – not just dissatisfaction with their own leaders, but the attractions of the genuinely pluralistic political structure of the Federal Republic and, above all, its triumphant market economy. Heym had also been initially sceptical of Gorbachev, convinced that vested interests in the Soviet Union would ensure progress was throttled, but as it became clear that the times were indeed changing, Heym himself changed gear. And his growing enthusiasm is evident in the rich flowering of his talents in that glorious year 1989.

During the period preceding the revolution, almost all Heym's published writing was closely focused on the GDR, on the pressures on its leadership, and on the pressures on the concept of socialism. As usual, he had no proper media outlet in the East, and he therefore had to express himself through Western media, especially television and the press. Much of the nonliterary material of this period anticipates and illuminates the fiction he was to write after the collapse of the Wall, and his short stories in particular illustrate the ambivalent and sometimes ambiguous attitude of an elderly man, now grown a little cynical, to the events of the *Wende*: a mixture of relief and disbelief, of satisfaction and foreboding, of hope and fear. These stories illustrate the attitude of a man who never wholeheartedly shared the November euphoria because he was fearful of the future, fearful as a result of years of opposition, persecution, and, not least, his detailed analysis in fiction of past revolutions in Germany. Heym had depicted the origins, development and aftermath of the Baden revolution of 1849 (*The Lenz Papers*), the setting up of a socialist republic in 1945 (*Schwarzenberg*), the Communist take-over in Czechoslovakia in 1948 (*The Eyes of Reason*), and the East German uprising of 1953 (*Five Days in June*); in each novel he showed himself cynically aware of how power shifts according to personalities, of the constant threat of restoration, of the erosion of idealism in face of the need to compromise, and of the personal tragedies and sacrifices demanded by dramatic change. These are features which he will yet again encounter in the aftermath of the *Wende*, which he will satirise in his short stories, but which he will largely overlook in his essays and interviews, where he still maintains his belief in the fulfilment of the socialist ideal.

Heym's reaction to changes was expressed in various forms. First, in fiction, in a number of satirical short stories which were collected under the title *Auf Sand gebaut. Sieben Geschichten aus der unmittelbaren Vergangenheit* (Built on Sand. Seven Stories from the Immediate Past, 1989). These are essentially GDR stories, completed before unification and devoted mainly to the impact of social and psychological change on Eastern citizens. Second, in essays for the press, also regularly satirical. Although he had always written short pieces of this sort, he wrote almost compulsively between January 1991 and January 1992; the best of these articles were collected under the title *Filz. Gedanken über das neueste Deutschland* (Sleaze. Thoughts about the Latest Germany, 1992). And, finally, Heym regularly gave interviews for the various media, both in Germany and elsewhere, in which he expressed in conversational terms his disappointment, fears, frustration, and sometimes his anger. Heym's media interviews often ran in parallel to his essays; owing to their spontaneous nature, they naturally lacked the sustained argument, the delicate irony, and the *pointes* of the latter, but in many of his utterances Heym is sharp and provocative: 'the bigwigs of yesterday are the bosses of today', for example.[1] The very fact he is so regularly sought out by journalists – far more than any other writer of East or West – is in itself an indication of his popularity and the relevance of what he has to say. The themes of these interviews are almost always related to the short stories of *Auf Sand gebaut* and to the essays in *Filz*: the bewildering new world, the growing unemployment in the East, the sell-off of Eastern assets, the destruction of all positive aspects of Eastern society, the rise of the 'elbow' as opposed to the 'heart'.

Since I have analysed aspects of *Auf Sand gebaut* elsewhere (Hutchinson 1997: 298–305), I shall deal with the collection only briefly here, focusing instead principally on the political essays. I shall then outline the election campaign. First, though, I shall sketch Heym's attempts to transform the GDR immediately before the *Wende*.

Heym was centrally involved in the 'quiet revolution', and the whole of 1989 was a hectic but exhilarating time for him. His autobiography *Nachruf* had appeared in the West at the end of the preceding year and had proved a tremendous publishing success. He was therefore still much in demand for Western readings and signings. He exploited this popularity to travel widely, not simply to read and sign books: he used every trip for an appearance on a television programme or for a newspaper interview. He always preferred television, because he knew this was the only way he could reach his Eastern audience. (He did not appear on GDR television or in GDR newspapers until the end of October.) He was an entertaining speaker, witty and well-prepared, and he ensured he was always controversial. That way he would constantly be in demand. He was forthright in his condemnation of his own government's behaviour, and yet he was also fiercely critical of aspects of his neighbour's. Even on his visit to Bad Sassendorf, as an official guest (invited by the premier of North Rhine-Westphalia Rau) to commemorate the fortieth anniversary of the Federal Republic, he castigated what he regarded as the evil aspects of capitalism. It is telling, incidentally, that Heym did not claim his own country as a socialist one. In this period he reverted to claims he made most strikingly in the sixties: that Stalinist elements needed to be removed from the East; that what currently prevailed was not genuine socialism (most strikingly in the essay 'Neue Hoffnung für die DDR', *Einmischung,* 1990: 242). This distinction was crucial, since it allowed Heym to plead for *true* socialism after the collapse of the SED (Socialist Unity Party). In this respect he was totally consistent. In his eyes, socialism had not been discredited by the failure of the GDR, since only a perverse form of it had been practised. This was a point, then, that he made in his interviews and speeches, hopeful that they would find their way back to his own country.

The points Heym made on television were certainly seen by viewers in the East, and he was given more coverage than ever before in the course of these months. The film of his novel *Collin,* firmly critical of cultural politics in the GDR, was shown on West German television at the end of 1988; *Schwarzenberg,* about a small group of revolutionary socialists, was shown in May; *Lenz oder die Freiheit,* about the Baden revolution of 1849, was shown over four separate evenings in July. The international media were constant visitors to his home, and his faultless command of English proved a great attraction to them. There were other events which kept him in the public eye. His novel *Ahasver* (which had appeared in the West in 1981) was actually published in the GDR, and there was to be a second edition in May. Eastern readers were, as ever, desperate to acquire copies of his novels.

By this stage Hungary was beginning to dismantle its barbed wire frontier with the West, and there was a large demonstration in Leipzig against the so-obviously rigged local election results. Heym gave an important and lengthy interview to *L'Unita,* the Italian communist publication. His key points were the pressing need for GDR citizens to be allowed to travel, and for the media to change their policy. What was the point of dissimulating if Western broadcasts were available as an alternative? His longest response here, though, was an attack on bureaucracy in the GDR, particularly the bureaucracy of the Stasi ('Warten auf Perestroika') (Waiting for Perestroika, in *Einmischung* 1990: 219–227). The points he made here were among those he kept repeating in the course of the next few months, as he lectured outside the GDR, conducted readings arranged by (Western) booksellers, appeared on West German 'talk shows', and visited other socialist countries. By this stage, of course, he was also urging his fellow countrymen to stay in their own land. This was not at all out of character, given Heym's long-standing condemnation of the West, and a point soon to be taken up by other true reformers in the GDR, those who during the demonstrations were to chant that they too wanted to stay – in contrast to the thousands who were now escaping. It was one of the key pleas of Pastor Friedrich Schorlemmer at the massive East Berlin demonstration on 4 November: 'Do stay here!'[2]

Heym's arguments in favour of staying are summarised in three carefully crafted and forceful essays, one in *Die Zeit*, the other two in *Der Spiegel*.[3] These re-emphasise the points he had been making in the previous two months and are partly based on tape-recorded conversations he had made with those who had fled the GDR and were in a West German refugee transit camp near Gießen.[4] He urged free elections, openness on the part of the leadership, and proper dialogue with the people. The minor changes of personnel at the top were not enough. Interestingly, he was already warning against unification – at a point well before the Wall had fallen and when no one else was openly contemplating it. Heym's case rested above all on hope, hope that a truly socialist society could yet be made from the old GDR. Significantly, though, he played down the material attractions of the West.[5]

Heym now began appearing on Eastern television, liaising more closely with other writers and intellectuals, and making frequent speeches. Together with Christa Wolf and Stephan Hermlin, he spoke to several thousand in the 'Erlöserkirche' (Church of the Redeemer) in East Berlin (Sunday 29 October) and on 4 November, of course, alongside such figures as Hein, Wolf and Schorlemmer, he gave his famous address to well over half a million in the Alexanderplatz and was hailed as the 'Nestor unserer Bewegung' (the Nestor of our movement). A statement by him and several other prominent figures, urging people not to leave the country, was read by Christa Wolf on GDR television on 8 November. On the night of 9 November he could barely sleep, and he went through the opened Berlin Wall at 4 o'clock in the morning.

The emphasis of Heym's statements now changed, with constant appeals to GDR citizens not to leave, pleas for a truly socialist society, fears about a resurgence of National Socialism, and warnings against unification. He was one of the principal signatories of 'Für unser Land' (For our Country), that call for a new GDR rather than a capitulation to Western materialism, and he readily accepted the invitation to make this public on behalf of the others.[6] Heym became deeply uneasy about the way the situation was developing and then, at the beginning of December, he expressed his turmoil of emotions in a piece entitled 'Aschermittwoch' (Ash Wednesday), a dramatic response to the surge of materialism engendered by the *Wende*. It was featured in *Der Spiegel* as well as in the Eastern *Junge Welt*, and it aroused anger among countless former admirers. One of his harshest critics was actually a former GDR writer in Western exile, Monika Maron, who firmly rebuked him for what she saw as impudence, indeed, arrogance in criticising GDR citizens' first experience of the West. She saw his response as typical of Eastern writers, who were dismayed that the people had not reacted in the way they had wanted them to: 'On this occasion the people have disappointed not their leaders, but their writers'.[7]

Heym was certainly not alone in his dismay that the path to socialism was being eroded by direct involvement with capitalism; GDR intellectuals as a whole were equally shaken. Christoph Hein, for example, who had emerged as one of the most outspoken in this period, was embittered by the way in which the chance of a socialist utopia was 'rejected' by the people.[8] However, after a brief period of disillusionment, Heym began again to write sarcastically of capitalism and to urge a return to a 'true' form of socialism. Not until the 'sell out' became earnest did he again find a serious reading public for his articles, even though his books, particularly *Nachruf,* were selling in vast quantities.

It is within this economic, political and psychological context, then, that Heym began to write his next sequence of short stories, pieces first published in the press and then included in the collection *Auf Sand gebaut* (1989). Like several major intellectuals of this period, Heym was in various respects disorientated and deeply disappointed, in a state probably best described as post-*Wende* shock. We cannot, therefore, expect in these stories a sense of GDR-nostalgia, but rather an eye for human folly, shortsightedness, materialism; we must be prepared for a sense of superiority from the author, who can see and foresee what others cannot; and finally, we must not be surprised by a hint of misanthropy. We look here in vain, therefore, for stories about the drama of the marches, rallies and speeches; there is nothing to do with the heroic efforts of individuals, of the sudden bursts of energy and courage which overcame so many people, of the heroic, indefatigable work of the churches. True, many of these aspects are contained in that anthology which Heym had edited together with Werner Heiduczek, *Die sanfte Revolution*, a collection largely of first-hand accounts of the great year. But here, in *Auf Sand gebaut*, Heym is concerned with quite the opposite: he is dealing rather with aspects of GDR society which ensured its failure, and which, ironically, ensured an easy transition, for some individuals, to a cut-throat capitalist world.

The first story *does* have the potential for recreating the excitement of a key moment in GDR history: the invasion of Stasi Headquarters in the Normannenstraße on 15 January 1990. Heym, however, de-dramatises the situation. Members of the Stasi who remain are ridiculous, pedantic bunglers. Members of the public who invade are gentle, well-meaning individuals, full of restraint, encouraging each other not to be violent: 'No violence, *please*! No violence!'[9] These people, suggests Heym, have been patient too long. The same point is made in the next story, 'Außenstelle' (Outpost), where a newly formed 'Bürgerkomitee' (citizens' committee) is investigating a secret Stasi installation. The citizens are insecure, timid, embarrassed. It seems impossible that such figures could have carried out a successful revolution. The story can be seen as a critique of the half-heartedness of the 'citizens' movements' in general.[10]

Heym's unease with GDR citizens seems to have grown as 1990 developed, as membership of the SED shrank from 2.3 million to 0.7, as the March elections proved such a disappointment to all those brave and idealistic members of the citizens' groups which had been so important in the previous year, as the general populace's desired timetable for unification moved from 'some time in the future', to 'as soon as possible'. Heym viewed this move with anxiety. His newspaper articles and interviews of the period plead desperately for a retention of those aspects of socialism in which so many had truly believed, but the populace as a whole was clearly impatient with any sort of visionary, even with the most prominent of those who had been at the forefront in November. As Pastor Schorlemmer put it so suggestively in February, in an ironic allusion to Wolfgang Leonhard, 'the revolution is now dismissing its fathers'.[11] Interestingly, at the same time that Heym was writing and speaking for socialism, he was also writing short stories which suggested his belief in the future was not strong. For one of the principal accusations of the pieces in *Auf Sand gebaut* is that the GDR possessed a number of citizens who already thought along capitalist lines; whose experience of the 'niche society' had encouraged a survivalist, opportunist mentality in social structures which were riddled with contradictions and all-too-obvious weaknesses. The story which sums this up best is 'Rette sich wer kann' (Every Man for Himself), Heym's original idea for the title of the whole collection. Here the ease with which GDR enterprises are assimilated into Western industrial empires is seen to be possible only because the Eastern managers are able to adapt effortlessly. They can do so, because they were thinking in capitalist perspectives well before the *Wende.*

In all these stories, as well as in the pieces he was to write in the following year, Heym treats a great range of issues. He is less concerned with the constitutional changes in Germany, the political and ideological; much more with the economic, the psychological, the emotional. He responds in a literary way with short stories, in a journalistic way with newpaper contributions; and in a personal way with a succession of interviews. There are slight hints of glee as his predictions are proved correct, but more commonly we find sadness and regret, sometimes bitterness. The writing is always committed and personal. It was usually intended to offend authority and to give encouragement to others. The tone of indignation is more common now than ever before, the sense of injustice stronger. What is different now, for Heym, is that there is no great ideal behind the changes which are being implemented: self-interest is what dictates all current developments.

One of the points which exercised Heym in this period was that the West was not concerned for the well-being of those in the East, and one of the most telling images he used was that of the mastiff and the pug ('Eine andere Welt', *Filz* 70). Imagine, he suggests, that common situation in the park, where the mastiff turns on the yapping little pug and we expect disaster. But the pug quickly throws itself on its back in capitulation and the glorious victor, tiring of his success, soon turns away in disgust. The mastiff is no happier for his easy victory, while the pug, although he has survived, is doomed to a future of servitude. The analogy captures well the sense of discomfort and ignominy experienced by many easterners in the aftermath of unification; the feeling they were 'second class' citizens. Another lively parallel Heym makes is that of East Germans with the eponymous hero of Voltaire's *Candide*, that figure who is always prepared to see the good side of humanity, who never suspects malice, and whose generous actions are severely punished by experience of the real world ('Candide', *Filz* 89–95). He makes a point which was later to be made by many others: that GDR citizens *should* have known the true nature of capitalism, for they had been lectured on it often enough by their leaders. But they had come to mistrust everything their leaders had told them, hence their refusal to believe those leaders' diatribes against the West.

Unification meant relative riches for some, relative disappointment, uncertainty, psychological distress for others. As Heym put it in a form of open letter to the Chancellor, 'so here we are, we Easterners with our unemployment and our shattered dreams and you Westerners with your new and unexpected burden'.[12] The author, of course, is attracted only by the former, and a rough history of what he sees as the more unfortunate aspects of transformation can be traced through his next volume *Filz*, a collection of his most important newspaper publications between January 1991 and January 1992. There are fourteen of these pieces, and I should like to focus on the five most strident.

The decision to move the centre of government from Bonn seemed a vote of confidence in the former capital of the GDR, and it was welcomed by a great many Berliners. But Heym was cautious, and in 'Mich hat ja keiner gefragt' (But no one asked me), he questioned the obvious. He also used the opportunity to launch a general attack on governments, on their capacity to spend their people's money, and on the succession of German governments which had failed in Berlin. He was not positive about the future: 'And yet it seems to me, in the light of world history, as if regimes have been remarkably similar, ever since regimes have begun to exist – if not in the background which their members share, then nevertheless in their nature and their ostentatious way of behaving'.[13] His shrewdest observation, however, was actually about the likely profits of 'landowners and estate agents'. The piece is written with zest, but its affected jocularity undermines every apparently positive statement. Heym makes a blunt and disarming comment at one point: 'I know I won't be popular in many places for views like these'.[14] This sort of remark is never aimed at governments or those in authority: it is aimed at his everyday readers. And it is exactly the same point he made just after the collapse of the Wall and his condemnation of consumerism. Whatever one may think of Heym, he never goes out of his way to court popularity.

Xenophobia was an issue on which Heym was bound to be sensitive: driven from Germany over fifty years before, he had experienced discrimination from an early age. Not surprisingly, he responded immediately to the events at Hoyerswerda, the scene of a violent arson attack on foreign workers during which the skinhead mob was actually urged on by middle-aged observers. In 'Erinnerungen' (Memories) Heym's criticism was not simply directed at that older generation, which had experienced National Socialism at first hand, nor at a government which seemed reluctant to get to the roots of the problem, and which seemingly handled the victims in a shoddy manner. His concerns were broader and his tone was largely reflective: he emphasised the need to address the problem by facing rather than ignoring it, but he also saw the events in historical and international terms. The drama of Hoyerswerda also had another consequence for Heym: it confirmed his decision that his massive personal archive should not stay in Germany but that it should come to England.

It was precisely the English, however, who did provide the inspiration for another major change in East German society over which Heym expressed despair: privatisation of the countless state-owned enterprises.

'Treuhand aufs Herz' (Trusthand on heart) starts apparently neutrally, harmlessly, historically, with only slight sarcasm. But the tone is deceptively bland so that brief clauses can have more cutting an effect. For example, after the historical details on how the *Treuhand* (the trust agency created to carry out the privatisation) came into existence, comes the harsh comment 'So it's no longer a question of *preservation of national property*, but *privatisation and reorganisation*, in other words sell-off and destruction'.[15] Heym is concerned about unemployment, sale of the people's assets, and, in his final sentences, with those corrupt GDR politicians who have managed the transition to the new economy so effortlessly that they remain involved in decisions on the future of Eastern citizens. As he wittily puts it, 'you scratch my trust and I'll scratch yours'.[16]

Yet although Heym can preserve his sense of humour in many of his statements, there is one piece in which his serious-ness of purpose displaces wit: it is his article on the wave of dis-missals which followed analysis of the Stasi files. Now we might expect this to have been an area in which Heym would not have been anxious to protect any culprits. Ridding the GDR of the Stasi had been one of the greatest transforming experiences of the country, and Heym and his family had suffered far more observation and harassment than almost any others. But Heym, as usual, does not take a wholly personal view; he expands the individual case – of a doctor who was dismissed for alleged Stasi collaboration – in order to make a warning against generalisations, to make a grand survey of questionable 'justice', and to plead for the ancient concept of a fair trial.

The original newspaper article employed an aggressive title: 'Die Wahrheit, und nichts als die Wahrheit'[17] (The truth, and nothing but the truth). Heym begins factually and indi-rectly, combining both personal and abstract. He comments on the crucial role of the doctor in society, and his own indebt-edness to certain physicians; but he then turns from adulation of the profession to a condemnation of certain individuals. Using the Third Reich as an example, a common technique of his writing, he reminds his readers that a doctor always stood at the entrance to a concentration camp. Only after such reflections does the author adopt an anecdotal tone, shifting in his vocabulary from the general to the specific, and to the story of a certain Peter Althaus.

This man, he relates, was a gifted doctor who built his own dialysis machine and who was visited by the Stasi when he complained about the type of defective equipment which had been built by the GDR. His contacts with a particular Stasi officer developed into more of a personal friendship, but the officer moved to Berlin and Althaus met his successor only once, when the latter consulted him about an operation on his wife. Althaus thought no more about these contacts until July 1992, when, now as a Professor at the Charité in Berlin, he was suddenly given his notice. The reason: investigation of the Stasi files had supposedly proved him to be an 'inoffizieller Mitarbeiter' (unofficial collaborator [with the secret police]).

In the long discussion which then follows, and which pleads for the basic human right to a fair trial, Heym goes straight to the heart of the matter: how reliable is the evidence? The fact that it has come from a specifically German organisation is not, he suggests, any consolation. Sources of information are regularly tainted in some way by the personal involvement of the informant, and what sort of person would such an informant have been anyway? The aim of these informants was not necessarily the truth; more likely it was financial or personal gain. As he puts it, 'they were paid according to the length and the content of their reports, and the commanding officers were paid according to the number and rank of those they commanded. What sort of lying and falsifying and adapting must have gone on according to request and to need!'.[18]

Heym's article aroused considerable attention, and Joachim Gauck himself (head of the organisation controlling the Stasi files) felt obliged to respond to it – although not in a way which gave any former victims cause for comfort (Gauck: 1991). Heym was nevertheless vindicated: Althaus was eventually reinstated.

Heym had worked on documents often enough in the past to recognise the subjective nature of the source. Indeed, his greatest novel, *The King David Report*, draws so much of its rich irony from the author's ability to reveal the inconsistencies of the Bible, a document whose fallibility went unquestioned for so many centuries. When he saw his own Stasi file, Heym immediately had the idea of making a short story from part of it, entitled 'IM Frieda' (Unofficial Collaborator Frieda [the code name for a maid employed in the Heym household]). He then decided to publish only extracts from it, together with a novelistic diary he had written late in 1976, the period following the expulsion of the singer Wolf Biermann from the GDR: *Der Winter unsers Mißvergnügens. Aus den Aufzeichnungen des OV Diversant*[19] (The Winter of our Discontent. From the Notes of the Operational Files on 'Subversive').When he wrote his plea for justice in connection with the Stasi files, Heym did not know the full extent of what had been done to him. He was soon to find that his file was one of the largest in the whole country.

The final piece from *Filz* that I should like to consider is 'Seelenschmerzen' (Soul pangs), written just over two years after the Wall fell. It was delivered before a literary audience, and its tone is correspondingly reflective, witty and cutting. One of Heym's first points is the question of whether the events of October and November 1989 can accurately be termed a 'revolution'. Hitherto, specialists would never have hesitated to designate it such: 'previously, at any rate, no historian or sociologist would have hesitated to describe as a revolution events which led to the complete inversion of an economic system'.[20] But was it *really* a revolution? Heym's refusal to provide an answer to this question suggests, indirectly, his own regret at the way this supposed 'revolution' turned out. What he concerns himself with now, then, are the effects of the 'inversion', and since he is addressing writers, he emphasises the positive flowering of long frustrated media talent in the east, and the clearing out of certain inadequate individuals; yet the main focus, as we might expect from Heym, is not the positive achievements of unification, but the negative. In particular, he deplores the attempt to denigrate what was successful in GDR literature. With allusions which suggest he had above all Christa Wolf in mind, he laments the constant attacks on those who had previously been hailed as heroes, and the sniping of the gutter press against those who had previously stood bravely in the face of the might of the SED. The present activity is all part of a systematic campaign, he suggests, one which will remove all aspects of the GDR which could remind people of former achievements: universities, academies, schools, museums, hospitals, et cetera, 'absolutely everything which could give Eastern citizens occasion and opportunity to reflect on the values which they created, as well as on their own personal value'.[21]

There is, suggests Heym, no need to get rid of individuals, as was the practice in ancient times (a practice he exposed so convincingly in *The King David Report*); all one needs to do now is to demolish their reputation. His suggestion leads to an obvious conclusion: as soon as the past is recognised as unreliable, inadequate, false, then transformation to, and embracing of, the new society is complete.

Possibly out of a sense of political impotence, Heym fell relatively silent in 1992 and 1993. Apart from the occasional article and interview, he devoted himself intensively to what will probably be his final great novel – on the life of Karl Radek, that passionate subversive who was involved not only with the Russian revolutions of 1905 and 1917, but also with the German November revolution of 1918. Radek's life in the USSR, culminating in one of the famous Stalin 'show trials' of the thirties, was a warning of the dangers of communism as a form of government; but Radek's passion for truly communist revolution was a counterweight to the stampede towards capitalism just witnessed in the East.

Early in 1994, as the various parties began to select candidates for the November elections, Heym was approached by the leaders of the 'Partei des Demokratischen Sozialismus' (Party of Democratic Socialism, PDS). For many Eastern voters, the personnel and politics of this group bore too close a resemblance to those of its predecessor, the old SED, but the new party embraced two principles which clearly did have an appeal: it wished to provide a truly socialist alternative (which was not offered by the SPD), and it aimed to represent the people of the East. However uneasy Heym may have felt about joining forces with former SED members, he was certainly in favour of these particular goals; so although he did not join the party itself, he allowed his name to be put forward as its candidate. With the German proportional representation system slightly modified for these elections, the PDS needed to win three seats outright in order to gain further seats in proportion to their total vote. Given his very high profile and his reputation as a socialist who had nevertheless opposed the old SED, Heym represented one of the PDS's strongest hopes for a directly elected candidate.

From the start, Heym's decision to run aroused lively interest. He was attacked fiercely in certain quarters (notably by Konrad Weiß, prime mover of 'Für unser Land' and leader of 'Bündnis 90/Die Grünen', by Günter Grass, and by Christa Wolf). On the other hand, such figures as the late Heiner Müller and Fritz J. Raddatz warmly applauded his decision. The controversy suited Heym perfectly: it gave him a prominent media platform from which he could renew his criticism of the improper way in which he felt former GDR citizens had been treated. In an interview in the *Berliner Zeitung* of 17 February 1994, just after he had declared his decision, he claimed he wanted to achieve 'a true opposition from the Left. I want to do something for the people of the former GDR. The country was treated unfairly after the *Wende*. The population didn't just want primitive capitalism. Most of them would have liked socialism with the "KadeWe" [Kaufhaus des Westens, a large luxury department store in West Berlin]. What they got was unemployment and "Aldi" [an unglamorous discounter]'.[22]

Heym saw Parliament as excessively influenced by industry, banks and the churches, and he hoped his own participation could redress the balance. His principal concern was unemployment in the East, together with the high cost of rents and the social problems arising from unification. He wished a return to some form of political control over the economy. As he put it in a later interview: 'Everything shouldn't just be left to market forces, to pure profits; it must also be judged and organised for the benefit of all'.[23]

Despite his age (he turned 81 in April 1994), Heym ran a successful campaign against a distinguished rival (Wolfgang Thierse, former East German activist and a Deputy Leader of the SPD). His name drew the media from all over Germany (and overseas) to what was seen as a symbolic seat. On 10 November he took 40.6 per cent of the votes, against the 37 per cent cast for Thierse. As oldest member of the House it was his role to deliver the opening speech of the new parliament, and despite the crass attempt by a senior Christian Democrat opponent to discredit him on the eve of that speech, he pleaded for mutual tolerance and understanding between the eastern and western parts of the country – exactly five years after the collapse of the Wall (Heym, 1995a: 208–12).

Heym's speech also included some criticism of Western capitalism, as well as references to aspects of GDR life which he claimed could fruitfully be taken over for Germany's common future; but these ideas were couched in far more moderate language than had been the case in the essays, speeches and stories of the preceding five years. Nevertheless, many Westerners were annoyed by the speech, just as they had been by Heym's earlier attacks on aspects of a united Germany. They felt his approach betrayed ingratitude for what the West had done, particularly in view of the great economic strain which unification was placing on the economy. It would have been unrealistic, however, to expect Heym to have stopped protesting overnight, and indeed, to stop protesting at all. As I have pointed out, he had been attacking the Western government for many years, and in numerous respects his post-*Wende* work is merely a continuation of his earlier work.

Did Heym protest too much and too rudely, though, and were his hopes for a new Germany ill-founded? Yes, he possibly did protest too much, but this was a tactic he had learnt from American exile in the thirties and which stood him in

good stead throughout his period in the GDR. If he had not
protested loudly, vigorously and frequently, nothing would
have changed. Without the strident critic, even democratically
elected leaders can be tempted towards policies which they
know are questionable. Ironically, however, although the GDR
leadership always took Heym seriously, the Federal Republic
leaders have failed to do so. They have resented him, been irri-
tated by him, been annoyed by him, but they have not taken
his comments to heart. And Heym himself may not have fully
appreciated that progress in Western democracies is often
dependent more on consensus and indirect lobbying than on
frontal attack. He might also have drawn more comfort from
the fact that his own political success – election to the Bundestag and thus to 'Alterspräsident', father of the house – was a
triumph of democracy. A senior member of the Christian
Democrats may have attempted to embarrass him out of office
on the eve of his speech to Parliament, but an open society
meant that this attempt was exposed as crude and vindictive.[24]
Further, his speech was not only delivered to the 'Bundestag',
but nationwide on radio and television. As Peter Graves
pointed out in his review of *Radek*, 'if the morality of a system
may be judged in part by the way it treats its opponents, this
event should give pause for thought' (Graves 1995: 27).

Finally, has Heym's dismay at the transformation of the GDR
been wholly justified? In numerous respects, it has, but in others,
it has not. A man with his record was bound to experience unification differently from others. The GDR achieved many goals
– most notably in employment, in social services and in the eradication of poverty – but it achieved these at a price which many
in the West would not have been prepared to pay, and at a price
which many of the GDR's most talented citizens were not prepared to pay. Too many of its 'successes' were bound up with
suppression of individuality, the demand for conformity, the
need to accept that whatever the state did was right. Further, it
could never have realised certain aims without a massive secret
police, a high degree of force, sometimes brutality, and considerable moral blackmail. Above all, it could never have achieved
them if there had been an alternative available to its populace.[25]

As I have indicated, many Eastern intellectuals, particularly
writers, were dismayed by the call of their own society for
'immediate capitalism'. Yet the majority of these intellectuals
were enjoying a form of 'socialism' which was beyond the

reach of the vast majority of the populace, and their calls for the preservation of 'the best' aspects of GDR society were based on a utopianism fostered by an untypical experience of GDR living. In his analysis of Christoph Hein's reaction to the transformation, William Niven suggests that the author's uncritical commitment to utopian socialism 'causes him not just to blackball, or refuse to acknowledge, the present, but also to misread the past and to lose himself in speculative visions of the future' (Niven 1995: 700). There is a hint – but only a hint – of this in Heym, and although I do not want to suggest that this versatile writer-cum-politician is wrong to continue the work he can do best – as lone and courageous gadfly – by continuing to use the GDR as a yardstick, he will clearly weaken some of his arguments. For all the reservations many have expressed about Heym and his activities since November 1989, this independent, awkward, courageous, and charismatic outsider remains a dominating figure in the period under review. Untypical intellectual though he may be, his reactions to the transformation of his land are frequently representative not just of the intelligentsia, but of the populace as a whole.

Notes

1. 'Die Bonzen von früher sind die Bosse von heute' (interview with Peter Gärtner in *Hessische Allgemeine, Kieler Nachrichten* and *Weser-Kurier*, 9 November 1990).
2. 'Bleibt doch hier!' (Schorlemmer 1992)
3. Reprinted in *Einmischung* 1990: 239–44; 249–56; 259–64.
4. *Die sanfte Revolution*, pp. 52–78.
5. In her valuable discussion of Heym's activity during this period, Kristie A. Foell draws attention to a certain tension within Heym at this point: 'By October Heym is still certain that his fellow citizens are not acting only out of pecuniary interest, but he seems less willing to speculate about their concrete motivations: 'Dabei ist zu notieren, daß die Verlockung, die DDR zu verlassen, nicht nur von den größeren Fettaugen auf den westlichen Fleischtöpfen herrührt. ... [Z]umindest bei einigen der Ausgereisten könnten neben dem Fressen auch edlere Motive eine Rolle spielen.' ('We should note in this connection that the temptation to leave the GDR does not stem solely from bigger dollops of fat in the western fleshpots. ... Alongside greed, more noble motives could well have played a part, at least in the case of some of those leaving.') (*Einmischung*, p. 241) The classical image of the people of Israel's betrayal of their god, while used in the negative here, indicates Heym's fear that the people of Marx may betray their moral mandate as well.'(Foell 1994: 37–48).
6. Principally Konrad Weiß, Christa Wolf, and Schorlemmer himself; both the first version of the text and the longer (published) second are featured in Schorlemmer 1992: 302–5.

7. 'Diesmal ist nicht die Regierung vom Volk enttäuscht, diesmal sind es die Dichter' (Maron 1990: 68). Heym's image of a materialistic mob is discussed in Hutchinson 1997: 396–98, as well as in Foell 1994: 39–40. Heym later recognised his realistic depiction of the situation constituted a mistake: see his interview with Regina General in 1994 in R. General and W. Sabath, *Stefean Heym. Querkopf,* Berlin, Elefanten Press, p.52.

8. For a survey of this situation, but with principal reference to Christoph Hein, see Bernhard Spies 1994: 393–405. For a full study of Heym's reactions, see Niven 1995: 688–706. For a sharp critique of the way in which 'Wolf, Heym, Braun, and many other intellectuals discredited themselves by completely miscalculating the direction in which democratic processes would lead citizens of the GDR', see the Introduction to von Hallberg 1996: 5.

9. 'Keine Gewalt, *bitte*! Keine Gewalt!' (*Auf Sand:* 52. My italics.)

10. For a survey of the citizens' movement in this period, see Haufe 1993: 78–158.

11. Wolfgang Leonhard's autobiography of a life under Stalinism had appeared as *Die Revolution entläßt ihre Kinder* (The Revolution dismisses its Children).

12. '... nun sitzen wir da, das Ostelevisionolk mit seiner Arbeitslosigkeit und seinen zerbrochenen Hoffnungen und das Westelevisionolk mit seiner neuen, unerwarteten Bürde', in 'Treten Sie zurück, Herr Kohl!' (Resign, Mr Kohl!) published on 4 April 1991 and collected in *Filz* as 'Kleines Gespräch mit Herrn Dr. K.' (Short Conversation with Dr. K).

13. 'Und doch scheint mir, im Licht der Weltgeschichte, als ähnelten die Regierungen, seit es Regierungen gibt, einander doch sehr – wenn nicht im Background ihres Personals, so doch in Wesen und Gehabe' (*Filz* 28).

14. 'Ich weiß, vielerorts wird man mich nicht lieben für derlei Ansichten' (*Filz* 29).

15. 'Also nicht mehr *Wahrung des Volkseigentums,* sondern dessen *Privatisierung und Reorganisation,* soll heißen Ausverkauf und Vernichtung' (*Filz* 47. Italics in original.)

16. '... eine Treuhand wäscht die andere' (*Filz* 51).

17. First published in the *Berliner Zeitung* on 9/10 November 1991, the article attracted such attention that it was syndicated. It appeared in the *Westfälische Rundschau* as late as 18 December 1991, with the title 'Sogar bei der Inquistion ging es milder zu' (Even the Inquisition was more lenient).

18. '... bezahlt wurden sie nach Länge und Inhalt ihrer Berichte, und die Führungsoffiziere nach Anzahl und Rang der von ihnen Geführten. Was wurde da nicht erlogen und gefälscht und zurechtgeschneidert nach Wunsch und Bedarf!' (*Filz* 85)

19. 'Diversant' (subversive) was the Stasi code name for Heym. The work is prefaced by an introduction and concluded by a 'postscript', both of which include documents from the Stasi files relating to Heym's activities at the point of composition.

20. '... früher jedenfalls hätte kein Historiker und kein Soziologe sich gescheut, Ereignisse, die zur kompletten Umstülpung eines ökonomischen Systems führten, als Revolution zu bezeichnen' (*Filz* 97).

21. '... alles überhaupt, was den Ost–Menschen Anlaß und Gelegenheit geben könnte, über die Werte, die sie schufen, nachzudenken und über ihren eigenen Wert' (*Filz* 102).

22. '... eine wirkliche linke Opposition. Ich will etwas tun für die Leute in der Ex-DDR. Das Land ist nach der Wende unfair behandelt worden. Die Leute wollten nicht nur den primitiven Kapitalismus. Die meisten wünschten sich den Sozialismus und das KaDeWe. Was sie bekommen haben ist die Arbeitslosigkeit und Aldi' (interview with *Berliner Zeitung* 17 February 1994).

23. 'Es dürfte nicht alles den Marktkräften überlassen werden, nicht nur dem reinen Profit, sondern müßte auch nach dem allgemeinen Nutzen beurteilt und arrangiert werden' (interview with Reinhard Zweigler in *Leipziger Volkszeitung*, 17 May 1994; also in *Die andere Stimme: Stefan Heym*, ed. Wahlbüro der PDS, Berlin, Parteivorstand der PDS, 1994, pp. 34–36.).

24. Heym was accused of assisting the Stasi in connection with their investigations into Heinz Brandt, who had fled the GDR in 1958. The papers held in the Stasi archive were 'discovered' shortly before the day of Heym's speech and passed on to the Home Secretary, Manfred Kanther, who made them public.

It was clear Heym's action at the time in question – giving his local police station a mimeographed letter which had been posted in West Berlin and which had reputedly come from Brandt —had not been designed to help the Stasi, and Heym chose to instigate judicial proceedings against Kanther for making the case public before he himself had been informed of it. The complaint was taken up by the Public Prosecutor, and Heym himself confessed that this action was a hopeful sign for democracy: 'Das gibt mir das Gefühl, daß hier doch eine gewisse Hoffnung für Demokratie besteht' (This gives me the feeling that there actually are some hopes for democracy in this country) (Heym 1995c: 26).

25. For the best short survey of the GDR's achievements in relation to its limitations, see Fulbrook 1992: 89–96. Also relevant is the subsection 'Was the GDR inevitably doomed to fail?' in Fulbrook 1995: 279–83.

References

Dahrendorf, Ralf. 1965. *Gesellschaft und Demokratie in Deutschland*. Munich, Piper.

Foell, Kristie A. 1994.'Shaping History: Stefan Heym's Responses to German Unification'. *Colloquia Germanica*, vol. 27, pp.37–48.

Fulbrook, Mary. 1992. *The Two Germanies, 1945–1990. Problems of Interpretation*. Basingstoke and London, Macmillan.

——. 1995. *Anatomy of a Dictatorship. Inside the GDR 1949–1989*. Oxford, Oxford University Press.

Gauck, Joachim. 1991. 'Die Behörde ist eine faire Maklerin, Herr Heym'. *Berliner Zeitung*, 22 November.

Graves, Peter. 1995. Review of *Radek*, *Times Literary Supplement*, 13 October, p.27.

Hallberg, Robert von, ed. 1996. *Literary Intellectuals and the Dissolution of the State. Professionalism and Conformity in the GDR*. Chicago, University of Chicago Press.

Haufe, G. 1993. 'Die Bürgerbewegungen im Jahr 1990', in *Die Bürgerbewegungen in der DDR und in den ostdeutschen Bundesländern*, ed. G. Haufe and K. Bruckmaier, Opladen, Westdeutscher Verlag, pp.78–158.

Heym, Stefan. 1951. *The Eyes of Reason*. Boston, Little, Brown; German translation from the original English *Die Augen der Vernunft*. Leipzig, List, 1955.

——. 1964. *The Lenz Papers*. London, Cassell, 1964; German translation from the original English, *Die Papiere des Andreas Lenz*. Leipzig, List, 1963.

——. *The King David Report*. London, Hodder & Stoughton; German translation from the original English, *Der König David Bericht*, Munich, Kindler Verlag, 1972.

——. 1974. *5 Tage im Juni*. Munich, Gütersloh; Vienna, Bertelsmann; English translation from the original German, *Five Days in June*. London, Hodder & Stoughton, 1977.

——. 1984. *Schwarzenberg*. Munich, Bertelsmann.

——. 1988. *Nachruf.* Munich, Bertelsmann.

——. 1989. *Auf Sand gebaut. Sieben Geschichten aus der unmittelbaren Vergangenheit.* Munich, Bertelsmann.

——. 1990. *Einmischung. Gespräche. Reden. Essays.* Selected and edited by Inge Heym and Heinfried Henniger. Munich, Bertelsmann.

——. 1992. *Filz. Gedanken über das neueste Deutschland.* Munich, Bertelsmann.

——. 1995a. *Rede zur Eröffnung des 13. Deutschen Bundestages, Neue Deutsche Literatur,* vol. 43, January 1995, pp.208–12; English translation by Stefan Howald, 'Old Echoes in German Reichstag', *New Times,* 26 November 1994, p.4.

——. 1995b. *Radek.* Munich, Bertelsmann.

——. 1995c. Interview with *Bonner Illustrierte,* 'Ein gutes Zeichen für die Demokratie', in *Bonner Illustrierte,* June 1995, p.26

——. and Heiduczek, Werner. 1990. *Die sanfte Revolution. Prosa, Lyrik, Protokolle, Erlebnisberichte, Reden.* Leipzig, Kiepenheuer.

Hutchinson, Peter. 1997. 'Stefan Heym and the *Wende*', in: Robert Atkins and Martin Kane, eds., *Retrospect and Review. Aspects of the Literature of the GDR 1976–1990,* Amsterdam/Atlanta, Rodopi, pp.292–307.

Leonhard, Wolfgang. 1990. *Die Revolution entläßt ihre Kinder,* 2nd edn. Cologne, Kiepenheuer und Witsch (1955).

Maron, Monika. 1990. 'Die Schriftsteller und das Volk'. *Der Spiegel,* 7, pp.68, 70. Also in English translation in *New German Critique,* Special Number on German Unification, no. 52, Winter 1991, pp.31–41.

Niven, William. 1995. '"Das Geld ist nicht der Gral": Christoph Hein and the Wende'. *Modern Language Review,* vol. 90, pp.688–706

Schorlemmer, Friedrich. 1992. *Worte öffnen Fäuste: die Rückkehr in ein schwieriges Vaterland.* Munich, Kindler.

Spies, Bernhard. 1994. 'The End of the Socialist State: The Socialist Utopia and the Writers'. *Modern Language Review,* vol. 89, pp.393–405.

CHAPTER 8

Writers in Times of Change

David Rock

The End of Utopias

Most critical writers in the GDR were unlike their counterparts in other Eastern bloc countries in one important respect: they remained loyal to the ideology of the socialist society in which they lived. However, with the ubiquitous activities of the Stasi and the often unpredictable responses of the censor, their loyalties were increasingly strained during the late 1970s and 1980s, with several prominent writers being forced to go to the West. Hence the breakdown of the SED regime in 1989 was welcomed by the vast majority of GDR writers and also, of course, by those who had already left. For instance, in his short essay with the self-explanatory title 'Über die letzten Tage. Ein kleiner Einspruch gegen die große deutsche Euphorie' (On the last few days. A minor objection to the great German euphoria) (Becker 1990a: 90), Jurek Becker welcomed the collapse of 'actually existing' socialist states. Yet at the same time, he lamented the demise of his remaining hopes for socialism and its promise of a more humane form of society in the face of Western societies which offer no real alternatives because they lack goals or objectives and are driven only by consumerism. This loyalty to the ideas of socialism was shared by most GDR writers, even those who had been most critical. And not a single GDR author (as far as I know) envisaged a united Germany at the time, for, as Eckhard Thiele put it: 'It would have been a radical recantation of their GDR identity. The collapse of a vision of the world' (Thiele 1991: 155).[1] Most GDR writers were, then, initally loyal to their own utopian notions of socialism. And so, unlike most East German citizens, most writers were also initially for an independent GDR state but one with 'real' social and political reforms. Yet their aspirations for such a state were vague and did not go much beyond a profession of faith in a reformed, humane GDR after Honecker, and none of them was actually able to propose a concrete alternative to the GDR or the Federal Republic. Moreover, they soon became aware that they belonged to an extremely small minority in advocating independence.

The most prominent author of the younger generation to argue for an independent GDR in late 1989 was Christoph Hein. He was also the one most conspicuously involved in events, participating in protest vigils in East Berlin churches, addressing demonstrators in the Alexanderplatz on 4 November and giving numerous interviews for the media. Yet his works themselves can be read as evidence of the impossibility of a new, reformed, independent GDR. Indeed, Hein's relationship with 'actually existing socialism' had always been problematic. Though a professed socialist, he was never a member of the Party, and in his works, orthodox Party men are invariably negative figures, for one of the main themes which dominates Hein's fiction and the target of much of his criticism is Stalinism. In the speech 'Unbelehrbar Erich Fried' (dyed-in-the-wool Erich Fried) which he delivered when he was awarded the Erich-Fried prize in May 1990, he was quite explicit: 'With the appearance of Stalin, the system strayed onto the path which made its lack of future, its failure foreseeable' (Baier 1990:23).[2] Hein's novels, stories and plays, then, attest to the growing conviction amongst writers in the final years of the GDR that things could not go on without radical change. Indeed, Hein once claimed, half-jestingly, that in his works he had described the end of the GDR eleven times!

Yet why, for all the bleakness of his writing, was he still able in late 1989 to call himself a socialist, to appeal for a 'socialism which really deserves the name'[3] and to express the hope that the demise of the GDR might offer a chance to realise the very socialist ideals which had been distorted by the SED regime? Indeed, at the Alexanderplatz he urged his fellow GDR citizens not to miss the opportunity presented to them: 'At last we have a chance, now, for the first time, and we should exploit it and not waste it' (Hein 1990b: 219).[4] And he was not alone in his stance, indeed he was typical of the second generation of GDR writers who, for all their problems with 'actually existing socialism', still described themselves as socialists and were against capitalist values; and they include such prominent writers as Wolf Biermann and Jurek Becker, who had actually left the country either voluntarily or by expulsion. Nor was their criticism in 1989 reserved for the GDR: in the weeks before the opening of the Berlin Wall, several writers, including Hein, Heym and Becker, attacked the government of the Federal Republic for its colonialist attitude to the GDR.

The answer is that these persistent hopes for socialism, shared by many other GDR writers, were invested in a GDR which had never really existed. The most famous statement of these hopes was made by Volker Braun in his poem 'Das Eigentum' (Property). Even though he had been another consistent critic of the SED regime with works such as *Unvollendete Geschichte* (Unfinished Story), Braun laments the loss of this utopia designed for the GDR in his much quoted poem:

> Was ich niemals besaß, wird mir entrissen
> Was ich nicht lebte, werd ich ewig missen
>
> (What I never possessed is snatched from me/ What I never lived I will miss for ever) (Chiarloni and Pankoke 1991: 109).

The poem neatly encapsulates the quandary of those former East German writers who realised that the object of their utopian concerns was now in the process of vanishing from the face of the earth.[5] Hein himself, too, soon appears to have shared the realisation that utopian hopes were not going to be realised, for by March 1990, his inital optimism was gone. His prognosis for his country was now decidedly bleak and the responsibility for failure clear: 'The independence of the GDR has been frittered away and squandered – and not through the fault of West Germany. This washed-out system here has no chance of bringing about a unification in an upright and dignified manner. There will therefore be no agreement but a take-over by the FRG' (Baier 1990: 44).[6]

Volker Braun's poem is representative both of immediate post-1989 sentiments and of a main trend: much of the writing of former GDR writers in the first few years after the *Wende* was concerned not so much with the new realities confronting them in the shape of the new Germany, but with the old GDR, and more specifically with coming to terms with the loss of utopian hopes which, despite everything, many writers still invested in the GDR (Mohr 1994: 19). In their different ways, other prominent writers such as Stephan Hermlin, Stefan Heym, Christa Wolf, Heiner Müller, Christoph Hein, Fritz Rudolf Fries and Helga Königsdorf, significantly all so-called 'Reformsozialisten' (reform socialists), gave expression to what Wilhelm Emmerich has called 'die Erschütterung, schließlich das Ortloswerden der sozialistischen Vision' (the disruption of the socialist vision and ultimately its loss of a place of location) (Emmerich 1997: 457).

Hein's modern parable, the short story 'Kein Seeweg nach Indien' (No Sea Route to India) (Baier 1990: 13–19), published in June 1990, is of particular interest here. Written specifically in response to a survey about the role played by writers in the GDR, it offers an answer, albeit in narrative form, to the question as to whether the socialist utopia still has any validity. Its title is also an allusion to another story written fifteen years earlier which deals with the theme of utopia: Fritz Rudolf Fries's *Der Seeweg nach Indien* (The sea route to India), a story concerning the explorer Colón who, whilst eventually charting his disillusionment with the 'paradise' he discovers, is sustained by the hope that new worlds will be found and at the end sets off again in search of 'India , wherever that may be' (Fries 1978: 19).[7]

The very title of Hein's parable, 'No sea route to India', signals with a note of finality the failure of this search for new, better worlds, for utopia. Even the first sentence portends this failure: 'From the outset, the venture was ill-starred. Only the smallest minority of the crew were convinced by the Great Captain's vision and really expected to find a route to India across the sea. The rest of the crew hardly had any other choice after the great war' (Baier 1990: 13).[8] The subsequent events of his story parallel the history of 'actually existing socialism', from its inception to its demise, in the fate of a fleet of ships, whose Captain sets out with his 'ancient charts on which paradise was marked in' (Baier 1990: 13).[9] The condition of the ships swiftly deteriorates and, despite assurances from the captain that they are on course, stormy seas and increasingly bad conditions on board lead to mutinous unrest. Widespread surveillance ensues. Increasingly desperate crew members flee the ships at night and in the end, even the Great Captain himself gives up the search for 'paradise'. The people, 'das Volk', therefore eschew notions of utopia which lead nowhere and return to 'die alte Heimat' ('the old homeland', i.e. the capitalist West) where they stare with wide-open eyes at the wealth which confronts them. The residents on the mainland, however, are concerned when they see the dilapidated state of both ships and crew and wonder who is going to foot the bill when all these impoverished people disembark. Negotiations take place and strict conditions are laid down, with a lengthy period of quarantine being demanded to prevent 'die blühende Stadt' (the flourishing city) being contaminated by the 'verfaulten Kähnen' (rotten old tubs). A new slogan goes up with a harshly realistic message: 'Beyond the ocean lies not paradise but death' (Baier 1990: 17)[10] and any one who does not endorse the sentiment comes under suspicion of being 'a follower of the Great Captain or an informer' (Baier 1990: 17).[11] New pressure is thus placed on the returnees to adapt to the new situation.

Hein's story, then, confronts in the form of a parable both the history of 'actually existing socialism' and the reality of the new Germany: the sort of difficulties facing former citizens of the GDR as the sailors discover another regime in which pressure to conform, hypocrisy and blackmail of a kind prevail. Have they jumped from the frying pan into the fire? This is certainly one of the two awkward questions which Hein is posing. The other is: what has happened to the ships' writers? 'And the scribes? There were scribes on board too, weren't there?' (Baier 1990: 17)[12] The question concerns, of course, the part played by writers before the *Wende* (the narrator actually uses the word in the text at the point where the ship turns about) and their responses to the new situation. During the journey, their books, which were chronicles of actual conditions on the ships, were popular both on board and elsewhere for the ships' newspapers contained only propaganda. Of course, the writers were constantly under surveillance, some were even forced to leave the ships, others were locked up, but still they went on writing about the journey (i.e., real life in the GDR): 'They wrote about the course set by the fleet and pointed out that it had long since ceased to match the old charts. Thus they kept alive unrest and mistrust.' (Baier 1990: 18)[13] When the crew managed finally to turn the ship about, the writers were celebrated as 'the intrepid chroniclers of the ships of fools' (Baier 1990: 18),[14] but later, when they reach 'the old homeland', the people no longer take any interest in them. They only want to hear what the 'Stadkämmerer' (city treasurers) have to say, the ones who hold the purse strings, And the response of the writers? They just return to their desks and continue their work – undisturbed now, and as was ever the case, they continue producing 'sehr verschiedene Bücher' (widely differing books). At this point in the story, Hein returns to the question of utopia as the narrator reports that a dispute has arisen amongst the writers: some of them persisted in their belief in 'Indien oder Amerika oder auch Utopia' (India or America or even utopia), stating that the ship was simply on the wrong course. Others argued that their experiences had confirmed them in their view that beyond the ocean lay only 'verzweifelte Hoffnung' (desperate hope). But asked whether their journey was 'eine verlorene Zeit' (time wasted), they retort: 'We have had an experience. So we have been enriched. For all you need to live and to write are love and experiences' (Baier 1990: 18).[15]

This is the first time that personal experiences and, in particular, love are mentioned in the parable. Is this, then, an indication of the way forward for Hein, a note of hope in a world now devoid of utopias? If this was indeed to be the case for writers such as Kunze, Kunert, Hein (Steinecke 1993: 201) and, as we shall see, Becker, then it was certainly not for others such as Christa Wolf and Volker Braun, who were reluctant to abandon their utopian hopes. In her eulogy for Paul Parin when he received the Erich Fried Prize in Vienna on 4 June 1992, for instance, Christa Wolf praised Parin's writing for demonstrating his inability to give up the word 'Utopie' (utopia), unlike 'whole hordes of people who, once enlightened and emancipated, today, in anxious postmodern haste, not only feel obliged to abandon but also to loudly mock both this word and also all their earlier insights and hopes' (Wolf 1994: 177).[16]

Revised Views of the Function of Literature

The question of writers' motives in the new situation, raised and tentatively answered by Hein in 'Kein Seeweg nach Indien', is one of many which have preoccupied both GDR writers and literary commentators since the *Wende*. Another central question was precisely this: what did they write about now that the main object of their writing, the GDR, had ceased to exist? And was it now time to abandon the notion of art as social or political commentary or as something with a social message? Hein himself again offers some answers in his essay, with the English title 'A World Turning Point' (Hein 1991: 3–5), in which he expresses his view that literature and history run incongruently: 'When history apparently pauses, when a time and a country are oppressed and marked by petrified conditions, literature remains by no means likewise paralysed' (Hein 1991: 4).[17] Similarly, in times of great historical upheaval, 'when things around him become all too noisy',[18] it may be that the writer will remain silent: ' if necessary he will remain silent for silence too is part of writing, part of literature' (Hein 1991: 4).[19] In his own case, Hein declares: 'What moves me, what takes such a fierce hold on me that I overcome or even forget my fear of the blank sheet of paper before me, is entirely personal, to do with me. It is not the mantle of history which moves me and determines and changes my writing, it is my lover's garment' (Hein 1991: 5).[20]

These questions about the function of literature which Hein raises both here and in 'Kein Seeweg nach Indien' have been widely debated since 1989. In May 1992, for instance, a Third Bitterfeld conference was held to consider the issue of literature and society (earlier ones during GDR times had been organised in order to try to steer GDR writing in directions desired by the SED). Prominent political figures such as Friedrich Schorlemmer were now calling for more guidance from intellectuals and writers. But others, particularly some of the writers, were arguing that it was now time to abandon the notion of art as social or political commentary or as something with a social message. Christoph Hein, for instance, was not alone in expressing a sense of relief that art now no longer needed to function as a substitute for the press: literature, was thus relieved of a burden it had carried in the GDR which had really nothing to do with the true business of art: 'Now I see signs of newspapers dealing with politics and art being thereby relieved of the burden. This means that art is being led back to its real tasks'(Hein, 1990b, p.183).[21] For Hein, literature with a social/political function smacked too much of the situation in the former GDR, where pressure came not only from the censor but also from GDR readers who expected their writers to play quite specific roles. In March 1990, for instance, he commented: 'Readers wanted to hear me sticking a knife into Honecker's body. There was a demand not only for the critically committed writer, but also the extremely political writer. And that is a danger for literature. A Proust would not have had a chance in the GDR' (Baier 1990: 44).[22]

The debate as to whether writers still had a social role to play was given a fresh and positive momentum when, in autumn 1992, the 'Bundesministerium für Bildung, Wissenschaft, Forschung und Technologie' (Federal Ministry for Education, Science, Research and Technology) in Bonn made concerted efforts to promote 'the cultural fusion of two formerly divided Germanies' (Schemme 1994: 4)[23] by organising several writers' conferences with the rather optimistic sounding theme 'Chancen für eine menschlichere Gesellschaft' (opportunities for a more humane society), culminating in the recently published anthology of writers' responses to the New Germany, *Von Abraham bis Zwerenz* (see Chapter 9).

The Changed Position of Writers

The first conference was held in September 1992 in Prora on the island of Rügen and was made up largely of a representative if motley cross-section of former GDR writers, from loyal hard-liner Erik Neutsch to disillusioned former communist Gerhard Zwerenz who left the GDR back in 1957. Many old enemies such as Hermann Kant and Helga Schubert now found themselves confronting one another again, albeit in more democratic circumstances, eliciting from Schubert the comment that she saw it as a mark of 'progress in society when people like you (Kant) who hindered democratic processes in the past now sit here with completely equal rights' (Schemme 1994: 12),[24] even though, as she adds, they will remain enemies.

In Prora, many former GDR writers voiced their dismay at the fact that their 'Leseland DDR', their captive GDR readership (and most critical writers had a huge following), also disapppeared with unification. This had been anticipated by Jurek Becker in his provocative essay 'Die Wiedervereinigung der deutschen Literatur' (Arnold 1992: 77–86), where he warned of the probably dismal prospects for former GDR writers in the new Germany, whose reading public would have quite different expectations from GDR readers with their desire to find their political concerns addressed in works of oppositional writers. Former GDR readers quickly changed their reading habits, for they no longer needed the critical voices of authors to represent their interests in the face of a press which had functioned exclusively as the mouthpiece of the SED.

Western readers, too, offered no compensation: in Prora, writers complained generally about the complete disregard for their works in the West. Waltraut Lewin, for instance, declared that there was 'No interest from the West in stories of the East – not even the ethnological curiosity of the colonist' (Schemme 1994: 27).[25] Jurek Becker's subsequent best seller *Amanda herzlos* (1992) has, of course, given the lie to such complaints, though Becker's success was doubtless partly due to the fact that he was already a well established and prominent writer in the Federal Republic. Yet what is undisputable is that GDR writers have had to adjust to a new pressure: the pressure from the censor (and the Stasi) has been replaced by that of market forces. More minor GDR authors, who owed their popularity in the GDR largely to their critical stance towards the SED regime, have doubtless been affected too by the increasing reluctance of publishers in the Federal Republic in recent years to publish what Karl-Heinz Jakobs has called 'the left-wing body of thought collected between book covers'.[26] Branded as communists, they have not enjoyed the success of earlier dissidents such as Biermann, Loest and Kunert whose long established popularity was partly founded upon Western interest in writers who opposed the 'actually existing' GDR. In the words of Günter de Bruyn: 'As a critical GDR author you were always in a very favourable position: you were read in the GDR because you were critical, you gained recognition in the West because you were critical – regardless of how good you were; that is now suddenly all over' (de Bruyn 1992b: 71).[27] The slim hopes for lesser known former GDR-critical authors rest probably with the multitude of minor publishing houses seeking to establish themselves in the east since unification (by January 1990, for instance, there had been 230 applications to start up new publishers), though the high failure rate of such ventures offers limited grounds for optimism.

One can have less sympathy perhaps with the predicament of conformist authors such as Eberhard Panitz and Günter

Görlich, the latter of whom had been on the Central Committe of the SED and remained chairman of the Berlin section of the GDR Writers' Union until 1990. Such authors have, not unsurprisingly, found it difficult to find publishers either in the East or in the West. They sought to remedy this in 1992 by founding their own publishing house in Berlin with the (particularly for English ears) grotesque name 'Spottless-Verlag'.[28] The fact that the ideological and political ballast carried by such authors makes any serious literary confrontation with their new situation well nigh impossible, is borne out by the title of Görlich's first publication, *Die verfluchte Judenstraße* (The Cursed Street of Jews), a story which virtually amounts to a return to the anti-fascist subject matter of much GDR literature of the 1950s. Nevertheless, in 1995 Jochen Vogt cited some evidence of a regional Eastern 'subsystem' of literature connected to specific GDR mainstream traditions, which he called 'eine Art literarischer PDS' (a sort of literary PDS) (Vogt 1995: 43), with an approximately twenty per cent share of the reading public of the former GDR. Vogt suggests that a divided literary market appears to be slowly emerging and gives as examples not only the hugely successful third volume of Erwin Strittmatter's trilogy *Der Laden* (The Shop, 1992), but also the healthy sales figures (in the East) for Christa Wolf's collection of essays and speeeches *Auf dem Weg nach Tabou* (On the Way to Tabou, 1994). Even the arch-hardliner Hermann Kant, reviled by many of his fellow writers during GDR times,[29] had a best seller in east Berlin with his novel *Der Kormoran* (The Cormorant) when it appeared in 1994. Further evidence of the danger of a literary gap emerging between East and West was offered by an article in *Der Spiegel* in 1996, entitled 'Berlin: Die Kluft zwischen West- und Ostintellektuellen' (Berlin: the gulf between intellectuals in East and West). Several Eastern writers assert that the demarcation line between intellectuals from East and West Germany is nowhere more sharply pronounced than in Berlin, where their mutual reserve, hitherto regarded as merely a temporary phase in the process of gradual convergence, has hardened. Daniela Dahn, the essayist, believes that paradoxically 'the process of convergence was abruptly broken off by unity' (Aust 1996: 168).[30] Thus Bert Papenfuß, one of the Prenzlauer Berg poets, now coedits a journal with the explicit title *Sklaven* (Slaves) which is aimed solely at readers in the East, eschewing the potentially

lucrative book market in the West on the grounds that Papenfuß prefers to work 'ehrenamtlich' (in an honorary capacity),
waging a 'Kulturkampf' (cultural struggle) against the West
which is for him a 'geistige[s] Flachland' (spiritual lowland).

Confronting the New Germany

Developments in Berlin, though sharply contoured, do appear
to be indicative of the wider scene evolving: in the main, most
GDR writers are suffering, or have suffered, what Antonia
Grunenberg has called 'eine kulturelle und persönliche
Tragödie' (a cultural and personal tragedy), since for them, not
only has a system collapsed but also their illusions: 'Not only an
illusion about the future of mankind but also an illusion about
the power of writers and the role of literature' (Schemme 1994:
31).[31] Wolfgang Schemme, who edited the proceedings of the
first conference in Prora, reports that the tenor of some of the
sessions was best characterised by the phrase 'Alles läuft schief!'
(It's all going wrong) (Schemme 1994: 21), as many of the writers took the opportunity to express their bitter disappointment
at social and political developments since the *Wende*. The young
poet Uwe Kolbe, for instance, often a fierce critic of the SED
regime, who had left the GDR in 1988, saw the frantic pace of
unification as an 'assault on the newly gained self-confidence of
GDR citizens' (Schemme 1994: 22).[32] Erik Neutsch viewed the
manner in which unification had taken place simply in terms of
the West having its revenge on the GDR. And Eberhard Panitz,
following Christoph Hein's line of criticism before the *Wende*,
spoke of unification in terms of economic colonialisation by the
West and loss of cultural identity. Their comments were in tune
with statements by prominent writers elsewhere. Wolf Biermann, for instance, like Günter Grass in the West and Stefan
Heym and Christa Wolf in the GDR, had warned against rushing too hastily into unification, and produced his own grotesque
parody of unification in his 'Ballade von Jan Gat unterm Himmel in Rotterdam' (Ballad of Jan Gat Beneath the Sky in Rotterdam): 'It's just that two halves of a pig/ don't make a
fatherland./ Reunification is for me like a brutal melodrama, a
monstrosity of a love-match. The affluent German, an ugly
beau, marries his wretched battered cousin from the poor-
house' (Heym and Heiduczek 1990: 412).[33]

Another discernible theme in the comments of several writers is the feeling of a loss of identity both in the sense of 'Heimatlosigkeit', a loss of the GDR as their homeland, and in terms of the inhibitions involved in feeling part of a new Germany and of simply being a German, 'ein Deutscher sein', after living in a state which had defined itself as anti-fascist and regarded the profession of specifically German sentiments as taboo. As Helga Schubert put it: 'Feeling German in some way or other was the greatest of taboos, it immediately had something National Socialist, something fascist about it' (Schemme 1994: 35).[34] Indeed, GDR propaganda, particularly in the 1950s and 1960s, had painted a picture of the Federal Republic not only as gaudy capitalist 'Klassenfeind' (class enemy), but also as the sinister successor state of the Third Reich; and parallel to this it had created its own official, squeaky-clean image as a state whose very roots lay in anti-fascism, as Jurek Becker wryly commented in an interview in 1994: "Of the 10,000 anti-fascists there may have been in Nazi-Germany, eight million lived in the GDR' (Doerry and Hage 1994: 195).[35] Some indication of the complexity of reactions to the problem of 'being German' emerged when GDR writers of different generations were asked in 1989 what they associated with the word 'Deutschland'. I cite just two examples from the younger and older generations. Uwe Kolbe, born in 1957, commented: 'For the major part of my life I associated nothing at all with the word Germany. The "Germany, united fatherland" of the national anthem, whose text we children of the Ulbricht era still had to learn, inevitably remained an abstraction' (Barthelemy and Winckler 1990: 56).[36] For Günter de Bruyn, on the other hand, born in 1926, the word is loaded with problematic historical associations: 'First and foremost I associate with this word a very wide range of historical ideas, extending from German culture to German crimes. I prefer not to use the word in relation to the present to avoid the misconception that I might mean the German Reich with its 1937 borders' (Barthelemy and Winckler 1990: 57).[37]

There were different reasons for Jurek Becker's difficulties with the word 'German'. A survivor of the Polish ghetto and concentration camps, Becker consistently reacted with considerable vehemence to any arguments in favour of German unification. For instance, in November 1988, a time when it still seemed a very remote possibility, Becker attacked Martin

Walser's case in favour of unification as coming dangerously close to revanchism and for being impervious to, as Becker put it, 'Faschismus-Reste, ... von denen ich mich umzingelt fühle!' (vestiges of fascism which I feel surrounded by) (Becker 1988: 61). In later articles, such as the very bleak essay, 'Mein Vater, die Deutschen und ich' (My father, the Germans and me) (Becker 1994a: 57), Becker focused on the question of the upsurge of right-wing extremism throughout the new Germany, relating it to his own experiences as a survivor of the ghetto and concentration camps, and suggesting several reasons for it, not least the vacuum left by the demise of the only alternative system to capitalism combined with the 'Mißmut' (sullenness) and 'Bitterkeit' (bitterness) of most East Germans, stemming from their disillusionment with Western values. Becker saw right-wing extremism resulting, too, from a mixture of the new and the old: on the one hand, there was the prevalent 'Gesellschaft-szustand' (state of society) which was characterised by 'Zukunftsangst, Perspektivenlosigkeit, Endzeitstimmung' (fear of the future, lack of prospects, an apocalyptic mood); and on the other, there were 'Nazibestandteile', fascist elements which had survived, above all in the West, where they had never really been eradicated after the Second World War, but also in the East: 'As we, the people of the GDR, never really dealt with our past in a *self*-critical way, we lost sight of what was fascistic about our own conditions and in our own behaviour.'[38] It was, then, not the fall of the Wall, he concluded, which spread the 'bacillus' to the new *Bundesländer.* 'German unification was at very least also the unification of potential right-wing radicals with those already active'.[39]

Becker did not, however, reserve his criticism for the new Germany: he wrote several polemics against former citizens of the GDR. In 'Zum Bespitzeln gehören zwei. Über den Umgang mit der DDR-Vergangenheit' (For spying you need two. On ways of dealing with the GDR past) (Becker 1990c: 35–36), he attacked the lack of resistance, the cowardice, the same 'Anpassung' (conformity) and 'Unterwerfungsbereitschaft' (submissiveness) which he pilloried in his novel *Schlaflose Tage* (Sleepless Days) and in stories such as 'Der Verdächtige' (The Suspect) and 'Allein mit dem Anderen' (Alone With the Other One) back in 1978, and which he ridiculed most grotesquely in *Amanda herzlos* (1992) in the words of the cynical West German lawyer Kraushaar who explains how he had the misfortune to marry an East German, for: 'these people are spoiled for life in the wild. They are used to living in enclosures, anything unexpected makes them panic. There is something cow-like about them, they chew their cud, gape at the horizon and want to be milked punctually.'(Becker 1992: 299).[40] In the aforementioned essay, Becker also asserted that former GDR citizens were now attempting to deny their submissiveness: 'The special zeal with which the Stasi-harassments are now being denounced and pursued seems to me like an attempt on the part of many of them to deny the reality of their own submissiveness' (Becker 1990c: 36).[41] The old opportunists were still at work, he added, and now it was the past which they were manipulating: 'That's probably what the opportunists like so much: the fact that their obedience has been forgotten overnight and that they appear as victims who have had an insuperable power breathing down their neck. This power was indeed breathing down their neck, and it was also mighty, but was it really *insuperable?*' (Becker 1990c: 36)[42] Hence Becker saw the GDR of the eighties essentially in terms of 'a communal work': 'Actually existing socialism was a communal work, created by the party leadership, their henchmen and the many who obeyed them.' (Becker 1990c: 36).[43]

On the other hand, in his article entitled 'Der Defekt ist der Normalfall' (Defects are the norm) (Becker 1993: 86–8), he suggested that, given similar historical circumstances, the behaviour of the West Germans would have been just as 'würdelos' (lacking in dignity) as that of the majority of East Germans. Indeed, in the figure of a West German resident of East Berlin, the reporter Stanislaus Doll, Becker demonstrated in *Amanda herzlos* that opportunism and conformity were not exclusively GDR characteristics, for Doll, too, has to admit that he is a 'Krämerseele' ('petty-minded little man') compared to Amanda, his East German lover (Becker 1992: 343).

However, even though Becker commented widely on the new Germany since the *Wende,* his long-awaited 'Einheitsroman' (novel about unity) failed to appear. He felt under severe pressure from critics to produce such a novel: 'For three years I have seen the critics in Germany drumming with their fingers on the table: Where is the German novel about unity? This can really paralyse any poor devil who sits down in front of a blank piece of paper. In many writers' studies, expectation hangs in the air like a terrible toxic cloud' (Doerry and Hage

1994: 197).[44] Not only did Becker not write an 'Einheitsro-man', he found it difficult, too, despite being in the West for almost twenty years, to write about life in the West in his prose works, his novels and short stories still focusing on his GDR experiences. Asked whether one of his recent characters, a writer from the West, was identical with his author, he retorted: 'No, Steinheim is a man from the West, and I have to invent people from the West. Up to now, I have not managed to be one myself' (Doerry and Hage 1994: 195),[45] and he described his seventeen years in the West as a transitional period: 'This transitonal period just will not end. Up to now I have not managed to write prose which is set in the West. I can't get rid of the feeling that here I am interfering in the affairs of strangers' (Doerry and Hage 1994: 195).[46] Becker remained convinced that the experiential differences of peo-ple in the two Germanies would separate them for some time to come, and even in 1994, he still referred to the east as 'DDR': 'I say the GDR because I am convinced of the fact that what people associate with these three letters will be there for a long time to come' (Doerry and Hage 1994: 195).[47]

When Becker's novel *Amanda herzlos* appeared in 1992, most reviewers and critics were expecting *the* novel of the post-*Wende* period. After all, here was a writer who, perhaps more than any of his contemporaries, had occupied a unique vantage-point in terms of East-West German relations during the late seventies and throughout the eighties. Most of them were disappointed. True, the novel begins at a point shortly before the author left, certainly a time of great upheaval in the GDR, but it also ends before things really started – on 3 Janu-ary 1989, a time heralding the great changes which were to fol-low. His choice of the date for the ending of the novel, January 1989, was quite deliberate, with Becker refusing to write the *Wende*-novel of epic proportions which many expected of him. Yet the political developments of the late eighties, 'die Unruhe im Land' (unrest in the country) (Becker 1992: 276), as it is referred to at one point, do form the backdrop to the novel which, set during the final twelve years of the GDR, takes the form of a 'Liebesroman' (romantic novel) whose plot, whilst focusing on three lovers, is an ironic mirror of the broad his-torical backcloth: Amanda's unhappy first marriage to the 'East' (with the rigidly doctrinaire GDR-conformist Weniger), is followed by her affair with a fellow-dissident (the writer Het-

mann) and the novel ends with her second marriage, this time
to the 'West' (in the shape of the ever-adaptable and appropriately named Doll for whom love can conquer all). The plot,
then, anticipates the political events which were to follow –
beyond the time-frame of the novel. Dreams of material fulfilment and happiness in this new union were ironised by Becker
in his parody of both the conventional happy ending and of
ensuing unification itself. In Amanda's description of the cor-
nucopia of delights which await her young son Sebastian,
bananas become the ironic symbol of the 'Übergangszeit'
(transitional period).

Becker's reluctance to write novels about the new Germany
was not experienced by all former GDR writers. Indeed, on the
contrary, Klaus Schlesinger declared his inability to write about
the GDR any longer except in terms of his bitter defiance of
Western attempts to interpret the past for him: 'The only thing
that can provoke me into wasting time with a few sentences
about the non-existent GDR at the moment is my own defiance. I simply can't stand listening to the spruced up twits on
the talk-shows trying to explain to me how I've been living for
thirty years and why it wasn't worth it' (Schlesinger 1993: 1).[48]

If Becker was unable to write his 'Wenderoman', then several
other writers were. A number of recent novels have dealt with
the events of 1989: Wolfgang Hilbig's *Ich* (I, 1993), Erich Loest's
Nikolaikirche (St. Nicholas's Church, 1995) and Thomas Brussig's *Helden wie Wir* (Heroes Like Us, 1995b). The difference in
narrative strategies employed by writers to confront recent
events is well illustrated in the two contrasting novels by Brussig and Loest. The latter, using a traditional narrative form, mirrors the radically changing times of the final GDR years in the
fortunes of the various members of a single, representative family and has been praised as one of the best literary analyses of
the first phase of the *Wende* (Emmerich 1997: 500). In contrast,
Brussig's immensely popular novel, topping the best-seller lists
in both East and West, gives his readers a highly original comic-
grotesque treatment – from an assumed Stasi perspective – not
only of the events leading up to the so-called 'gentle revolution'
of 1989, but also of its consequences, including the cowardly
behaviour of some Stasi informers since the *Wende*. On seven
tapes and in response to a questionnaire by the *New York Times,*
the 'hero' and first-person narrator Klaus Uhltzsch records,
from a post-*Wende* perspective, the story of his life in the GDR

and his remarkable claims about his personal contribution to events in late 1989. A Stasi collaborator and a typically uncritical, inhibited product of authoritarian GDR society, Uhltzsch grotesquely transposes any potential feelings of guilt into fantasies about his own omnipotence, expressed via an abundance of references to genitalia. Whereas his abject subservience to the state and willingness to carry out even the most senseless of commands is given particularly groteque shape in his putative blood transfusion, performed in order to keep Honecker alive, his complementary sexual megalomania reaches its grotesque climax in his claim that it was not 'das Volk' (the people) which brought down the Wall, but his own penis! Injured on 4 November, the day of the big demonstration on Berlin Alexanderplatz, Uhltzsch undergoes an operation that subsequently causes his penis to grow to an enormous size which so impresses the border guards that they open the Wall. For Uhltzsch, then, the fall of the Wall and, in its wake, of the SED-regime itself, was the result not of the 'peaceful revolution' but an accident related to a single individual: the 'people' of the GDR were too passive to effect any such event themselves.

Why was the novel such a success in both East and West? For the author himself, the reason for its popularity lay in the provocative approach to the subject, as he argued in his article 'Halb so wild und doppelt so schön', (Half as wild and twice as nice) (Brussig 1996). Readers in the East were encouraged to laugh at their own painful past, those in the West at prejudices which they themselves were unable to voice in the prevailing climate of the time. Brussig's provocative portrayal of recent events was well received by most critics too. Ian Wallace, for instance, praises both its memorable inventiveness and its challenge to common perceptions in both East and West in targeting the 'heroes' of 1989: the GDR people and, as a leading subgroup, the intellectuals (Wallace 1996/7: 4–5). Yet some East German reviewers criticised the lack of any sense of guilt and responsibility in Brussig's treatment of GDR history. For instance, overlooking the distancing effect of the humorous, grotesque dimensions of the first-person narrator and Brussig's intention to shake his East German readers out of any 'Ostalgie' (nostalgia for East Germany), as he explained in an interview entitled 'Wer saß unten im System? Icke' (Who was at the bottom of the pile in the GDR system? Me) (Brussig 1995c), Martin Ahrends suggested that the novel could be read as a

'Generalabsolution aller Mittäter und Mitläufer' (general abso-
lution of all accomplices and fellow travellers) (Ahrends 1996).
Some critics in the West, on the other hand, were unhappy
with the intertextual cross-references to Christa Wolf's story
Was bleibt which permeate Brussig's novel: it is Uhltzsch's Stasi-
colleagues, for instance, who have the job of observing the first-
person narrator of Christa Wolf's story! Yet Brussig's criticism
is directed not so much at Wolf herself as at what she (and her
readers) represented for Brussig, namely an older generation
with a tendency to escape the drab everyday reality by
indulging in utopian fancies of what might be (Brussig 1995a).

Other works which look beyond the old GDR in theme and
subject-matter in the first years after the *Wende* are Stefan
Heym's *Auf Sand gebaut* (Built on Sand, 1990, see Chapter 7),
Brigitte Burmeister's *Unter dem Namen Norma* (Under the Name
of Norma, 1994) and Thomas Rosenlöcher's prose works, *Die
verkauften Pflastersteine. Dresdener Tagebuch* (Paving Stones Sold
Off. Dresden Diaries, 1990) and *Die Wiederentdeckung des Gehens
beim Wandern. Harzreise* (The Rediscovery of Walking when
Rambling. Journey through the Harz, 1991). Burmeister shows
that feelings of superiority are the distinguishing characteristic
even of well-meaning West Germans in their dealings with
their East German fellow-citizens. When the heroine tells a
completely fabricated story about her complicity in unofficial
Stasi operations to a well-bred West German acquaintance, his
reaction reinforces what Norma expects of Western attitudes,
with their assumption of the 'collective depravity of those who
stayed in the GDR. ... We are stereotypes in the eyes of west
Germans' (Burmeister 1994: 252).[49]

In Rosenlöcher's diary of events in Dresden from September 1989 up to the first free election in March 1990, honest
self-mockery and self-deflation mingle with ironic comment
on ridiculous aspects of the commercial take-over of East by
West signalled in the title, as the writer records his private
responses to the comprehensive changes taking place around
him and oscillates between fear and hope, revulsion and fascination: he tells everyone of his 'Kaufhausekel' (revulsion for
department stores) yet admits his incessant inability to resist
the consumer temptations of the West: 'You too enjoy bathing
in chic and glitter' (Rosenlöcher 1990: 56).[50] The serious
undertone to Rosenlöcher's often light-hearted treatment of
monumental historic events is provided by the sense, shared

by Hein in 'Kein Seeweg nach Indien', that certain things have not changed: the pressure to conform, the 'Zwang' (compulsion) is still there, allbeit in new circumstances, as well as the same old cowardice in the face of such pressure. Describing a meeting in Berlin between forty affluent and hence self-righteous West German writers and their forty East German counterparts, Rosenlöcher is astounded to discover that the former are all 'Ja-Sager' (yes-men), apart from three or four 'Restlinke' (residual lefties) whose stuttering opposition is of no avail in the face of such unanimity. Rosenlöcher is equally self-critical: 'I feel the way I always did. As if I'd stumbled into a meeting of the Unity Party: incapable of the slightest opposition. Sweating with cowardice under the prevailing compulsion to think in terms of unity' (Rosenlöcher 1990: 101).[51] The serious message which emerges from Rosenlöcher's humorous text echoes the situation of many writers who had remained in the GDR: they were uneasy not only about the past and their role in it, but also about the future which, even in late 1989, was starting to look far from rosy. Rosenlöcher's next prose work, *Die Wiederentdeckung des Gehens beim Wandern. Harzreise,* a chronological continuation of *Die verkauften Pflastersteine,* begins with the currency union on 1 July 1990, or as the writer puts it: 'The Deutschmark had been introduced' (Rosenlöcher 1991:9).[52] The heavier coins are unfamiliar and he has to count them out like 'a foreigner in his own country which admittedly never belonged to him either' (10).[53] 'Seeing that Germany was to become one again' (9),[54] Rosenlöcher resolves to follow in the satirical footsteps of his famous forbear, Heinrich Heine, and make a journey on foot through the Harz. The reality of the West becomes increasingly apparent to this not-so-happy wanderer from Saxony for wherever he goes, he encounters 'das Signum der Sieger' (the sign of the victors): Western money, Western luxury goods, Western beer, West Germans and Western cars – 'weh dem, der hier zu Fuß ging' (woe betide anyone going on foot here)! The charm of Rosenlöcher's texts consists in his capacity for directly confronting the new German situation with satire, irony and gentle humour which draws much of its effect from the sense of the topsy-turviness of history. For instance, when once again the writer overhears the apologist for the new (this time capitalist) values, he comments: 'Already before this, and for forty years, the briefcase-man had talked about initial difficulties. It was unbelievable, however, what demands world-history made of one! The new age of all things had suddenly become the old one. Whilst the old age, which had long since been overcome, was suddenly, as the new age, creating new initial difficulties.' (16)[55]

The appearance of his 1993 novel *Das Napoleon-Spiel* led to Christoph Hein being hailed by some critics[56] as one of the first GDR authors to confront aspects of the new Germany. Yet Hein does so very indirectly and in an entirely unorthodox way which disappointed those critics who were expecting either Hein's 'Abrechnung' (settling of accounts) with the GDR or a novel which attempted to deal directly with the social and political realities of the new 'Bundesländer' (Federal States). What they got was the confession of a murderer who believes that he has committed the perfect murder. 'It is a killing not a murder' explains the accused, a respected lawyer, in an unrepentant letter to his defence counsel which he writes from prison as he awaits his trial. The 'killing' is carried out in order to score a win against both conventional ethical strictures and prevailing legal processes. The narrator is a cynic who has one all-consuming passion, the 'game' and sees life as a series of 'game-situations': power, money and sex are merely 'game-materials' and retain their attraction only until he has mastered the rules of the particular game. His only fear is boredom: 'Without these games our short lives are so terribly boring' (Hein 1993: 207).[57] Hence, like his model, Napoleon, who marched off to Moscow because there were no other suitable opponents left, he devises a series of games in order to escape the threat of boredom, seeking the ultimate 'magnificent game for a great player. A player like Napoleon' (11).[58] His quest culminates in the 'unfortunately imperative … killing of Bernard Bagnall … on the evening of June 21' (13).[59]

The novel received widespread critical attention, much of it negative for the reasons cited above, and provoked widely divergent interpretations. It was read by West German critics such as Bernhard Spies as a negative continuation of GDR utopian ideas in a protagonist who is the 'negative mirror image of the former positive outlook' (Spies 1994: 404): Spies sees the protagonist as a type who embodies the renunciation of Hein's hopes that individual subjectivity might form the basis of a humane utopia. On the other hand, former East German intellectuals/critics viewed *Das Napoleon-Spiel* as a text treating 'quite a different reality to the one in the GDR'

(Hartinger 1995: 62).[60] Some saw it predominantly as an exposure of the real nature of success and of successful individuals in bourgeois capitalist society since the days of Napoleon. Other former GDR academics such as Walfried Hartinger stress Hein's presentation of the moral vacuum in which politics operate: 'Politics too appears as a big game, no longer emanating from moral principles' (Hartinger 1995: 63).[61] Hartinger sees the novel, too, as a metaphor for the emptiness of modern consumer-driven societies.

If *Das Napoleon-Spiel* is arguably not concerned with some sort of settling of accounts with the GDR, does this mean, then, that Hein is, as Bernhard Spies has argued, one of the first authors, 'to produce a substantial text dealing with the reality of Germany both divided and united'? (Spies 1994: 404) Here I would advocate caution, for the central issues of the novel are concerned with hypothetical matters, with a constructed situation and the position adopted by the central character, rather than with the new social and political reality. Though the mentality of the main character can be, and has been, interpreted as a grotesque reflection of Western-style decadence (Spies 1994: 404), the situation which Hein constructs could occur, if indeed at all, in any social context. Even Hartinger, for instance, concedes: 'Hein is working his way towards a field yet to be discovered' (Hartinger 1995: 62).[62]

New Modes of Portrayal

We have noted above that Jurek Becker restricted the concerns of his prose writing to life in the GDR. However, he did deal with the new German situation in the television series *Wir sind auch nur ein Volk* (We, too, are only a people). Why television? The main reason for his change of medium relates to his GDR upbringing which shaped his earlier view that literature should have a social purpose: 'I cherish the hope that literature is something which can contribute to making a society in which it takes place more sensitive. More sensitive means more sensitive to disfigurement, more sensitive to violence, more alert to injustice' (Pfeiffer 1984: 17).[63] This hope faded somewhat in the light of his experiences in the West, particularly post-unification. In *Warnung vor dem Schriftsteller*, for instance, he admitted: 'Even if it is true that my views were considerably influenced by reading books, I don't rate the influence of literature very highly' (Becker 1990b: 15);[64] and in 'Die Wiedervereinigung der deutschen Literatur' he warned GDR writers of the danger of self-delusion in this matter: 'It may have been self-deception if they believed hitherto that they were able to exert an influence on societal developments through their texts; but even more absurd is the hope that they will be able to do this in future when all around them will be the West' (Arnold 1992: 85).[65] If Becker now had serious doubts about the ability of writers to influence society through books, there was another possibility: television appeared to him to be the one medium in the new Germany where writers could actually have a direct influence on their public, a view later substantiated by both the popularity of his own series and by the considerable influence on public opinion in Germany exerted by Loest's *Nicolaikirche* in 1995, when the novel was adapted for television by Frank Beyer (Soldat 1997: 145).

When explaining his reasons for writing *Wir sind auch nur ein Volk*, Becker acknowledged not only his desire to entertain but also a more serious intention: to open people's eyes (particularly in the West) to the realities of the new Germany:

> Quite a few things are said and shown which appear to me to be appropriate with regard to our German situation. ... The fact that so many West Germans are convinced that the GDR would not have been possible if they had been there; that their characters are so steadfast and their spines so rigidly constructed that the authorities over there would never have been able to bend them as they did the people in the GDR. Or I would like to open people's eyes to the fact that the different views and behaviour of East and West Germans will exist for as long as the conditions in which they live are so different.(Doerry and Hage 1994: 96)[66]

These points were underlined by Otto Meissner, the producer, in his short summary of the series: 'Of the many subjects ... we were not so much interested in the theme of coping with and reappraising the GDR past, rather we were above all exercised with the question as to how the Germans, after 40 years' separation and division into two states, might be able to find common ground again. ... We were preoccupied with the question of conveying to the majority of the 60 million West Germans, in an amusing, entertaining way, some idea of the everyday lives of former citizens of the GDR.' (Meissner 1994: IV/3).[67]

The title of Becker's television series, *Wir sind auch nur ein Volk,* was of course yet another and this time ironic modification of the famous phrases of the *Wende*, when the original opposition slogan of the 'sanfte Revolution' (gentle revolution), 'Wir sind das Volk', became the nationalistic 'Wir sind ein Volk'. Becker explained his own variation thus: 'The title is intended to indicate that the author is making a plea for a more sober approach: he is saying that the elation of celebrating unification is past. Get your feet back on the ground, that's the best place to be.' (Doerry and Hage 1994: 200)[68] Whilst the title was an indication of the author's light-hearted approach to the subject, it signalled, too, a vein of humour far removed from the harsh, mocking satirical tones of 'Motzki' and 'Trotski', the two controversial television sitcoms featuring stereotypical characters: the West German Friedhelm Motzki, a 'foul-mouthed bigot in the Alf Garnett mould' (Rinke 1995: 236), and the East German antidote, Herbert Trotski. For all the laughter that Becker's characters evoke, they are, without exception, all allowed to retain their dignity.

The plot focuses directly on 'German-German' issues: *Wir sind auch nur ein Volk* is a television series within a television series. The directors of ARD television decide that it is time to put on a series about everyday life in a typical East German family, a series which will be 'our contribution to furthering the mutual understanding of the people in East and West' (Becker 1994b: 11).[69] The directors insist on commissioning the successful novelist Steinheim, who is attracted by the fee offered but has to admit a seemingly insurmountable problem: not only has he never been to East Germany, he has never even met an 'Ossi' and declares, with his author's tongue firmly in his cheek: 'It is a bit of a problem writing about something you haven't got a clue about' (Becker 1994b: 33).[70] He accepts the contract, however, on condition that the televison company find a typical East German family for him to observe at close quarters: 'I would need a typical family in the East in whose house I could live for a while in a mouse-hole, as it were. And who would initiate me into the mysteries of the East, without feeling disturbed by my presence' (Becker 1994b: 35).[71] Yet he is not optimistic: 'they would have to be in a position to offer me something different from the depressing stuff that appears in the newspaper every day. In a word – such a family does not exist at all' (Becker 1994b: 35).[72] The film producer knows better, however, pointing out that the East is 'voll von typischen Ostfamilien' (full of typical Eastern families), and encounters no difficulty in finding the Grimms who consist of four members, three unemployed males and one working female: Benno, an unemployed 'Dispatcher', a term which baffles all the 'Wessis'; his wife Trude, a teacher, who explains: 'I am one of the few teachers at our school not to lose their job. I'm considered to be unincriminated, whatever that means' (Becker 1994b: 49);[73] their son Theo, like his author a former student of philosophy; and Opa Blauhorn, a pensioner. The Grimms agree to be used as guinea pigs 'zu Studienzwecken' (for the purpose of study) despite Theo's misgivings about the venture: 'I suspect that in this television thing, we are supposed somehow to play the role of insects that somebody wants to look at under a magnifying glass, and I don't feel very happy about it. But if it pays well ...' (Becker 1994b: 52)[74]

However, after a couple of visits from the writer, they overhear a telephone call in which Steinheim informs his wife that the television-people will have to get him a more inspiring family: instead of being supplied with the material for 'wahnsinnig originelle Geschichten' (incredibly original stories), he is merely 'Zeuge von tausend Alltäglichkeiten' (witness to a thousand commonplace events). Afraid to jeopardise their fee for 'das Sich-Beobachten-lassen' (having themselves watched), the family decide to spice up Steinheim's 'studies' in order to sustain his interest in them, and a series of comical episodes ensues designed to initiate their guest from the West into many of the mysteries of life in the former GDR. For instance, when Steinheim expresses the desire to meet a real, live former Stasi-collaborator, the Grimms, uncertain which of their acquaintances were definitely working for the Stasi, employ an actor-friend to play the role, and the latter, despite lamenting the absence of a script, gives an inspired performance, an on-the-spot improvisation of the stock Stasi-man.

It is interesting to compare Becker's literary treatment of the Stasi issue, his wry, humorous approach, with Wolf Biermann's advice on how to come to terms with the real-life experience of betrayal. For the latter, the only way is to do it via a brutal literary treatment, 'with an aesthetic cosh': 'The only way you can still strike these rogues dead is with the aesthetic cosh and in alliance with the muses'.[75] Biermann offered the following advice to Karl-Heinz Jakobs on how to best respond to the revelation that a friend had spied on him for years: 'In my opinion you should write a great novel on this theme. That would be the only possible way to boot it into touch. ... Your fiasco with this fellow Dahnke is as banal and cosy as a well-farted-on farmhouse chair which only becomes exciting when Van Gogh paints it. ... Write it down in durable language – and floor the bastard!' (cited by Wallace 1994: 126–7).[76] This is strong and no doubt therapeutic medicine as far as Jakobs is concerned, but is it a recipe for serious literature? I think not. Becker, on the other hand, as critics' favourable responses would indicate, managed to bridge the gap between 'Literatur und Unterhaltung' (literature and entertainment) precisely by eschewing the sort of literary hatchet job called for by Biermann. Becker's weapon was a gentle one, namely comic irony. And by giving the Stasi issue and other problems humorous treatment, he deterred such above-cited indulgence in bitter revenge whilst also avoiding the sort of 'Ostalgie' (nostalgia for East Germany) prevalent elsewhere, which loses sight of the reality that was the GDR.

To conclude, the situation which Becker created in *Wir sind auch nur ein Volk* afforded him the opportunity to focus on realities, on the difficulties facing East Germans in the new political situation, but also to expose prejudices and false assumptions of 'Insektenforscher aus'm Westen' (insect-researchers from the West) as the Grimms' son Theo calls them. As in Loest's *Nicolaikirche*, a family situation was employed to reflect social and political problems at first hand, but through delicate irony, Becker gave both the conventional family model, and the wider problems thereby reflected, humorous treatment, avoiding Loest's occasional tendency to cliché. For instance, during his stay in the East German houshold, Steinheim, for all his wit and culture, is ultimately exposed as the typically naive West German, unversed in the circumstances and sensibilities of the former GDR and its people and all too frequently concealing his own ignorance under an air of easy superiority. Even the scriptwriter, then, needs considerable time and effort before he is able to come to a balanced, realistic appreciation of the family. His initial impression, for instance, leads him to the assumption that an East Berlin family is no different from any other, be they in Hessen, Bavaria or Thuringia! Such naive oversimplifications are soon corrected, as Becker himself commented in the *Spiegel* interview: 'Later he realises that this is wrong. The difference ensues from the fact that the Grimms are from the acceded area, not the old federal states. They have to find their feet in a completely new situation. The place where they have always been living is now suddenly the West' (Doerry and Hage 1994: 195).[77]

Yet the strength of Becker's script lies not so much in the plot and the central themes set against the backcloth of 'deutsch-deutsche Probleme' (German-German problems) as in the sensitively drawn characters themselves, who really do come alive, and in the humour they generate. We experience, as Steinmann himself does, a 'close-up' of this family, 'with its cares, its joys, its dreams, its farts and its belches too' (Becker 1994b: 30).[78] Indeed, Becker lamented the lack of literature in Germany which deals simply with the ordinary, the everyday: 'In Germany more frequently than elsewhere, authors suffer the constraint of being expected to investigate the ultimate and most dreadful mysteries of life. Too seldom do they try to write a *book*, too often the book to end all books. It seems to me that they lack the courage to be more commonplace' (Doerry and Hage 1994: 197–8).[79] Becker's concern, then, was not so far removed from Christoph Hein's: he was more interested in stories about people than in historical/political events, as he commented in 1992, with reference to *Amanda herzlos*: 'My concern is not with the GDR but with stories I want to tell' (Steinert et al. 1992).[80] And Becker admitted that it was his move to the West which changed him in this respect: 'Without a doubt, since I have been living here in the West, I have become more private. To the extent that I previously considered myself to be a social being, I now consider myself more and more to be a separate individual, of course with social interests and aspects too, no question about that' (Arnold 1992: 12).[81] Thus Becker tended to focus his gaze on private experience rather than sociopolitical circumstances, giving us what Günter de Bruyn has called 'DDR-Innenansichten' (inside views of the GDR) (de Bruyn 1992a: 155). In his stories from the late 1970s, for instance, he exposed the extent to which individuals in the GDR had internalised authoritarian character traits. And in most of his works, through the fine details of people's everyday lives and experiences, the broader picture of social and political issues is gradually reflected, as two critics have observed of *Amanda Herzlos*: 'As if quite by the way, the reader learns more and more about everyday life in the GDR' (Köpf 1992);[82] 'It is precisely the casualness with which he introduces numerous facets of GDR-history which makes his depiction credible and impressive' (Dobrick 1992).[83]

With many former GDR writers such as Christoph Hein and Jurek Becker, then, literature has been returning to what Hein called 'ihre eigentlichen Aufgaben' (its real tasks) (Hein 1990b: 23), employing a discourse rooted in personal, individual experiences of the ordinary and the everyday, and moved not by the 'Mantel der Geschichte' (mantle of history) but 'das Hemd der Geliebten' (the lover's garment) (Hein 1991: 5). It may well be the case that the kind of literature that focuses on these 'Innenansichten' will turn out to be a particularly appropriate vehicle for probing the complex business of coming to terms with the new Germany.

Notes

1. 'Es wäre der radikale Widerruf der DDR-Identität gewesen. Der Zusammenbruch einer Vision'.

2. 'Mit dem Erscheinen Stalins geriet das System auf jenen Weg, der seine Zukunftlosigkeit, sein Scheitern absehbar machte'.

3. 'Sozialismus, der wirklich den Namen verdient' (speech at Berlin Alexanderplatz, 4 November 1989).

4. 'Endlich haben wir eine Chance, wir haben sie erst jetzt, und wir sollten sie ... für uns nützen und sie nicht vertun'.

5. Braun's sentiments, shared by many writers, have persisted well beyond the immediate post - *Wende* period. For instance, in his last interview before his death in March 1997, Jurek Becker's final words were an expression of regret at the loss of what could have been: 'The fact that the GDR went under is no great loss, the GDR didn't deserve any better. But the fact that what the GDR could have been, I suspect, went under as well – this I do regret. ('Daß die DDR untergegangen ist, darum ist es nicht schade, diese DDR hatte es nicht besser verdient. Aber daß das, was die DDR hätte sein können, nach meiner Vermutung, untergegangen ist, darum tut es mir sehr leid') (Koelbl 1997: 216).

6. 'Die Selbständigkeit der DDR ist hier verludert und vertan worden – und nicht durch die Schuld Westdeutschlands. Dieses marode System hier hat keine Chance, aufrecht und mit Würde eine Vereinigung herbeizuführen. Es wird deshalb auch kein Agreement geben, sondern eine Übernahme durch die BRD'.

7. 'Indien, wo immer das liegt'.

8. 'Das Unternehmen stand von Beginn an unter einem schlechten Stern. Nur der kleinste Teil der Mannschaft war von der Vision des Großen Kapitäns überzeugt und erwartete tatsächlich, einen Weg nach Indien über das Meer zu finden. Dem Rest der Mannschaft blieb nach dem großen Krieg kaum eine andere Wahl'.

9. '... uralten Karten, auf denen das Paradies eingezeichnet war'.

10. 'Hinter dem Ozean liegt nicht das Paradies, sondern der Tod'.

11. '... ein Anhänger des großen Kapitäns [...] oder ein Spitzel'.

12. 'Und die Schreiber? Es waren doch auch Schreiber an Bord?'

13. 'Sie schrieben über den eingeschlagenen Kurs der Flotte und verwiesen darauf, daß er schon lange nicht mehr mit den alten Karten übereinstimmt. So hielten sie die Unruhe wach und das Mißtrauen'.

14. '... die unerschrockenen Chronisten der Narrenschiffe'. Hein described himself as a chronicler of events in the GDR.
15. '... wir haben eine Erfahrung gemacht. Wir sind also reicher geworden. Denn alles, was man braucht, zum Leben und zum Schreiben, sind Liebe und Erfahrungen'.
16. '... ganze Scharen einstmals aufklärerisch, emanzipatorisch Gesinnter heute in angstvoller postmoderner Eile nicht nur dieses Wort, sondern all ihre früheren Einsichten und Hoffnungen nicht nur fahren lassen, sondern grell belachen müssen'.
17. 'Dort, wo Geschichte scheinbar verharrt, wo versteinerte Verhältnisse eine Zeit und ein Land bedrücken und kennzeichnen, verharrt die Literatur keineswegs in der gleichen Erstarrung'.
18. '... wenn es um ihn herum allzu laut wird'.
19. '... notfalls wird er auch schweigen, denn auch das Schweigen gehört zum Schreiben und zur Literatur'.
20. 'Was mich bewegt, so heftig erfaßt, daß ich meine Angst vor dem weißen Blatt Papier überwinde oder sogar vergesse, liegt ganz bei mir und in mir. Es ist nicht der Mantel der Geschichte, der mich berührt und mein Schreiben bestimmt und verändert, es ist das Hemd der Geliebten'.
21. 'Jetzt sehe ich Anzeichen dafür, daß sich die Zeitungen mit Politik befassen und die Kunst dadurch entlastet wird. Damit wird Kunst wieder auf ihre eigentlichen Aufgaben zurückgeführt'.
22. 'Die Leser wollten hören, wie ich dem Honecker das Messer in den Leib stoße. Gefragt war nicht nur der kritisch-engagierte, sondern der extrem politische Schriftsteller. Und das ist eine Gefahr für die Literatur. Ein Proust hätte keine Chance in der DDR'.
23. '... das kulturelle Zusammenwachsen zweier ehemals getrennter "Deutschländer"'.
24. 'Fortschritt in der Gesellschaft, wenn Leute wie Sie (Kant) damals demokratische Verfahren verhindert haben ..., jetzt völlig gleichberechtigt hier sitzen'.
25. 'Kein Interesse des Westens an Geschichten des Ostens – nicht mal die ethnologische Neugier der Kolonisten'.
26. '... linkes Gedankengut, in Buchdeckeln versammelt'.
27. 'Als kritische DDR-Autor war man in jedem Fall in einer recht günstigen Lage: Man wurde in der DDR gelesen, weil man kritisch war; man wurde im Westen anerkannt, weil man kritisch war – unabhängig davon, wie gut man war; das ist jetzt plötzlich vorbei'.
28. The German word 'Spott' means 'mockery'.
29. Cf. Jurek Becker's 'Brief an Hermann Kant', written in 1979 but published in Arnold, 1992, pp.51–59.
30. 'Der Prozeß der Annäherung wurde durch die Einheit abrupt abgebrochen'.
31. 'Nicht nur eine Illusion über die Zukunft der Menschheit, sondern auch eine Illusion über die Macht der SchriftstellerInnen und die Rolle der Literatur'.
32. 'Anschlag auf das eben gewonnene Selbstbewußtsein der Bürger der DDR'.
33. 'Bloß machen zwei halbe Schweine noch / kein Vaterland. / Ich erlebe die Wiedervereinigung wie ein brutales Rührstück, eine geklotzte Liebesheirat. Der Wohlstands-Michel, ein häßlicher Beau, heiratet sein elendes verprügeltes Cousinchen aus dem Armenhaus'.
34. 'Es ist das größte Tabu gewesen, sich in irgendeiner Weise deutsch zu fühlen, das hatte sofort etwas Nationalsozialistisches, Faschistisches'.

35. 'Von den 10 000 Antifaschisten, die es in Nazi-Deutschland gegeben haben mag, lebten acht Millionen in der DDR'.

36. 'Mit dem Wort "Deutschland" verband ich die längste Zeit meines Lebens überhaupt nichts. Das "Deutschland, einig Vaterland" der Nationalhymne, deren Text wir Kinder der Ulbricht-Zeit noch lernten, es mußte uns ein Abstraktum bleiben'.

37. 'In erster Linie verbinde ich mit diesem Wort historische Vorstellungen in ihrer ganzen Breite, die von deutscher Kultur bis zu deutschen Verbrechen reichen. Auf die Gegenwart bezogen benutze ich das Wort möglichst nicht, um das Mißverständnis zu vermeiden, ich meinte das Reich in den Grenzen von 1937.'

38. 'Da wir, die DDR-Menschen, uns nie *selbst*kritisch mit unserer Vergangenheit beschäftigt haben, ging uns der Blick für das Faschistoide an unseren eigenen Verhältnissen und in unserem eigenen Verhalten verloren.'

39. 'Die deutsche Vereinigung war jedenfalls auch die Vereinigung der potentiellen mit den bereits praktizierenden Rechtsradikalen.'

40. '... diese Leute sind für ein Leben in freier Wildbahn verdorben. Sie sind es gewohnt, in Gehegen zu existieren, alles Unerwartete versetzt sie in Panik. Sie haben etwas Kuhiges, sie malmen ihr Gras, glotzen den Horizont an und wollen pünktlich gemolken werden.'

41. 'Der besondere Eifer, mit dem die Stasi Schikanen nun angeprangert und verfolgt werden, scheint mir für viele wie ein Versuch, die eigene Unterwürfigkeit ungeschehen zu machen.'

42. 'Das könnte den Opportunisten so gefallen, daß ihre Fügsamkeit über Nacht vergessen ist, daß sie als Opfer dastehen, denen eine unüberwindliche Macht im Nacken gesessen hat. Im Nacken saß ihnen diese Macht wohl, und stark war sie auch, aber *unüberwindlich?*'

43. 'Der real existierende Sozialismus war ein Gemeinschaftswerk der Parteiführung, ihrer Handlanger und der vielen Gehorsamen'.

44. 'Seit drei Jahren sehe ich in Deutschland die Kritiker auf den Tisch trommeln: Wo ist der deutsche Einheitsroman? Das kann den armen Hund, der sich hinsetzt vor ein leeres Blatt Papier schon lähmen. In vielen Schriftstellerzimmern schwebt die Erwartung wie eine fürchterliche, giftige Wolke.'

45. 'Nein Steinheim ist ein Westmensch, und einen Westmenschen muß ich erfinden. Es ist mir bis heute nicht geglückt, einer zu sein'.

46. 'Die Übergangszeit will und will nicht aufhören. Es ist mir auch bis heute nicht gelungen, Prosa zu schreiben, die im Westen spielt. Ich werde die Empfindung nicht los, ich mische mich hier in die Gelegenheiten fremder Leute ein'.

47. 'Ich sage DDR, weil ich davon überzeugt bin: das, was man mit diesen drei Buchstaben assoziiert, wird es noch lange geben'.

48. 'Das einzige, was mich im Moment herausfordern kann, ein paar Sätze über die verschwundene DDR zu verlieren, ist mein Trotz. Ich kann es einfach nicht mehr hören, wenn mir die geleckten Affen aus den Talk-Shows erklären wollen, wie ich dreißig Jahre gelebt habe und warum es sich nicht gelohnt hat.'

49. 'kollektiver Verdorbenheit der Dageblieben. ... Wir sind für Westdeutsche Stereotypen'.

50. 'Auch du badest dich gern in Schick und Glanz'.

51. 'Mir geht es, wie es mir schon immer ging. Als wäre ich in eine Versammlung der Einheitspartei geraten: Unfähig zum geringsten Widerspruch. Schwitzend vor Feigheit unter dem herrschenden Zwang zum Einheitsgedanken'.

52. 'Die Deutsche Mark war eingeführt worden.'

53. 'ein Fremder im eigenen Land, das mir freilich auch nie gehörte'.

54. 'da Deutschland wieder eines werden sollte'.
55. 'Schon einmal, vierzig Jahre lang, hatte die Aktentasche von Anfangs-schwierigkeiten gesprochen. Was einem die Weltgeschichte aber auch abverlangte! Ausgerechnet die neue Zeit war plötzlich die alte geworden. Während die alte Zeit, die längst überwunden war, plötzlich als die neue Zeit neue Anfangs-schwierigkeiten machte.'
56. E.g. Spies 1994: 393–405.
57. 'Ohne diese Spiele ist unser kurzes Leben doch entsetzlich langweilig'.
58. '... grandioses Spiel für einen großen Spieler. Einen Spieler wie Napoleon.'
59. '... leider unerläßichen ... Tötung Bernhard Bagnalls ... am Abend des 21. Juni.'
60. '... ganz andere Realitäten [als] DDR-Wirklichkeit'.
61. 'Auch Politik erscheint als großes Spiel, kommt sie doch nicht mehr aus moralischen Grundsätzen'.
62. 'Hein arbeitet sich einem Feld entgegen, das noch entdeckt werden will'.
63. 'Ich habe die Hoffnung, daß Literatur etwas ist, was dazu beitragen könnte, eine Gesellschaft, in der sie stattfindet, sensibler zu machen. Sensibler bedeutet, sensibler für Verunstaltung, sensibler für Gewalt, aufmerksamer für Unrecht.'
64. 'Auch wenn es wahr ist, daß meine Ansichten durchs Bücherlesen wesentlich beeinflußt wurden, schätze ich die Wirking von Literatur nicht sehr hoch ein'.
65. 'Es mag Selbsttäuschung gewesen sein, wenn sie bisher glaubten, mit ihren Texten Einfluß auf gesellschaftliche Entwicklungen nehmen zu können; noch absurder aber ist die Hoffnung, daß ihnen dies in Zukunft möglich sein wird, da alles um sie herum Westen wird'.
66. 'Es wird einiges gesagt und gezeigt, was mir im Hinblick auf unsere deutsche Situation angemessen vorkommt. ... Daß so viele Westdeutsche überzeugt davon sind, die DDR wäre mit ihnen nicht zu machen gewesen. Daß sie charakterlich so gefestigt und rückgratmäßig so beschaffen sind, daß man sie nie so hätte verbiegen können wie die Leute in der DDR. Oder ich möchte den Blick dafür öffnen, daß die unterschiedlichen Ansichten und Verhaltensweisen der Ost- und Westdeutschen so lange exisitieren werden, so lange die Lebensbedingungen so unterschiedlich sind.'
67. 'Von den vielen Stoffen ... interessierten uns weniger die Bewältigung und die Aufarbeitung der DDR-Vergangenheit, uns bewegte vor allem die Frage, wie die Deutschen nach 40 jähriger Trennung und staatlicher Spaltung wieder zueinander finden könnten. ... Uns beschäftigte die Frage: Wie kann man auf amüsante, unterhaltsame Weise der Mehrheit von 60 Millionen Westdeutschen einen Begriff vom Alltagsleben der ehemaligen DDR-Bürger vermitteln?'
68. 'Der Titel will andeuten, daß der Autor für mehr Nüchternheit plädiert: Das Hochgefühl der Vereinigungsfeierlichkeiten ist vorbei, will er sagen. Kommt auf den Teppich zurück, dort ist der beste Platz!'
69. '... unseren Beitrag, das gegenseitige Verständnis der Menschen im Osten und Westen zu fördern.'
70. 'Es ist nicht ganz unproblematisch, über etwas zu schreiben, wovon man keine Ahnung hat.'
71. 'Ich bräuchte eine typische Familie im Osten, bei der ich sozusagen für eine Weile im Mauseloch leben darf. Die mich einweiht in die Geheimnisse des Ostens, ohne sich durch mich gestört zu fühlen.'
72. '... sie müßten in der Lage sein, mir etwas anderes zu bieten als das deprimierende Zeug, das jeden Tag in der Zeitung steht. Mit einem Wort – so eine Familie gibt es überhaupt nicht'.

73. 'Als eine der wenigen Lehrerinnen an unserere Schule bin ich nicht arbeitslos geworden. Ich gelte als unbelastet, was immer das bedeutet'.

74. 'Ich habe den Verdacht, daß wir bei dieser Fernsehsache irgendwie die Rolle von Insekten spielen sollen, die sich einer unter die Lupe ansehen will, und sehr wohl ist mir nicht dabei. Aber wenn's gut bezahlt wird ...'

75. 'Diese Lumpen erschlägt man nur noch mit dem ästhetischen Knüppel und im Bündnis mit den Musen'.

76. 'Nach meiner Meinung solltest Du einen großen Roman über dieses Thema schreiben. Das wäre der einzig mögliche *Befreiungsschlag*. ... Dein Fiasko mit diesem Dahnke ist so banal und gemütlich wie ein vollgefurzter Bauernstuhl, der erst aufregend wird, wenn Van Gogh ihn malt. ... Schreib es in haltbarer Sprache auf. Und schreib ihn nieder, den Hund'.

77. 'Später merkt er, daß das nicht stimmt. Der Unterschied ergibt sich schon daraus, daß die Grimms zum Beitrittsgebiet gehören, nicht zum Stammgebiet. Sie müssen sich in einer vollkommen neuen Situation zurechtfinden. Da, wo sie seit jeher wohnen, ist plötzlich Westen'.

78. 'Mit ihren Sorgen, mit ihren Freuden, mit ihren Träumen, mit ihren Fürzen und nicht zuletzt mit ihren Rülpsern'.

79. 'In Deutschland leiden Autoren häufiger als anderswo unter dem Zwang, daß ihre Bücher den letzten ungeheuerlichsten Geheimnissen des Lebens nachspüren sollten. Man will zu selten ein *Buch* schreiben und zu oft *das* Buch der Bücher. Es fehlt, so scheint mir, der Mut, alltäglicher zu sein'.

80. 'Es geht mir nicht um die DDR, sondern um Geschichten, die ich erzählen will'.

81. 'Ganz zweifellos habe ich mich, seit ich hier im Westen lebe, privatisiert. In dem Maße, wie ich mich vorher für ein gesellschaftliches Wesen gehalten habe, halte ich mich mehr und mehr für ein einzelnes Wesen, sicher mit gesellschaftlichen Interessen und Aspekten, keine Frage'.

82. 'Wie nebenher erfährt der Leser immer mehr über den Alltag in der DDR'.

83. 'Gerade die Beiläufigkeit, mit der er zahlreiche Facetten der DDR-Historie plaziert, macht seine Schilderung glaubwürdig und eindrucksvoll'.

References

Ahrends, Martin. 1996. 'Generalabsolution. Thomas Brussig auf der Suche nach dem großen Wir'. *Freitag*, 12 April.

Arnold, Heinz Ludwig. 1991. *Christoph Hein: text und kritik*. Munich, Verlag text + kritik.

——. 1992. *Jurek Becker: text und kritik*. Munich, Verlag text + kritik.

Aust, Stefan. 1996. 'Berlin: Die Kluft zwischen West- und Ostintellektuellen'. *Der Spiegel*, 26, 24 June, pp.168–71.

Baier, Lothar, ed. 1990. *Christoph Hein: Texte, Daten, Bilder*. Frankfurt am Main, Sammlung Luchterhand.

Barthelemy, Francoise, and Winckler, Lutz, eds. 1990. *Mein Deutschland findet sich in keinem Atlas*. Frankfurt am Main, Luchterhand.

Becker, Jurek. 1988. 'Gedächtnis verloren – Verstand verloren. Antwort an Martin Walser'. *Die Zeit*, 18 November, p.61.

——. 1990a. 'Über die letzten Tage. Ein kleiner Einspruch gegen die große deutsche Euphorie'. *Neue Rundschau*, 101, no. 1, p.90.

——. 1990b. *Warnung vor dem Schriftsteller*. Frankfurt am Main, Suhrkamp.

——. 1990c. 'Zum Bespitzeln gehören zwei. Über den Umgang mit der DDR-Vergangenheit'. *Die Zeit*, 3 August, pp.35–36.

——. 1992. *Amanda herzlos*. Frankfurt am Main, Suhrkamp.

——. 1993 'Der Defekt ist der Normalfall. Der Schriftsteller Jurek Becker über Arroganz und Opportunismus in Ost- und Westdeutschland'. *Der Spiegel*, 47, 36, pp. 86–8.

——. 1994a. 'Mein Vater, die Deutschen und ich'. *Die Zeit*, 20 May, p.57.

——. 1994b. *Wir sind auch nur ein Volk 1–3*. Frankfurt am Main, Suhrkamp.

Biermann, Wolf. 1990. 'Die schweigende Mehrheit hat eindlich das Sagen', in Stefan Heym and Werner Heiduczek, eds., *Die sanfte Revolution*, Leipzig and Weimar, Gustav Kiepenheuer Verlag , p.412.

Boeger, Wilhelm and Lancaster, Helga, eds. 1995. *Von Abraham bis Zwerenz*. Fulda, Parzeller.

Brussig, Thomas. 1995a. 'Thomas Brussig: "Feiglinge wie ich". Frankfurter Buchmesse: Gespräch mit dem jungen Autor aus dem ehemaligen Ost-Berlin'. *Münchener Merkur*, 14/15 October.

——. 1995b. *Helden wie wir*. Berlin, Verlag Volk und Welt..

——. 1995c. '"Wer saß unten im System? Icke" Interview mit Thomas Brussig'. *Wochenpost*, 21 September.

——. 1996. 'Halb so wild und doppelt so schön'. *Das Sonntagsblatt*, 22 March.

de Bruyn, Günter. 1992a. 'Intimes aus der DDR'. *Der Spiegel*, 32, pp.155–59.

——. 1992b. *Politische Meinung*, no.276, November, p.71.

Burmeister, Brigitte. 1994. *Unter dem Namen Norma*. Stuttgart, Klett-Cotta.

Chiarloni, Anna and Pankoke, Helga, eds. 1991. *Grenzfallgedichte. Eine deutsche Anthologie*. Berlin, Aufbau.

Dobrick, Barbara. 1992. 'Eine unsichtbare Frau'. *Deutsches Allgemeines Sonntagsblatt*, no.35, 28 August.

Doerry, Michael, and Hage, Volker. 1994. '"Zurück auf dem Teppich!" Der Schriftsteller Jurek Becker über seine neue Fernsehserie, über deutsche Dichter und die Nation'. *Der Spiegel*, 50, 12 December, pp.195–200.

Emmerich, Wolfgang. 1997. *Kleine Literaturgeschichte der DDR: Erweiterte Neuausgabe*. Leipzig, Gustav Kiepenheuer Verlag.

Fries, Fritz Rudolf. 1978. *Der Seeweg nach Indien. Erzählungen*. Leipzig, Reclam.

Hartinger, Walfried. 1995. 'Texte nach der Wende'. *Berliner LeseZeichen*, vol. 3, nos. 6/7, June/July, pp.46–76.

Heidelberger-Leonard, Irene. 1992. *Jurek Becker*, Frankfurt am Main, Suhrkamp Verlag.

Hein, Christoph. 1990a. *Als Kind habe ich Stalin gesehen. Essais und Reden*. Berlin/Weimar, Aufbau.

——. 1990b. *Die fünfte Grundrechenart. Aufsätze und Reden 1987–1990*. Frankfurt am Main, Luchterhand.

——. 1991. 'A World Turning Point', in Heinz Ludwig Arnold, *Christoph Hein: text und kritik*. Munich, Verlag text + kritik.

——. 1993. *Das Napoleon-Spiel*. Berlin/Weimar, Aufbau.

Heym, Stefan, and Heiduczek, Werner, eds. 1990. *Die sanfte Revolution. Prosa, Lyrik, Protokolle, Erlebnisberichte, Reden*. Leipzig, Gustav Kiepenheuer Verlag.

Hilbig, Wolfgang. 1993. *Ich*. Leipzig, Reclam.

Koelbl, Herlinde. 1997. 'Das ist wie ein Gewitter. Das letzte Interview mit Jurek Becker'. *Der Spiegel*, 13, pp.210–16.

Köpf, Gerhard. 1995. 'Einer stellt sich selbst ein Bein'. *Die Welt*, no. 190, 15 August.

Loest, Erich. 1995. *Nikolaikirche*. Leipzig, Linden Verlag.

Meissner, Otto. 1994. "Programm extra" zum Pressedienst Erstes Deutsches Fernsehen/ARD, 50, p. IV/3.

Mohr, Heinrich. 1994. 'Mein Blick auf die Literatur in der DDR'. *Aus Politik und Zeitgeschichte. Beilage zur Wochenzeitung Das Parlament*, vol. 10, 11 March, pp.12–22.

Pfeiffer, Helmut. 1984. *Deutsche Autoren heute 6*. Bonn, Inter Nationes.

Rinke, Andrea. 1995. 'From Motzki to Trotzki: Representations of East and West German cultural identities on German television after unification', in Osman Durrani, Colin Good and Kevin Hilliard, eds., *The New Germany: Literature and Society after Unification*, Sheffield, Sheffield Academic Press, pp.231–51.

Rosenlöcher, Thomas. 1990. *Die verkauften Pflastersteine. Dresdener Tagebuch.* Frankfurt am Main, Suhrkamp Verlag.

——. 1991. *Die Wiederentdeckung des Gehens beim Wandern. Harzreise.* Frankfurt am Main, Suhrkamp Verlag.

Schemme, Wolfgang. 1994. *Schriftsteller der DDR nach der Vereinigung.* Bonn, GFP Gesellschaft für Projektentwicklung und Liegenchaftesverwaltung.

Schlesinger, Klaus. 1991. 'Literatur'. *Die Zeit,* 4 June, supplement, p.1.

Soldat, Hans-Georg. 1997. 'Die Wende in Deutschland im Spiegel der zeitgenössischen deutschen Literatur'. *German Life and Letters*, vol.L, no.2, April, pp.133–54.

Spies, Bernhard. 1994. 'The end of the Socialist German State: The Socialist Utopia and the Writers'. *Modern Language Review*, 89, pp.393–405.

Steinecke, Hartmut. 1993. 'From Two German Literatures to One Literature'. *London German Studies*, vol. V, pp.198–206.

Steinert, Hajo, Arnold, Heinz and Isenschmid, Andreas. 1992. 'Ich will kein Scharfmacher sein. Gespräch mit dem Autor Jurek Becker'. *Süddeutsche Zeitung*, no.174, 30 July.

Thiele, Eckhard. 1991. 'Identität und Widerruf', in Heinz Ludwig Arnold and Frauke Meyer-Gosau, eds., *Literatur in der DDR. Rückblicke: text und kritik*, Munich, Verlag edition text + kritik.

Vogt, Jochen. 1995. 'Orientierungsverlust oder neue Offenheit? Deutsche Literatur in Ost und West vor und nach 1989'. *Berliner LeseZeichen*, 6/7, pp.30–45.

Wallace, Ian. 1994. 'Writers and the *Stasi*'. *German Monitor*, 33, pp. 126–7.

——. 1996/97. 'East German writers look back at the GDR: Two recent examples'. *Institute of Germanic Studies: Friends Newsletter*, pp. 3–9.

Wolf, Christa. 1994. *Auf dem Weg nach Tabou. Texte 1990–1994.* Cologne, Verlag Kiepenheuer und Witsch.

CHAPTER 9

Von Abraham bis Zwerenz. An Anthology for Unification?[1]

Martin Kane

The euphoria which accompanied the coming together of the two German states evaporated with remarkable rapidity. As the West German economists Rudolf Hickel and Jan Priewe have noted, Helmut Kohl's vision of 'blühende Landschaften' (blossoming landscapes) – delivered in a speech on 18 May 1990 to mark the signing of the treaty on the monetary, economic and social union of the two Germanies – was soon replaced with the prospect of something infinitely less enticing.[2] Intellectuals, of course, are no less subject to the vicissitudes of economic and political upheaval than any other section of the populace, and it was inevitable that East Germany's writers would not be spared the often traumatic repercussions of unification. The tribulations of the 'Transformationskrise' (crisis of transformation) (Hickel and Priewe 1994: 21) – the awkward adjustment to new and harsh realities – would be as much a determinant of the cultural as of the social and political spheres, leaving the writer, like all his fellow citizens, prey to feelings of disorientation and often hopelessness. Asked discreetly about his financial and professional expectations at a public reading he gave in Canterbury in summer 1990, the East German poet and editor Richard Pietraß replied, 'Ich bin ratlos' ('I don't know where to turn').

His response would have mirrored the sentiments of many fellow writers who, in the take-over of east German publishing by market-orientated West German enterprises, had seen the outlets for their work swallowed up, almost overnight. As Ruth

Rehmann has observed in her instructive account of forays into the literary world of the former GDR, not even the so-called Christian publishing houses – or rather, those firms dedicated to publishing Christian literature – were free of the rapacious profit principle. She notes of the bitter experience of an East German publisher at the hands of his Western 'partners': 'The negotiations, he said, were an instructive experience. They pressurized and squeezed us dry as if we were bankrupts. ... But that's nothing new, even though one might perhaps have expected a little more loyalty from our brothers in Christ' (*AbisZ*: 1661).[3] This extract from Ruth Rehmann's *'Unterwegs in fremden Träumen'* – *Begegnungen mit dem anderen Deutschland* ('Travelling in Foreign Dreams' – Encounters with the Other Germany) is to be found in the anthology *Von Abraham bis Zwerenz*, which was published by the Bonn Ministry of Education, Science, Research and Technology in 1995 and brings together over three hundred contributions by 104 writers from East and West Germany. Intended, as its subtitle indicates, to give impetus to 'the intellectual and cultural unification of Germany', *Von Abraham bis Zwerenz* not only offers a unique insight into how German writers have responded to developments since 1990, but also, in its frequent excursions into the past, throws light on the historical, social and psychological roots of present problems. This chapter will consider the ways in which the contributors to the three volumes of the anthology have portrayed, and reacted to, an unsettling passage of recent German history, and will pay particular attention to questions of identity and to the frequency with which writers have been able to bring an unexpectedly wry and humorous perspective to bear.

In an interview in *Sinn und Form* in 1991, Heiner Müller, keeping faith with his reputation as the GDR's most provocative playwright, described the act of unification as a form of colonisation in which 'the economically over-, but culturally underdeveloped civilisation of the former Federal Republic was trying, by defamation and administrative means, to eliminate the culture of the GDR which had grown out of the resistance to Stalinist colonisation' (Müller 1991: 667).[4] Any act of colonisation will always involve as a first prerequisite the eradication of the identity of the colonised. To fully impose themselves, the vanquishers must deprive the vanquished of all that might remind them of who and what they are. Applied to the former GDR, this is nowhere more graphically illustrated than in the wholesale clearout, after the *Wende*, of millions of East German books from libraries and book stores and the consigning of them, quite literally, to the rubbish dump. Klaus Michael reports how in May 1991 students of the Friedrich Schiller University in Jena, alerted by a photograph in the *Süddeutsche Zeitung*, had investigated the tip in Hainichen near Espenheim and found some fifty thousand tons of books buried there:

> Under rotten potatoes, building rubble and wrecked cars they found a mountain of books. What came to light was in no way just the detritus of a dead epoch, Socialist Unity Party pamphlets, or Honecker's speeches, but also whole piles of books ranging from editions of Goethe, Schiller, Shakespeare, Hegel, and Rosa Luxemburg, through to children's literature and volumes by Helga Königsdorf and Christoph Hein. (Michael 1991: 34)[5]

Not quite perhaps the Nazi book burnings or *Fahrenheit 451*, but 'ein Kulturskandal ohnegleichen' (an unparalleled cultural scandal) (Dieter Mucke, *AbisZ*, 1366) which not only stirred uneasy echoes of the past, but also seemed to many East German writers to reflect what was happening in every other area of life in the former GDR:

> From the state of things in 1989/90 I could only conceive of German unification as a swallowing up of the GDR by the FRG, in which everything which ran counter to the political, cultural, legal and economic maxims and interests of the FRG had to be abandoned or smashed. ... Our books, millions of them, ended up on the rubbish tip, along with millions of men and women, the lives they led and their places of work... (Eberhard Panitz, *AbisZ*, 1462).[6]

This is the context in which the achievement of *Von Abraham bis Zwerenz* has to be examined and measured. Namely, as an act of intellectual rescue and restitution, which has its physical counterpart in the heroic efforts of 'Bücherpastor' (book pastor)[7] Martin Weskott in the subsequent months of 1991 to salvage from the rubbish dumps of Leipzig and elsewhere some 500,000 GDR books, transport them to his parish in Katlenburg, and offer them to libraries, institutions and interested individuals in exchange for a modest donation to the 'bread for the world' campaign.

The anthology and its aims also have to be seen in the framework of a series of conferences (again a Bonn initiative) which sought to bring together East and West German writers, academics and educationalists. The first of them, held at Prora on the island of Rügen from 25 to 26 September 1992, seems to have been less a blow for all-German cultural harmony than what Kerstin Hensel called 'Hahnenkämpfe' (cock fights) between dissident exiled writers and those who had chosen to remain in the GDR (*AbisZ*, 678). The resurrection of old grievances, going back in some cases to the 1960s, demonstrated that some of the most agitated debates since the *Wende* have been conducted between GDR writers themselves, reminding us that 'the gulf between those who remained in the GDR and the "dissidents"' is probably deeper than that between them and the authors originally from West Germany' (Schemme 1994: 17).[8] The second of these conferences, held in Klingenthal, Alsace, from 17 to 21 May 1993 was more focused in its theme, concentrating on literature and the environment, while the third, from 14 to 17 November 1994, saw the launching of the anthology and, very appropriately, took place in Pastor Martin Weskott's Katlenburg.

The invitation of the editors of *Von Abraham bis Zwerenz*, Helga Lancaster and Wilhelm Boeger, to authors from East and West to volunteer a selection of texts of their own choice has produced a vibrant mixture of published and unpublished work – poems, prose pieces, playlets, texts for film and radio, extracts from novels, essays, reflections and reportages. Supplemented by detailed biblio- and biographical details, and the authors' responses to questions designed to elicit a view of dramatically changed cultural and political circumstances, this anthology offers a most inviting dip into not only the current all-German literary scene, but also, in the case of many of the contributors, into what has been written in the post-1945 period as a whole. While a handful of the authors have experienced an upturn in their fortunes, a large proportion – a result of the fact that those from the East are in the majority – are notably unsanguine about the future. Few have seen their expectations of unification realised; virtually none – in response to being asked how much solidarity they feel there is to be found amongst German writers – find any source of comfort in their colleagues. Typical of the answers are the following: 'Writers are in no way nicer, if anything they are worse than other people. They are envious, resentful, and bear grudges …' (Matthias Biskupek, *AbisZ*, 123)[9]; 'The outlook for solidarity among writers is poor' (Hans Christoph Buch, *AbisZ*, 248)[10]; 'It doesn't exist' (Stephan Hermlin, *AbisZ*, 688); and, tersest of all, './.' (Günter Ullmann, *AbisZ*, 2096). The tensions which reverberate in these comments have the same source as the acrimonious debates (themselves symptomatic of wider problems)[12] within the East and West German PEN about who should, and should not, on the basis of their past involvement with the darker side of the GDR's cultural life and its relationship with the State, be allowed to be a member. The gloom, however, which emanates from the writers themselves when addressing questions about both their own personal situation and the wider consequences of unification is one thing; the variety and robustness of what they contribute to these three volumes is, as we shall see, quite another.

One of the concerns of discussion about the two German literatures in the 1980s was to detect points of convergence. As the shackles of Socialist Realism were loosened, it was sometimes argued, the two literatures – apart from local reference – had become increasingly indistinguishable. It would be difficult to use *Von Abraham bis Zwerenz* to support this thesis. If there is one thing that links the vastly heterogeneous sweep of texts gathered here, it is the documentation of differences of background, heritage, lifestyle and – above all – of assumptions. What emerges most strongly from these very differently conceived and executed literary texts is the preoccupation with the particularity of the East German experience, the insistence on an East German identity in all its aspects, both positive and negative. This is perhaps no more than one might expect from a collection in which contributors from the former GDR predominate. What constantly surprises, however, is how many of their colleagues from the Federal Republic leap to the defence and support of these same principles.

This brings us to what West Germans as a whole (although not West German writers and intellectuals, who, once again, find themselves out on a limb) have apparently understood least about their East German cousins: the fact that, for all the faults and derelictions inherent in the socialist system and its often cruel mechanisms of social deformation, the forty years in which the GDR existed had forged a difference in presuppositions and outlook, a sense of separateness, which, although temporarily drowned out by the chants of *Wir sind ein Volk* (We are one people) in the streets of Leipzig and elsewhere in November 1989, seemed increasingly worth holding on to as citizens of the GDR saw themselves, their institutions, and their culture, swept up and consigned to the dustbin of history.

It is on this very point that literature, in pinning down and fixing the rapidly fading singularity of the GDR, has had a vital role to play in helping East Germans to understand themselves. It might also offer some useful insights to those West Germans who have occasionally been inclined to insensitivity. Some confirmation of this argument is to be found in a *Neue Deutsche Literatur* review of Bernd Schirmer's bizarre and amusing satirical novel *Schlehweins Giraffe*, an extended extract of which is included in the anthology. In the penultimate chapter of the novel, the narrator abandons the politically compromised giraffe he has taken in tow (the beast had been photographed licking lumps of sugar from the hand of Erich Honecker – an act not only of comic, but also much wider symbolical significance), to attend a reading by a fictional writer, Ralph B. Schneiderheinze. Schneiderheinze introduces his new work, a fairy tale, in which a fat and wealthy prince seduces and marries a simple 'Mädchen aus dem Volk' (girl from the people), depriving her in the process of everything which had made her what she was. The tale is clearly a thinly veiled allegory of unification:

> She had to bend to his will in everything, nothing of herself remained, and after he had taken her honour, and her pride, and her dignity, and her joy, and her will, and her memory, and her little house and garden, he also took her beauty, and found her ugly (Schirmer 1992: 144).[13]

In discussion of this episode from the novel, the *NDL* (New German Literature) reviewer makes an interesting point: 'German unification brought together people who were related by blood, but who were complete strangers. *We* did not know *them*, and *they* knew little of *us*. But we *have* to know what we are like …' (Wendisch, *NDL* 1992: 152).[14] This last sentence is crucial as a formulation of the task which East German writers have now taken upon themselves to articulate the social and psychological particularity of a society which has been devoured by its neighbour, but which still nevertheless lingers on in its sense of a discrete identity.

What must be stressed, however, is that this process is not pursued in a sense of melancholic nostalgia in which the bad is forgotten and the good suffused in a rosy glow. The writers represented in *Von Abraham bis Zwerenz* are unfailingly remorseless in exposing the psychological and social distortions wrought by 'actually existing socialism'. They are committed to a process of understanding and attempting to come to terms which approaches a vexed and complex subject from a variety of perspectives: the seemingly detached narrative voice of a Christoph Hein short story may illuminate one corner of a murky past, an impassioned, unforgiving address to the Humboldt University from Jürgen Fuchs quite another. Invariably, however, and whatever the approach, history and the legacy of ideology are unravelled and elucidated through the often painful disclosing of individual lives and fates. In Hein's 'Die Vergewaltigung' (The Rape), for instance, a successful lawyer has identified herself so much with the values of the regime and its version of history that, when reminded by her husband that as a child she had witnessed her grandmother's rape by Soviet soldiers – a taboo subject in the GDR – she not only denies it, but accuses him of being a fascist for having even raised the subject (*AbisZ*, 666–70). While Jürgen Fuchs, in his dual identity as practising psychologist and sometime dissident and persecuted GDR writer, offers with 'Die Schnürsenkel von Torgau oder Der Verlust der humanen Orientierung' (The Torgau Shoelaces or The Loss of Humane Orientation) a different, but equally poignant perspective on the particular case. The climax of this corruscating and wide-ranging calling to account is the private record, by one of the casualties, of the routine cruelties inflicted on the inmates of the Torgau juvenile offenders prison. It is prefaced with a survey of the infamies of the GDR system as a whole and its all too willing collaborators, and of the baleful long-term effects of the 'absence of civil courage and the presence of spineless subservience and withdrawal into the private sphere'.[15] In his plea for the rehabilitation of the victims – the unjustly persecuted, exiled and oppressed – Fuchs is very specific:

> I want the social democrat who did not join the Socialist Unity Party and was imprisoned in Bautzen to experience acknowledgement of the injustice done him, to be able to document why he was imprisoned and had to suffer what he did. ... I also have in mind the Christian who wouldn't compromise, the liberal, the eurocommunist, the conscientious objector, the teller of political jokes, the refugee not allowed back into the country for twenty years (*AbisZ*, 539).[16]

Hein (born in 1944) and Fuchs (born in 1950) are anxious, in their varying ways, to link questions of GDR identity and its attendant skeletons closely to a quest for the past and an examination of the psychological consequences ('the loss of humane

orientation') of suppressing the truth in the name of ideological exigency and purpose. Their approach is understandably
different from that of the older generation of established writers in the anthology – those who had prospered, to greater or
lesser extent, in the GDR, and now find themselves stranded
in a world which has swept away the ideals to which they, for
better or worse, had committed their lives. Several of these
have submitted pieces to *Von Abraham bis Zwerenz* which help
to clarify the circumstances which led to the embracing of
those ideals. There is a crucial extract, for instance, from
Dieter Noll's *Die Abenteuer des Werner Holt* (The Adventures of
Werner Holt), a novel dealing with the effect on youth of fascism and militarism, and one familiar to all GDR schoolchild-
ren for whom it was required reading (and none the worse for
that). In an episode depicting the desperate plight of a dwindling Wehrmacht unit during the last days of the war, the
eponymous hero finds himself caught not only between
advancing American and Soviet troops, but also at the centre
of an ideological conflict – anchored in the inimical philoso-
phies of two of his comrades – between fascism and militarism
on the one hand and a humane socialism on the other. The
unmistakably didactic purpose with which the novel is written,
and an implicit Marxist perspective pointing inexorably to the
morally superior social order which socialism will deliver,
leave the young Werner Holt with no real choice to make.

It is the same choice, of course, which was made by many
other writers of Noll's generation (Franz Fühmann is the other
outstanding example). Formed and scarred as they were by
Hitler's fascism, socialism was the only serious option in the post-
war world. We find similar justification for the embracing of this
philosophy in the passages from Stephan Hermlin's *Abendlicht*
(Evening Light), which give graphic insights into developing
social and political tensions and the rise of fascism in the 1930s
and seemed (at least until recent revelations shifted a supposedly
autobiographical text into the realm of eloquent, but falsifying
fiction)[17] to offer persuasive testimony as to why a young man of
bourgeois origins and a social conscience might, in the post-war
world, see socialism as the only rational alternative.

It is there again in the contribution of Elfriede Brüning,
born in 1910, a communist of the old school and survivor of
the Nazi period, but someone who did not always profit in the
GDR from the advantages such a biography might bring. In

her autobiography *Und außerdem war es mein Leben* (And Besides, it was My Life), she covers some of the same historical and ideological ground as Hermlin, and offers us here its final chapter, 'Verlust der Illusionen' (Loss of illusions). Contemplating the official day of unification, and with it the final demise of a world to which her whole life had been dedicated, she writes: 'We did not want to spend the 3 October 1990 in Berlin. They would again be letting off celebratory rockets. We were not in the mood for it.' And a little later: 'Should I mourn the dead, or envy them because they were no longer able to experience this day? What has become of the hopes we once had? Were we nothing more than idle dreamers? Idealists remote from reality?' (*AbisZ*, 216 and 218).[18]

This is a reflective, resigned and mildly embittered response to events which Volker Braun, of a much later generation (he was born in 1939), and even more firmly embedded in the literary and political fabric of the GDR, albeit at times uncomfortably, grapples with in two interviews and a clutch of corruscating poems and prose pieces which lament the failings of socialism, but are also scathing in the contemplation of a meretricious and predatory capitalism. Virtually all of Braun's work in the last decade and a half of the GDR (the expatriation of the gadfly political balladeer Wolf Biermann in 1976 is, of course, a vital turning-point)[19] is suffused by a sense of loss as he experiences the stifling of utopian aspiration by a socialism increasingly in the grip of Stalinist inertia and inflexibility. Asked here what he had liked best about the old GDR he replies: 'The possibility of critical, oppositional participation, through working together (in the theatre, for instance) to "want something" in common. It was always work on a utopia.' Asked what annoyed him most about it he answers: 'That this work was visibly getting us nowhere: was messed up, frustrated by "consolidation"' (*AbisZ*, 157–58).[20]

As this anthology demonstrates again and again, he is far from alone in his disenchantment. Eva Strittmatter, for instance, contributes a handful of poems from the 1970s which trace her diminishing trust and faith in the system, and, for obvious reasons, could not be published then. In the poem 'Wollust' (Voluptuousness), for instance – the title refers to the possibility of sensual escape which the incantatory power of words may offer – she writes: '... All ties are crumbling./ All belief has been perverted by politics./ One is losing friend upon friend:/ Secret, sinister murder in cold blood./ I would like to call everyone brother/ And know not in whose service he is/ Who comes and goes in my house/ Seeking perhaps to ensnare and trap me' (*AbisZ*, 2048).[21] Inklings here of the petty treacheries which would unsettle and ultimately destroy so many friendships in the former GDR; uncanny hints and suspicions which the opening of Stasi files after 1990 would only confirm. What the poem does not reveal, of course, is how much, if anything, she knew of the dubious affiliations of her own husband, Erwin, who – as has recently come to light – between 1958 and 1964 reported negatively to his Stasi contact on numerous of his colleagues: Anna Seghers, Erich Loest, Stephan Hermlin, Peter Hacks, Stefan Heym, Arnold Zweig and Peter Huchel.[22]

Not the least intriguing aspect of systematically working one's way through *Von Abraham bis Zwerenz,* is that the alphabetic ordering of the contributors juxtaposes authors of quite different status, and from very diverse corners of German literary life. For all (in part, because of) their developing scepticism, Eva Strittmatter and her husband Erwin were two of the best known and most widely-read writers in the GDR, as well as being the recipients of numerous official honours. It is one of the many thought-provoking coincidences of the anthology that we find these two 'approved' authors alongside a figure such as Gabriele Stötzer-Kachold, one of the GDR's most challenging and innovative woman writers. Castigator of patriarchal arrogance as it emanated from both individual males and from the state itself, and, as a consequence of her political views, unable to publish in the GDR, Gabriele Kachold (as she was known then) was subject to frequent harassment by the authorities, and in 1977 found herself imprisoned for a year, with disastrous consequences for her health.[23]

She was one of the younger generation of East German writers in the 1980s, who lived their lives very much at the periphery of GDR society, and for whom linguistic experimentation was a way of deconstructing the 'Herrschaftssprache', the autocratic language of power, in a society in which, as she writes in the introductory notes to the texts she has submitted to the anthology, 'the literary critical system ... was a politicised trauma directed against the articulation of any expression of personal feeling' (*AbisZ*, 1986).[24] In remedying this, in her often perilous search for authenticity of experience and feeling –

'truthfulness as a permanent tightrope walk above the abyss' as one critic has put it[25] – Gabriele Stötzer-Kachold takes language into new territory, transporting the turbulence of her invariably painful emotions and experience onto the page in a spontaneous, breathless cascade of words. In his foreword to a volume of her prose finally published in 1989 in the *Außer der Reihe* series, Gerhard Wolf had seen her as articulating the silent desperation of a whole generation: 'Perhaps no other woman in these years has dared to express herself in such an utterly vulnerable and reckless manner, with no regard for the rules of the game. ... The gaping mouth, the unbridled gesture ... bear witness to what until now remained unsaid, was suppressed or simply passed over in silence by this generation.' [26]

Stötzer-Kachold's writing grates the bone. The remorseless search to find herself through uninhibited expression of her feelings, and to come to terms with the inflictions of an unforgiving, male-dominated and brutal system, is a way, she has argued, not only of creating her own self, but also, by extension, of remaking the world. The fortitude she demonstrates in not only coping with what life has thrown at her, but writing about it so compellingly, evokes intense admiration. However, working through the extended shriek of her prose is not a particularly cheering experience. Humour, the lighter touch, are not part of her vocabulary.

This could not be said of this anthology as a whole. It is clear that many of its contributors, in opting for the comic as an approach to the fraught passage of recent German social and political history have remembered Brecht's observation that comedy 'interessiert sich gerade für ernste Dinge' (is interested precisely in serious matters), and often comes closer than tragedy to rendering what is really of import (Brecht 1975: 130–32). The so-called 'Ossie/Wessie' jokes which proliferated in the wake of unification – jokes by East Germans sometimes directed at their own doziness and provinciality, but more usually about the perceived arrogance and condescending ways of West Germans – find a kind of literary counterpart in many of the satirical pieces in these volumes. In Matthias Biskupek's 'Eiserne Pfanne' (Iron Pan) (*AbisZ*, 137–38), for instance, an extravagent burlesque at the expense of Western capitalist values, in which an entrepreneurial spirit from the former GDR builds a fast food empire out of inauspicious beginnings (a handful of dried rolls) and rises to become Germany's first woman Chancellor. Humour, here the mocking of the spurious notion held out by Helmut Kohl of an economic miracle supposedly open to all, may be seen as a way of asserting identity by fighting back. But the assertion, through humour directed against the shortcomings of the GDR, of identity in its less positive aspects is also well in evidence in this anthology. Adolf Endler's 'Brunhilde Humperdinck/Materialien für eine Biographie' (Brunhilde Humperdinck/ Material for a biography), for instance, a wicked send-up of the GDR's policies on popular culture, in which it is argued, tongue-in-cheek, that Marxist pop songs would have been a more persuasive reason for leaving the country than political oppression, is an indispensable reminder of a relatively harmless corner of GDR life which might otherwise have been forgotten (*AbisZ*, 440–49).

The political humour – wry, ironical, satirical – which has clearly flourished with the end of censorship brought by the demise of the GDR, was of course to be found even before the state collapsed. Christoph Hein's *Die Ritter der Tafelrunde* (The Knights of the Round Table, 1989), with its depiction of King Arthur and his court in a state of advanced mental sclerosis, was an unmistakable and clever satire on the political entourage of Erich Honecker in terminal decline. Historical setting here offered an enlightening perspective on the present, a technique which Stefan Heym had deployed earlier to such telling effect in *Der König David Bericht* (The King David Report, 1974) and his novel *Ahasver* (1981).

Heym, of course, was one of the first off the mark to comment in fictional form on the repercussions of the fall of the Wall. Always a wily observer, it was unlikely that he would be caught unawares by the inconstancy, opportunism and capacity for sheer self-deception displayed by his fellow GDR citizens as they prepared to face up to unification. In the seven wry tales which make up *Auf Sand gebaut* (Built on Sand) – two of which are included in the anthology – Heym scrutinised partly pathetic, partly singularly unappetising characters who embodied to perfection the disappearance overnight of a way of life and beliefs which only months before had seemed set in stone: the former Party elite vying for jobs in the new capitalist order of things, and glibly manipulating its terminology – 'joint venture', 'public relations' – as easily as the old communist slogans and shibboleths; the poets and writers privileged by the SED regime disavowing in panic their awards and honours; stalwarts of the Stasi sliding effortlessly into fresh and well-remunerated niches.[27]

What Heym, along with other sharp-eyed *Wende* observers in this anthology – Matthias Biskupek, for instance, with a tale of rapacious exploitation of Vietnamese workers masquerading as philanthropy – does supremely well, is to catch the voice and postures of the weather-vane opportunists and scoundrels who are abroad in the new Germany, and using their slippery talents to adjust unproblematically to a time of transition. In operating in satirical and comic mode, they favour an approach which can be seen in the response of a significant number of other former GDR writers who seem to have taken up the challenge implicit in Volker Braun's ironic comment on living with the savage repercussions of unification: 'A glorious, wild, brutal life, if we only have the humour for it ...' (*AbisZ*, 162).[28]

Without the opportunity here to more than hint at the role which humour has had to play in illuminating the post-unification landscape, one might, nevertheless, again draw attention to Bernd Schirmer's *Schlehweins Giraffe* (1992), as well as to novels by Barbara Sichtermann, Thomas Brussig, Reinhard Wosniak, Matthias Biskupek, Heinz-Dieter Ziesing, and, above all, by Fritz Rudolf Fries. His *Die Nonnen von Bratislava* (The Nuns of Bratislava) is an unrestrained political romp which breaches the laws of probability in cavalier, but illuminating fashion. Fries's narrator is a reincarnated version, and bears the name of Mateo Alemán (1547–1614), author of the first picaresque novel *Guzmán de Alfarache*. Pressed into service by the Stasi, and endowed with multiple identities and biographies, he is whisked through a rapidly changing series of locations – Seville, Bruges, Montpellier, Moscow, Warsaw, Berlin, Bratislava and Mexico City. Throughout, however, the novel is kept anchored in present all-German realities with pointed and satirical observations and reflections on skinheads and asylum seekers, as well as the machinations of the *Treuhand* and Stasi. Its climax – a plot to blow up the Bonn water works and restore and proclaim the old East German order in the Palast der Republik – develops into a rambunctious satire on 'Ostalgie'. Written as a film scenario which plunders both Goethe's Walpurgisnacht and the more extravagant corners of Heiner Müller, it builds into what Fries himself has described as the characteristic mixture in his novel of 'Slapstick und Wehmut' (slapstick and melancholy).[29]

That breadth of reading and cultural interests (and particularly his familiarity with franco- and hispanophone literature) which always kept Fries free from the whiff of provinciality sometimes found in GDR literature, 'the urge again and again to demonstrate the presence of the great amidst the small, and what is distant in the near at hand'),[30] serves him well in *Die Nonnen von Bratislava* in the playing of exuberant games of historical and literary intertextuality. As perfectly befits a hispanist, Fries uses the licence of the picaresque form to comb history for revealing repetitions and patterns. The narrator's counterpart, for instance, Dr Alexander Retard, who resurfaces from Fries's *Alexanders Neue Welten* of 1982 as an 'abgewickelter DDR-Wissenschaftler' – a sacked GDR academic now turned itinerant Goethe-Institut lecturer given to polymath extemporisation – evokes sly parallels between the effects of intellectual repression in sixteenth- and seventeenth-century Spain and the GDR. As one critic has put it, however, what is at stake here is not primarily a search for historical truth, but 'a witty and humorous game with history, and particularly with its supposed analogies'.[31] This playfulness enables Fries to develop a provocative argument about the writer then and now as heretic, and moves him into that controversial area of debate about the extent to which an artist's resourcefulness and creativity might be not stifled, but stimulated by having to write in oppressive circumstances.

In attempting to formulate an adequate overall response to *Von Abraham bis Zwerenz,* it is not easy to do more than hint at the range and compass of what in effect is a whole library in miniature. From its first author, Peter Abraham, to its last, Gerhard Zwerenz, and despite the fact that there are important names missing – no Hans Magnus Enzensberger, Jurek Becker or Bert Papenfuß-Gorek – this highly ambitious anthology is a literary resource of incalculable value, bringing together an unparalleled assortment of German writers of different experience, outlook, and generation (the oldest Jan Koplowitz, born 1909, the youngest, Miriam Margraf, born 1964), the majority of whom, as has been noted, from the former GDR.

But what of the West German contingent? Günter Grass is there, not represented by an extract from his latest and controversial novel about unification, but by a cycle of thirteen sonnets which give reflective, lyrical form to the deep misgivings, which he has frequently expressed elsewhere, over the indecent haste (the 'Kopflose Eile' as he calls it) in which the two German states had been united. There are perceptive essays by Peter Schneider, formulator, in *Der Mauerspringer* (The Walljumper), of the prophetic term 'the Wall in the head' which he foresaw, as early as 1982, would still continue to separate the citizens of East and West long after the physical barrier dividing the two German states had come down. Christoph Meckel, best known perhaps for a single poem (reproduced here), 'Der Pfau' (The Peacock, 1962), with its excoriating view of the German economic miracle of the 1950s, continues, in a short piece which looks at the country through the eyes of a Turkish guest worker, to cast a jaundiced glance at the heartlessness behind German material prosperity.

And finally, Dieter Lattmann and Friedrich Christian Delius, who both take up cudgels on behalf of the GDR. In giving his response to unification, Lattmann – novelist, sometime President of the West German Writers Union and, from 1972 to 1980, an SPD member of the Federal Parliament – sees an invaluable opportunity lost. The emphasis on economics and material matters had ignored those forces for reform in both Germanies which would have led to mutually beneficial renewal. In his extract 'Der Hausmeister' (The Caretaker, [*AbisZ*, 1090–104]) from the novel *Jonas vor Potsdam* (Innaron Verlag, Zürich, 1995) five decades of German history roll past the cellar window and the keeper of the boilers of a Berlin building whose changing occupants – by turns, the Nazi *Reichsluftfahrtministerium*, the Soviet Military Administration, the GDR's ruling Socialist Unity Party, and finally the *Treuhand* – testify to the historical upheavals to which he has been a passive, and worm's-eye, witness.

This telling of history from a personal, East German perspective, is used again by F.C. Delius in his story *Die Birnen von Ribbeck* (The Pears of Ribbeck, 1991). It is reminiscent in technique of Volker Braun's *Bodenloser Satz* (Groundless Sentence, 1989), an epitaph – composed of a single sentence stretching out over thirty nine pages – both to the GDR and Braun's own failed utopian vision. Delius's story (its title and setting take their cue from a celebrated poem by Theodor Fontane) is built out of the interior monologue – simultaneously narrative account, accusation and judgement – in which an ageing inhabitant of the village of Ribbeck contemplates a descending horde of West German visitors. As he catches them in pursuit of Fontane's pear tree, patronizing the natives with cakes and ale, and sizing up their property, he reflects in a single whirr of recollection, in which history and personal experience become inextricably intertwined, on a lifetime in Ribbeck spent under the different tyrannies of feudalism, National Socialism and Communism. The achievement of Lattmann and Delius in these two pieces is to slip sympathetically and convincingly into the skin and the experience of their East German protagonists. In doing so, they make their own distinctive contribution to *Von Abraham bis Zwerenz,* and to the principal achievement of this anthology, the understanding of what it was to be, then and now, a German living beyond the Elbe.

Notes

1. References to works from this collection are made with the abbreviation *AbisZ* and the page number.
2. 'Nach unserer Auffassung sind die Aussichten für Wirtschaftswachstum, Beschäftigung und Abbau der Arbeitslosigkeit in beiden Teilen Deutschlands düster, düsterer jedenfalls, als in den meisten vorliegenden und zu optimistischen Prognosen angenommen wird. Die Einigungskrise wirft ihre Schatten auf die gesamten 90er Jahre, vermutlich auf einen noch viel längeren Zeitraum.' (In our view the prospects for economic growth, jobs and the reduction of unemployment in both parts of Germany are grim, grimmer at least than is assumed in most of the existing and overoptimistic forecasts. The unification crisis casts its shadow over the whole of the nineties, and probably over a much longer period). In: Hickel and Priewe 1994: 273.
3. 'Die Verhandlungen ... haben ihm lehrreiche Erfahrungen vermittelt. Sie haben uns gedrückt und ausgewrungen, als wären wir Bankrotteure.... Aber das weiß man schon, wenn man auch vielleicht von den Brüdern in Christo etwas mehr Loyalität erwartet hätte.'
4. '... die ökonomisch über- und kulturell unterentwickelte Zivilisation der ehemaligen Bundesrepublik versucht, die in der ehemaligen DDR im Widerstand gegen die stalinistische Kolonisierung gewachsene Kultur durch Diffamierung und administrativ auszulöschen.'
5. 'Unter faulen Kartoffeln, Bauschutt und Autowracks fanden sie einen Bücherberg. Was zum Vorschein kam, waren keinesfalls nur Altlasten einer zu Ende gegangenen Zeit, SED-Schriften oder Honecker-Reden, sondern auch stapelweise Ausgaben von Goethe, Schiller, Shakespeare, Hegel, Rosa Luxemburg bis hin zu Kinderbüchern und Bänden von Helga Königsdorf und Christoph Hein.'
6. 'Ich konnte mir die deutsche Vereinigung nach Lage der Dinge 1989/90 nur als die Vereinnahmung der DDR durch die Bundesrepublik vorstellen, wobei alles, was den politischen, kulturellen, juristischen und wirtschaftlichen BRD-Maximen und Interessen zuwiderlief, auf der Strecke bleiben oder niedergemacht werden mußte. ... Unsere Bücher, Millionen, landeten auf der Müllkippe, und Millionen Männer und Frauen, ihr gelebtes Leben und ihre Arbeitsstätten ...'

7. See: Lancaster 1996: 6.

8. '... der Graben zwischen den in der DDR Verbliebenen und den "Dissidenten" womöglich noch tiefer ist als der zwischen jenen und den originären West-Autoren'.

9. 'Schriftsteller sind keineswegs nettere, höchstens schlechtere Menschen. Also sind sie neidisch, mißgünstig, nachtragend ...'

10. 'Mit der Solidarität unter Schriftstellern ist es schlecht bestellt'.

11. 'Die gibt es nicht'.

12. See, for instance, Hofmann *Die Zeit*, 1995: 3.

13. 'Sie mußte in allem ihm zu Willen sein, es war schon nichts mehr von ihr übrig und geblieben, und nachdem er ihr die Ehre und ihren Stolz und ihre Würde und ihre Freude und ihren Willen und ihre Erinnerung genommen hatte und ihr Gärtlein und ihr Häuslein, nahm er ihr auch noch ihre Schönheit, er fand sie häßlich.'

14. 'Die deutsch-deutsche Vereinigung hat zwar Blutsverwandte, aber Fremde zusammengeführt. *Wir* kannten *sie* nicht, und *sie* wußten wenig von *uns*. Wir *müssen* aber wissen, wie wir sind.'

15. 'Abwesenheit von Zivilcourage und die Anwesenheit von Kuschverhalten, Unterordnung und Rückzug ins Private'.

16. 'Ich will, daß der Sozialdemokrat, der nicht in die SED ging und in Bautzen saß, noch erlebt, daß ihm Unrecht geschah, daß er dokumentieren kann, warum er saß, was er erleiden mußte. ... Ich meine auch den Christen, der keine Kompromisse machte, den Liberalen, den Eurokommunisten, den Wehrdienstverweigerer, den Politische-Witze-Erzähler, den Flüchtling, der zwanzig Jahre Einreisesperre hatte.'

17. See, for instance, Corino, *Die Zeit* 1996: 9–11. Hermlin might perhaps have avoided the obloquy heaped on him by Corino and others, had he adopted the strategy employed by Peter Weiss in discussing his *Die Ästhetik des Widerstands*. In describing the work as a 'Wunschautobiographie', Weiss acknowledges that its proletarian hero and narrator is a politicised and *fictionalised* version of his own younger self. Unlike Hermlin, he makes no secret of the fact that it is not *his* life which is being unfolded here, but an extended speculation about what his life might have been, had he been born into a proletarian rather than a petty borgeois milieu. See, 'Es ist eine Wunschautobiographie. Peter Weiss im Gespräch mit Rolf Michaelis über seinen politischen Gleichnisroman', *Die Zeit*, 10 October, 1975, Literatur, 5.

18. 'Wir wollten den 3. Oktober 1990 in Berlin nicht verleben. Sie würden wieder Raketen loslassen, Freudenraketen, aber uns stand nicht der Sinn danach. ... Soll ich die Toten bedauern oder sie eher beneiden, weil sie den heutigen Tag nicht mehr erleben können? Was ist aus unseren Hoffnungen von ehemals geworden? Waren wir doch bloß Phantasten? Realitätsferne Idealisten?'

19. Although, as some have argued, not the only turning-point. See, for instance, Dennis Tate's essay, 'Keeping the Biermann Affair in perspective. Repression, resistance and the articulation of despair in the cultural life of the GDR', in Atkins and Kane 1997: 1–16.

20. 'Die Möglichkeit kritischer, widerständiger Anteilnahme, also in der gemeinsamen Arbeit (z.B. am Theater) gemeinsam "etwas zu wollen". Es war Arbeit immer auch eine Utopie. ... Daß diese Arbeit zusehends ins Nichts lief: verwurstet, verunmöglicht durch die "Konsolidierung".'

21. '... Alle Bindungen sind brüchig geworden./ Allen Glauben hat Politik pervertiert./ Freunde um Freunde, die man verliert:/ Heimlich unheimliches Meuchelmorden./ Ich möchte Bruder sagen zu allen/ Und weiß nicht, in wessen

Diensten steht,/ Wer ein in mein Haus und aus ihm geht/ Und fängt mich vielleicht in Schlingen und Fallen'.

22. See Walther 1996: 631–36. Erwin Strittmatter's cooperation with the Stasi seems to have come to an end in July 1964, when, '[D]ie Zusammenarbeit ... schließlich ganz zum Erliegen [kam]' (co-operation ... finally came to a complete standstill) (Walther, 635).

23. She is generally accepted to be the model for the young woman writer who visits the narrator of Christa Wolf's *Was bleibt.*

24. '... das literaturkritische system ... war ein politisiertes trauma gegen jegliche persönliche gefühlsäußerung'.

25. 'Wahrhaftigkeit als permanente Gratwanderung über dem Abgrund' (Meusinger 1992: 365).

26. 'Vielleicht hat sich hier in diesen Jahren keine Frau so rückhalt- und wehrlos, das heißt auch so wagehalsig auszusprechen versucht, ohne sich an die bekannten Spielregeln zu halten. ... Der aufgerissene Mund, die zügellose Geste ... geben Zeugnis davon, was bisher von dieser Generation noch nicht gesagt wurde, was unterdrückt, geleugnet oder einfach verschwiegen worden ist' (Gerhard Wolf, foreword to Stötzer-Kachold, 1989).

27. Heym is not alone in homing in on, and deploying to satirical effect, the whole new vocabulary which the *Wende* has brought with it. See, for instance, in Bernd Schirmer's *Schlehweins Giraffe*: 'Wir müssen umdenken. Das ist auch wieder so ein Wort, umdenken. Ich schreibe es auf. Ich schreibe alle neuen Wörter auf. ... Umdenken, einklagen, Seilschaft, Altlast, Warteschleife, Wendehals, herunterfahren, abwickeln, abschmelzen, Treuhand, filetieren. Ich sammle diese neuen Wörter. ... Ich sammle die neuen Wörter, die jetzt Konjunktur haben. Wende. Wendehals. Mauerspecht. Wahnsinn. Aber mit dem Wahnsinn ist es vorbei. Arbeitsbeschaffungsmaßnahmen. Marketing. Holding. Outfit. Stasisyndrom. Wegbrechen. Wohlstandsmauer. Die neuen Wörter sind ein gefundenes Fressen für ausgeflippte Germanisten' (Schirmer 1992: 18 and 28). (We have to rethink our ideas. That is another of those expressions, 'rethinking out ideas'. I'll make a note of it. I make a note of all new expressions. ... 'Rethinking our ideas', 'sueing for compensation', 'old pals' network', 'legacy of the past', 'holding pattern', 'turncoat', 'run down', 'wind up', 'slim down', 'privatisation trust', 'asset stripping'. I collect these new expressions which are enjoying a boom at present. 'Transition'. 'Turncoat'. 'Wallwoodpecker'. 'Crazy times'. 'But the crazy times are over'. 'Work creation measures'. 'Marketing'. 'Holding'. 'Outfit'. 'Stasi syndrome'. 'Breaking away'. 'The wall of affluence'. The new expressions are meat and drink for freaked-out Germanists.)

28. 'Ein herrliches, wildes, brutales Leben, wenn wir nur erst den Humor dazu haben ...'

29. '"Dies ist der lezte deutsche Gesellschaftsroman". Slapstick und Wehmut: Ein Interview mit dem ostdeutschen Schriftsteller Fritz Rudolf Fries anläßlich seines neuen Romans *Die Nonnen von Bratislava*', in *Frankfurter Rundschau*, 4 October 1994, Feuilleton, 12.

30. 'Der Zwang, immer wieder im Kleinen das Große, im Nahen das Ferne zu zeigen'. (See Konrad Franke, 'Die Giraffe war eine Altlast', in *Süddeutsche Zeitung*, 30 September 1992, 'Beilage', 6).

31. 'Ein geistreich-humorvolles Spiel mit Geschichte, insbesondere ihre vermeintlichen Analogien'. Michael Basse, '"... und die Gegenwart haben wir nie besessen". Die Roman-Antwort des literarischen Zeitreisenden Fritz Rudolf Fries auf die Wende', in *Süddeutsche Zeitung*, 5 October 1994, L8.

References

Atkins, Robert and Kane, Martin, eds. 1997. *Retrospect and Review. Aspects of the Literature of the GDR 1976–1990*, Amsterdam/Atlanta, Rodopi.

Biskupek, Matthias. 1996. *Der Quotensachse*. Leipzig, Gustav Kiepenheuer Verlag.

Boeger, Wilhelm and Lancaster, Helga, eds. 1995. *Von Abraham bis Zwerenz* Fulda, Parzeller.

Braun, Volker. 1990. *Bodenloser Satz* Frankfurt am Main, Suhrkamp Verlag.

Brecht, Bertolt. 1975. 'Bemerkungen', in *Der aufhaltsame Aufstieg des Arturo Ui*. Frankfurt am Main, edition suhrkamp (8th edn.).

Brüning, Elfriede. 1994. *Und außerdem war es mein Leben*. Berlin, Elephantenpreß-Verlag (1998. DTV, Munich).

Brussig, Thomas. 1995. *Helden wie wir*. Berlin, Verlag Volk & Welt.

Corino, Karl. 1996. 'Dichtung in eigener Sache'. *Die Zeit*, 4 October, pp. 9–11.

Fries, Fritz Rudolf. 1994. *Die Nonnen von Bratislava. Ein Staats- und Kriminalroman*. Munich and Zürich, Piper Verlag.

Hein, Christoph. 1989. *Die Ritter der Tafelrunde. Eine Komödie*. Frankfurt am Main, Luchterhand Literaturverlag.

Hermlin, Stephan. 1979. *Abendlicht*, Berlin and Weimar, Aufbau-Verlag.

Heym, Stefan. 1990. *Auf Sand gebaut. Sieben Geschichten aus der unmittelbaren Vergangenheit*. Munich, C. Bertelsmann Verlag.

Hickel, Rudolf and Priewe, Jan eds. 1994. *Nach dem Fehlstart. Ökonomische Perspektiven der deutschen Einigung*. Frankfurt am Main, S.Fischer Verlag.

Hofmann, Gunter. 1995. 'Schmerzen einer deutschen Familie. Die neue Unversöhnlichkeit unter den Schriftstellern ist eine Chiffre für den Zustand der Republik'. *Die Zeit*, 29 September, p. 3.

Lancaster, Helga. 1996. 'Zum Geleit'. *Berliner Lesezeichen*, vol. 4, no. 3/4, p. 6.

Meusinger, Annette. 1992. 'Verordnete Sprachlosigkeit und die Artikulation außerhalb des offiziellen Diskurses – "zügel los" Texte von Gabriele Kachold', in G. Meyer, G. Riegel, D. Strützel, eds., *Lebensweise und gesellschaftlicher Umbruch in Ostdeutschland*, Jenaer Reden und Schriften Neue Folge, vol. 3, Erlangen, Verlag Palm & Enke, Jena, Universitätsverlag, pp. 365–71.

Michael, Klaus. 1991. 'Neue Verlage und Zeitschriften in Ostdeutschland'. *Aus Politik und Zeitgeschichte*, B 41–42/91, 4 October, p. 34.

Müller, Heiner. 1991. 'Was wird aus dem größeren Deutschland. Fragen von Alexander Weigel'. *Sinn und Form*, vol. 43, pp. 666–69.

Noll, Dieter. 1960. *Die Abenteuer des Werner Holt*. Berlin and Weimar, Aufbau-Verlag.

Rehmann, Ruth. 1993. *"Unterwegs in fremden Träumen" – Begegnungen mit dem anderen Deutschland*. Munich, Hanser Verlag.

Schemme, Wolfgang. 1994. *Chancen für eine menschliche Gesellschaft. Schriftsteller der DDR nach der Vereinigung*. Bonn, published by GFP Gesellschaft für Projektentwicklung und Liegenschaftsverwaltung.

Sichtermann, Barbara. 1995. *Vicky Victory*. Hamburg, Hoffmann und Campe Verlag.

Schirmer, Bernd. 1992. *Schlehweins Giraffe*. Frankfurt am Main, Vito von Eichborn Verlag.

Stötzer-Kachold, Gabriele. 1989. *zügel los*. Berlin and Weimar, Aufbau-Verlag.

Tate, Dennis. 1997. 'Keeping the Biermann Affair in perspective. Repression, resistance and the articulation of despair in the cultural life of the GDR', in Robert E. Atkins and Martin Kane, eds., *Retrospect and Review. Aspects of the Literature of the GDR 1976–1990*, German Monitor no. 40, Amsterdam, Rodopi, pp.1–16.

Walther, Joachim. 1996. *Sicherungsbereich Literatur. Schriftsteller und Staatssicherheit in der Deutschen Demokratischen Republik.* Berlin, Ch. Links Verlag.

Wendisch, Agathe. 1992. 'Kein Buch mit sieben Siegeln'. *Neue Deutsche Literatur,* vol. 40 , no. 9, pp. 151–153.

Wosniak, Reinhard. 1995. *Sie saß in der Küche und rauchte.* Halle, Mitteldeutscher Verlag.

Ziesing, Heinz-Dieter. 1996. *Opoczynski. Das neue Leben des Erich O.* Berlin, Verlag Neues Leben.

CONCLUSION

David Rock

'Socialism departs and Johnny Walker arrives'
Volker Braun, *Die Zickzackbrücke*[1]

Heinrich Mohr coined the phrase 'verzweifelte Euphorie' (desperate euphoria) (Mohr 1994: 22) to describe the state of mind of GDR intellectuals when they suddenly rediscovered their badly damaged or already discarded hopes in 1989 as they solicited support for a 'sozialistische Alternative' (socialist alternative) to the GDR. And it was not just the 'Glanz der Utopie' (gleam of utopia) which flickered again in the mass demonstrations, but also fear: fear of the alternative facing them in the shape of capitalism. For Mohr, those authors and intellectuals who sought to reform socialism were 'die Verlierer ohne Abstrich' (the losers full-stop), for they failed to achieve their goals both before and after the *Wende*. Writers also lost their representative function as 'Ersatzöffentlichkeit' (a substitute public medium) which had placed them on a pedestal from which they conducted a counter-discourse 'between the lines' with their readers. Similarly, in the GDR, opposition groups coped with state-imposed restrictions and with their limited scope for activity by crediting themselves with a social significance which went beyond their actual effect. They saw themselves as being 'at the focal point of GDR history'. And as far as the churches are concerned, religion and politics now largely occupy separate functional niches, and though many former members of the church-based groups, such as Friedrich Schorlemmer, are currently involved in political parties and associations, some have withdrawn from political activity completely, having lost confidence in politics.

Yet the new situation has brought gains as well as losses, for gone are the old restraints and (for writers) the pressure from both readers and the censor. In their place is a new freedom for writers to voice their unique, individual experiences without restriction and for all 'protagonists of culture ... to explore not only the relationship between citizen and state but also the diversity of cultures and the range of identities that are alive in contemporary German society' (Kolinsky and van der Will 1998: 18).

There are few signs, though, that unification is the same thing as unity. Willy Brand's confident prediction of 1989: 'Jetzt wächst zusammen, was zusammengehört' (what belongs together will now grow together) now rings hollow. Indeed, Wilhelm Emmerich (Emmerich 1997: 522) has argued that intellectual and, above all, literary interests in East and West were in many ways closer *before* 1989 when Western readers discovered that writers such as Fühmann, Müller, Kunert, Wolf, Mickel, Fries, Becker, Braun, Hilbig and, above all, Hein were not only writing in a modern and innovative way, but also dealing with a central theme of direct relevance to them, namely that of the isolated and oppressed individual, alienated from society. Whereas after the *Wende* came not the union but the clash of the two literatures in the shape of the German-German 'Literaturstreit' (literature conflict) centred around Christa Wolf, when it also became apparent how little many on each side thought of the other's literature. In the words of Emmerich, 'the mythical GDR-identity has in many places even become reinforced rather than transformed' (Emmerich 1997: 525).[2] Literature is thus reflecting widespread signs of the emergence of a new Eastern consciousness, with 'Ostalgie' (nostalgia for the GDR) the defensive response to social changes.

What, then, are the implications now for GDR writers and intellectuals in the new culturally divergent Germany? There is still some evidence of a continuing fixation with the GDR. Ian Wallace (Wallace 1997: 3) has cited a statement by Kurt Drawert as representative: 'I can only see the present from out of the past: what I mean is that I look at the Federal Republic as if out of the window of a cell. And I am so proccupied with this view and with everything that was my life in the GDR that the Germany of the present is only of interest to me in terms of the way it differs from my experiences' (Herzog 1994: 70).[3] Others, such as Christa Wolf and Volker Braun, still feel some continuing loyalty, albeit with reservations, to the original political ideals of the GDR. But there are also some, such as Thomas Brussig and Günter de Bruyn, who celebrate the freedom of the new situation. There is evidence, too, in the works of writers such as Braun and Brussig, that a new era has begun for a literature that is politically and socially critical (Steinecke 1993: 201). Yet one could also point to a completely opposite trend, particularly in the great majority of exile writers, such as Kunze and Kunert, who expressed their relief that they were able at long last to turn to the real tasks of literature, namely the exploration of the 'basic questions of human experience' (Steinecke 1993: 201).

Clearly, then, GDR intellectuals and writers themselves reflect the cultural divergence of the new Germany with its many social and political problems, a society much less clearly defined than the one in the GDR. And herein lies, for Heinrich Mohr, the very source of optimism for the future of literature:

Writers' texts are fantasies about reality – fantasies of the most diverse kind. ... I expect that we will be reading exciting texts in the years to come, especially from authors from the former GDR too. Conditions are pointing in that direction. 'The happy man has no fantasies', said Freud. In united Germany, there are, and will be, many and very divergent ways of being unhappy. A fertile time for literature (Mohr 1994: 21–22).[4]

Notes

1. 'Der Sozialismus geht und Johnny Walker kommt.'
2. '... die mythische DDR-Identität ... hat sich ... mancherorts sogar wieder verfestigt statt sich zu verwandeln'.
3. 'Ich kann die Gegenwart nur aus der Vergangenheit heraus sehen, das heißt, ich schaue auf die Bundesrepublik wie aus dem Fenster einer Zelle. Und mit diesem Blick und mit allem, was mein Leben in der DDR war, bin ich so beschäftigt, daß mich das gegenwärtige Deutschland nur in seiner ... Differenz zu meinen Erfahrungen interessiert.'
4. 'Die Texte der Dichter sind Phantasien über die Wirklichkiet – Phantasien der allerverschiedensten Art. ... Ich nehme an, daß wir in den kommenden Jahren erregende Texte lesen werden, gerade auch von Autoren aus der "gewesenen"

DDR. Die Zustände sind danach. "Der Glückliche phantasiert nicht", meinte Freud. Im vereinten Deutschland gibt es – und wird es geben – viele und sehr verschiedenartige Weisen, unglücklich zu sein. Eine fruchtbare Zeit für Literatur.'

References

Braun, Volker. 1992. *Die Zickzackbrücke.* Halle, Eij Abriß-Kalender.

Emmerich, Wolfgang. 1997. *Kleine Literaturgeschichte der DDR: Erweiterte Neuausgabe.* Leipzig, Kiepenheuer und Witsch.

Herzog, Andreas. 1994. 'Erinnern und Erzählen. Gespräch mit Kurt Drawert'. *Neue deutsche Literatur,* no.1, pp. 70ff.

Kolinsky, Eva and van der Will, Wilfried. 1998. 'In Search of German Culture', in Eva Kolinsky and Wilfried van der Will, eds., in *The Cambridge Companion to Modern German Culture,* Cambridge, Cambridge University Press, pp. 1–19.

Mohr, Heinrich. 1994. 'Mein Blick auf die Literatur in der DDR'. *Aus Politik und Zeitgeschichte. Beilage zur Wochenzeitung Das Parlament,* vol. 10, 11 March, pp.12–22.

Steinecke, Hartmut. 1992. 'From Two German Literatures to One Literature'. *London German Studies,* vol. V, pp.198–206.

Wallace, Ian. 1996/97. 'East German writers look back at the GDR: Two recent examples'. *Institute of Germanic Studies: Friends Newsletter,* pp. 3–9.

NOTES ON CONTRIBUTORS

KARL CORDELL is Senior Lecturer in the Department of Politics at the University of Plymouth. He has published numerous articles on *die Wende* and its aftermath, and German-Polish relations, and is currently editing a book on the politics of ethnicity in Central Europe. He is the editor of *Ethnicity and Democratisation in the New Europe* (1998).

PETER HUTCHINSON is Fellow of Trinity Hall, University of Cambridge. He has a special interest in the literature of the GDR, on which he has published many articles, and has edited *Die DDR erzählt* (1973), Kafka: *Die Verwandlung* (1985), Frisch *Biedermann und die Brandstifter* (1986) and *Andorra* (1994), and *Von der DDR zu den fünf neuen Ländern* (1992). He is the author of *Literary Presentations of Divided Germany* (1977), *Games Authors Play* (1983) and *Stefan Heym. The Perpetual Dissident* (1992).

ROGER JONES lectures in German at Keele University. He has published extensively on nineteenth- and twentieth-century German literature and has a particular interest in the history of religion in the nineteenth century and in the interconnections between English and German literature.

MARTIN KANE was Reader at the University of Kent at Canterbury until he retired in summer 1998. He has published numerous articles on aspects of East and West German literature, and is the author of *Weimar Germany and the Limits of Political Art* (1987), and editor of *Socialism and the Literary Imagination. Essays on East German Writers* (1991) and *Retrospect and Review. Aspects of the Literature of the GDR 1976–1990* (1994).

STUART PARKES is Professor of German Literature and Society at the University of Sunderland. He has published widely on contemporary German literature in its social context. He is the author of *Writers and Politics in West Germany* (1986) and is co-editor of *Literature on the Threshold* (1990), *German Literature at a Time of Change 1989-1990, The Individual, Identity and Innovation. Signals from Contemporary Literature and the New Germany* (1994) and *Contemporary German Writers, Their Aesthetics and Their Language* (1996).

DETLEF POLLACK is Professor of Comparative Cultural Sociology, Europa-Universität Viadrina, Frankfurt/Oder. He has published numerous articles and books on politics and society in the GDR and the new Germany, including *Die Legititiät der Freieheit. Politisch alternative Gruppen in der DDR unter dem Dach der Kirche* (1990) and *Die Entzauberung des Politischen: Was ist aus den politischen alternativen Gruppen der DDR geworden* (1994).

DAVID ROCK lectures in German at Keele University. He has published extensively on nineteenth- and twentieth-century German authors, with special emphasis on the literature of the GDR. He is editor of *Jurek Becker. Five Stories* (1992) and co-editor of *Gerhart Hauptmann. Bahnwärter Thiel* (1992), and is currently completing books on Jurek Becker and German Minority Writers.

FRIEDRICH SCHORLEMMER is Studienleiter at the Evangelische Akadamie, Wittenberg (see Chapter 4 for biographical details).

SELECT BIBLIOGRAPHY

Anz, Thomas, ed. 1991. *Es geht nicht um Christa Wolf.* Munich, edition spangenberg.
Arnold, Heinz Ludwig, ed. 1991. *Christoph Hein: text und kritik.* Munich, Verlag edition text + kritik.
———. 1992. *Jurek Becker. text und kritik.* Munich, Verlag text + kritik.
———. 1993. *Feinderklärung. Literatur und Staatssicherheit: text und kritik.* Munich, Verlag edition text + kritik.
———. and Meyer-Gosau, Frauke, eds., 1991. *Literatur in der DDR. Rückblicke: text und kritik.* Munich, Verlag edition text + kritik.
Atkins, Robert and Kane, Martin, eds. 1997. *Retrospect and Review. Aspects of the Literature of the GDR 1976–1990,* Amsterdam/Atlanta, Rodopi.
Aust, Stefan. 1996. 'Berlin: Die Kluft zwischen West- und Ostintellektuellen'. *Der Spiegel,* 26, 24 June, pp.168–71.
Barthelemy, Francoise, and Winckler, Lutz, eds. 1990. *Mein Deutschland findet sich in keinem Atlas.* Frankfurt am Main, Luchterhand.
Baumann, Eleonore, et al., eds. 1990. *Fischer Weltalmanach. Sonderband DDR.* Frankfurt am Main, Fischer Taschenbuch Verlag.
Becker, Jurek. 1990. *Warnung vor dem Schriftsteller.* Frankfurt am Main, Suhrkamp.
Boeger, Wilhelm and Lancaster, Helga, eds. 1995. *Von Abraham bis Zwerenz.* Fulda, Parzeller.
Bohse, R. et al. 1990. *Jetzt Oder Nie-Demokratie!.* Berlin, Forum Verlag.
Brand, Karl-Werner. 1990. 'Massendemokratischer Aufbruch im Osten. Eine Herausforderung für die NSB-Forschung'. *Forschungsjournal Neue Soziale Bewegungen,* vol. 3, no. 2, p. 10.
Chiarloni, Anna and Pankoke, Helga, eds. 1991. *Grenzfallgedichte. Eine deutsche Anthologie.* Berlin, Aufbau.
Conrady, Karl Otto, ed. 1993. *Von einem Land und vom andern,* Frankfurt am Main, Suhrkamp.
Cordell, Karl. 1990. 'The Role of the Evangelical Church in the GDR'. *Government and Opposition,* 21, 1, winter, pp.48–59.
———. 1990b. 'Political Change in the GDR', *International Relations,* vol. 10, No.2, pp.161–66.
———. 1995. 'The Church: Coming to Terms with Change', in *Between Hope and Fear.* Keele, Keele University Press.
Corino, Karl. 1996. 'Dichtung in eigener Sache'. *Die Zeit,* 4 October, pp. 9–11.
Dahrendorf, Ralf. 1965. *Gesellschaft und Demokratie in Deutschland.* Munich, Piper.
Durrani, Osman, Good, Colin and Hilliard, Kevin, eds. 1995. *The New Germany: Literature and Society after Unification,* Sheffield, Sheffield Academic Press.
Emmerich, Wolfgang. 1997. *Kleine Literaturgeschichte der DDR: Erweiterte Neuausgabe.* Leipzig, Gustav Kiepenheuer Verlag.

Enzensberger, Hans Magnus. 1990. 'Gangarten'. *Kursbuch 100*, pp.1–10.

Findeis, Hagen, Pollack, Detlef and Schilling, Manuel, eds. 1994. *Die Entzauberung des Politischen: Was ist aus den politisch alternativen Gruppen der DDR geworden?*. Leipzig, Berliner Debatte und Evangelische Verlagsanstalt.

Foell, Kristie A. 1994. 'Shaping History: Stefan Heym's Responses to German Unification'. *Colloquia Germanica*, vol. 27, pp.37–48.

Fulbrook, Mary. 1992. *The Two Germanies, 1945–1990. Problems of Interpretation*. Basingstoke and London, Macmillan.

——. 1995. *Anatomy of a Dictatorship. Inside the GDR 1949–1989*. Oxford, Oxford University Press.

Goeckel, R. 1990. *The Lutheran Church and the East German State*. London, Cornell University Press.

Goodbody, Axel and Tate, Denis eds. 1992. *Geist und Macht: Writers and the State in the GDR*. Amsterdam/Atlanta, Rodopi.

Görtz, Franz Josef et al., eds. 1990. *Deutsche Literatur 1989*. Stuttgart, Reclam.

—— eds . 1993. *Deutsche Literatur 1992*. Stuttgart, Reclam.

Grabner W.J., et al. 1990. *Leipzig im Oktober*. Leipzig, Wichern-Verlag.

Grass, Günter. 1990. *Ein Schnäppchen namens DDR*. Frankfurt am Main, Luchterhand.

Gross, J. 1990. *Begründung der Berliner Republik*. Stuttgart, Deutsche Verlags-Anstalt.

Hallberg, Robert von, ed. 1996. *Literary Intellectuals and the Dissolution of the State. Professionalism and Conformity in the GDR*. Chicago, University of Chicago Press.

Hartinger, Walfried. 1995. 'Texte nach der Wende'. *Berliner LeseZeichen*, vol. 3, nos. 6/7, June/July, pp.46–76.

Haufe, G. and Bruckmaier, K., eds. 1993. *Die Bürgerbewegungen in der DDR und in den ostdeutschen Bundesländern*. Opladen, Westdeutscher Verlag.

Haufe, Gerda and Karl Bruckmeier, eds. 1993. *Die Bürgerbewegung in der DDR und in den ostdeutschen Bundesländern*, Opladen, Westdeutscher Verlag.

Heidelberger-Leonard, Irene. 1992. *Jurek Becker*, Frankfurt am Main, Suhrkamp Verlag.

Hein, Christoph. 1990. *Als Kind habe ich Stalin gesehen. Essais und Reden*. Berlin/Weimar, Aufbau.

——. 1990b. *Die fünfte Grundrechenart. Aufsätze und Reden 1987–1990*. Frankfurt am Main, Luchterhand.

Heym, Stefan. 1990. *Einmischung. Gespräche. Reden. Essays*. Selected and edited by Inge Heym and Heinfried Henniger. Munich, Bertelsmann.

——. 1992. *Filz. Gedanken über das neueste Deutschland*. Munich, Bertelsmann.

——. 1995. *Rede zur Eröffnung des 13. Deutschen Bundestages, Neue Deutsche Literatur*, vol. 43, January 1995, pp.208–12; English translation by Stefan Howald, 'Old Echoes in German Reichstag', *New Times*, 26 November 1994, p.4.

——. and Heiduczek, Werner. 1990. *Die sanfte Revolution. Prosa, Lyrik, Protokolle, Erlebnisberichte, Reden*. Leipzig, Gustav Kiepenheuer Verlag.

Hickel, Rudolf and Priewe, Jan eds. 1994. *Nach dem Fehlstart. Ökonomische Perspektiven der deutschen Einigung*. Frankfurt am Main, S.Fischer Verlag.

Hildenbrandt J. and Thomas G., eds. 1990. *Unser Glaube mischt sich ein*, Berlin, Evangelische Verlaganstalt.

Hirschmann, Albert O. 1992. 'Abwanderung und Widerspruch und das Schicksal der Deutschen Demokratischen Republik. Ein Essay zur konzeptuellen Geschichte', in *Leviathan*, 20, pp. 330–58.

Hochhuth, Rolf. 1995. *Wessis in Weimar*. Berlin, Verlag Volk & Welt.

Hofmann, Gunter. 1995. 'Schmerzen einer deutschen Familie. Die neue Unversöhnlichkeit unter den Schriftstellern ist eine Chiffre für den Zustand der Republik'. *Die Zeit*, 29 September.

Hutchinson, Peter. 1992. *Stefan Heym. The Perpetual Dissident.* Cambridge, Cambridge University Press.

Jackson, Paul. 1994. *DDR – Das Ende eines Staates.* Manchester, Manchester University Press.

Joas, Hans and Kohli, Martin, eds.. 1993. *Der Zusammenbruch der DDR. Soziologische Analysen.* Frankfurt am Main, Lang.

Joppke, C. 1993. 'Why Leipzig? "Exit" and "Voice" in the East German Revolution', *German Politics*, vol.2, No.3, pp. 393–414.

Kaelble, Hartmut, Kocka, Jürgen and Zwahr, Hartmut, eds. 1994. *Sozialgeschichte der DDR*, Stuttgart, Klett-Cotta.

Kolinsky, Eva and van der Will, Wilfried. 1998. *The Cambridge Companion to Modern German Culture.* Cambridge, Cambridge University Press.

Lancaster, Helga. 1996. 'Zum Geleit'. *Berliner Lesezeichen*, vol. 4, no. 3/4, p. 6.

Lease, G. 1992. 'Religion, the Churches, and the German Revolution of November 1990', *German Politics*, vol.1, No.2, pp. 264–73.

Leonhard, Wolfgang. 1990. *Die Revolution entläßt ihre Kinder*, 2nd edn. Cologne, Kiepenheuer und Witsch (1955).

Maron, Monika. 1990. 'Die Schriftsteller und das Volk'. *Der Spiegel*, 7.

Meyer, G., Riegel, G. and Strützel, D., eds. 1992. *Lebensweise und gesellschaftlicher Umbruch in Ostdeutschland*, Jenaer Reden und Schriften Neue Folge, vol. 3, Erlangen, Verlag Palm & Enke, Jena, Universitätsverlag.

Michael, Klaus. 1991. 'Neue Verlage und Zeitschriften in Ostdeutschland'. *Aus Politik und Zeitgeschichte*, B 41–42/91, 4 October.

Minnerup, Günter. 1994. 'The Political Opposition in the GDR'. *German Monitor: Reassessing the GDR*, 33, pp.67–82.

Mitter, A. and Wolle, S. eds. 1990. *Ich liebe euch doch alle! Befehle und Lageberichte des MFS: Januar–November 1989.* Berlin, Basis Druck.

Mohr, Heinrich. 1994. 'Mein Blick auf die Literatur in der DDR'. *Aus Politik und Zeitgeschichte. Beilage zur Wochenzeitung Das Parlament*, vol. 10, 11 March, pp. 12–22.

Müller, Heiner. 1990. "Zur Lage der Nation". Berlin, Rotbuch.

——. 1991. 'Was wird aus dem größeren Deutschland. Fragen von Alexander Weigel'. *Sinn und Form*, vol. 43, pp. 666–69.

——. 1992. *Krieg ohne Schlacht. Leben in zwei Diktaturen.* Cologne, Kiepenheuer und Witsch.

Niven, William. 1995. '"Das Geld ist nicht der Gral": Christoph Hein and the Wende'. *Modern Language Review*, vol. 90, pp. 688–706

Opp, Karl-Dieter and Voss, Peter. 1993. *Die volkseigene Revolution.* Stuttgart, Klett & Cotta.

Pollack, Detlef. 1990. 'Das Ende einer Organisationsgesellschaft. Systemtheoretische Überlegungen zum gesellschaftlichen Umbruch in der DDR'. *Zeitschrift für Soziologie*, 19, pp. 292–307.

——, ed. 1990. *Die Legitimität der Freiheit. Politisch alternative Gruppen in der DDR unter dem Dach der Kirche*, Frankfurt am Main, Lang.

Probst, Lothar. 1993. *Ostdeutsche Bürgerbewegungen und Perspektiven der Demokratie. Entstehung, Bedeutung und Zukunft.* Cologne, Bund Verlag.

Rehmann, Ruth. 1993. *"Unterwegs in fremden Träumen" – Begegnungen mit dem anderen Deutschland.* Munich, Hanser Verlag.

Reid, J.H. 1990. *Writing without Taboos.* New York/Oxford/Munich, Berg.

Rock, David. 2000. *Jurek Becker: A Jew Who Became a German?* Berg, Oxford and New York.

Rosenlöcher, Thomas. 1990. *Die verkauften Pflastersteine. Dresdener Tagebuch.* Frankfurt am Main, Suhrkamp Verlag.

Rüddenklau, Wolfgang. 1992. *Störenfried. DDR–Opposition 1986–1989.* Berlin, Basis-Druck.

Rüß, Gisela, ed. 1976. *Dokumente zur Kunst-, Literatur- und Kulturpolitik der SED 1991–1974.* Stuttgart, Seewald.

Sandford, John. 1983. *The Sword and the Ploughshare. Autonomous Peace Initiatives in East Germany.* London, Merlin Press.

Schemme, Wolfgang. 1994. *Schriftsteller der DDR nach der Vereinigung.* Bonn, GFP Gesellschaft für Projektentwicklung und Liegenchaftesverwaltung.

Schorlemmer, Friedrich. 1992. *Versöhnung in der Wahrheit,* Munich, Knaur.

——. 1992. *Worte öffnen Fäuste.* München, Kindler Verlag.

——. 1993 *Bis alle Mauern fallen,* Munich, Knaur.

Schulze, R., ed. 1990. *Nach der Wende,* Berlin, Wichern-Verlag.

Sievers, H.J. 1991. *Stundenbuch einer deutschen Revolution.* Göttingen, Vandenhoeck & Ruprecht.

Soldat, Hans-Georg. 1997. 'Die Wende in Deutschland im Spiegel der zeitgenössischen deutschen Literatur'. *German Life and Letters,* vol.L, no.2, April, pp. 133–54.

Spies, Bernhard. 1994. 'The End of the Socialist State: The Socialist Utopia and the Writers'. *Modern Language Review,* vol. 89, pp. 393–405.

Steinecke, Hartmut. 1993. 'From Two German Literatures to One Literature'. *London German Studies,* vol. V, pp.198–206.

Strauß, Botho. 1993. 'Anschwellender Bocksgesang'. *Der Spiegel,* 6, pp.202–7.

Swatos jr., W., ed. 1994. *Politics and Religion in Central and Eastern Europe.* London, Praeger.

Torpay, John. 1992. 'Two Movements, Not a Revolution. Exodus and Opposition in the East German Transformation, 1989–1990'. *German Politics and Society,* 26, pp. 21–42.

Unterberg, Peter. 1991. *'Wir sind erwachsen, Vater Staat!', Background, foundation and effect of Neues Forum in Leipzig.* Diploma Thesis for the Faculty of Social Sciences, Bochum Ruhr University.

Vester, Michael, Hofmann, Michael and Zierke, Irene, eds. 1995. *Soziale Milieus in Ostdeutschland. Gesellschaftliche Strukturen zwischen Zerfall und Neubildung.* Cologne, Bund Verlag.

Vinke, Hermann, ed. 1993. *Akteneinsicht Christa Wolf.* Hamburg, Luchterhand Literaturverlag.

Vogt, Jochen. 1995. 'Orientierungsverlust oder neue Offenheit? Deutsche Literatur in Ost und West vor und nach 1989'. *Berliner LeseZeichen,* 6/7, pp. 30–45.

Wallace, Ian. 1994. 'Writers and the *Stasi*'. *German Monitor,* 33, , pp. 126–7.

——. 1996/97. 'East German writers look back at the GDR: Two recent examples'. *Institute of Germanic Studies: Friends Newsletter,* pp. 3–9.

Walser, Martin. 1993. 'Deutsche Sorgen'. *Der Spiegel,* 26, pp.40–47.

Walther, Joachim, et al., eds. 1991. *Protokoll eines Tribunals.* Reinbek bei Hamburg, Rowohlt.

—— 1996. *Sicherungsbereich Literatur. Schriftsteller und Staatssicherheit in der Deutschen Demokratischen Republik.* Berlin, Ch. Links Verlag.

Watson, Roger. 1993. 'Flüstern und Schreien: punks, rock music and the revolution in the GDR'. *German Life and Letters,* vol. XLVI, no.2, April, pp. 162–75.

Wendisch, Agathe. 1992. 'Kein Buch mit sieben Siegeln'. *Neue Deutsche Literatur*, vol. 40 , no. 9, pp. 151–153.

Wielgohs, Jan. 1993. 'Auflösung und Transformation der ostdeutschen Bürgerbewegung'. *Deutschland Archiv*, 26 , pp. 426–434.

Wielgohs, Jan and Schulz, Marianne. 1991. 'Von der illegalen Opposition in die legale Marginalität. Zur Entwicklung der Binnenstruktur der ostdeutschen Bürgerbewegung'. *Berliner Journal für Soziologie*, 1, p. 385ff.

Wimmer, Micha, Proske, Christina, Braun, Sabine and Michalowski, Bernhard, eds. 1990. *'Wir sind das Volk!' Die DDR im Aufbruch*. Munich, Heyne.

Wolf, Christa. 1994. *Auf dem Weg nach Tabou. Texte 1990–1994*. Cologne, Verlag Kiepenheuer und Witsch.

Woods, Roger. 1986. *Opposition in the GDR under Honecker 1971–85*. Basinstoke/London, Macmillan.

INDEX